TESTIMONIALS

Part history, part thriller, part biography, Bob West-brooks writes a compelling story of the Covid crisis, uncovering the pervasive and international fraud which accompanied it and the damning decisions by our national leadership. The reader relives what government did right and what it too often did wrong. It is a must-read manual for how to respond to future crises. Everyone should read it because everyone experienced it. It cannot be put down."

–**Richard Kessler**, Ph.D., Retired Staff
Director of the Senate Homeland Security
and Governmental Affairs Committee and
House Foreign Affairs Committee

Government officials and all taxpayers need to read this compelling personal account of one of the greatest anti-fraud challenges in history. Were the American people ripped off? This book proves it conclusively. However, it also recounts what could have happened without the "watchdogs" doing their duty. Thanks to Bob Westbrooks and his PRAC team for an "Agile Government" approach to oversight."

–**G.Edward DeSeve**, Special Assistant
to President Barack Obama and then
Vice President Joe Biden

In the 19th century, Alexis de Tocqueville wrote that the success of the U.S. experiment was based on the ability of its citizens to practice "self-interest well understood" – to act in a way that maximized both their individual and collective interest. Bob Westbrooks' account illustrates how the COVID-19 pandemic, and the disinformation surrounding it, exposed and accelerated the erosion of this unique American quality. His insight is a wake-up call for why uniting under a common set of facts is essential for rebuilding our public trust and democratic social fabric.

–**Asha Rangappa**, Former FBI Special Agent and Senior Lecturer at the Jackson School of Global Affairs

The American people owe a debt to a host of public servants who served during the pandemic. As a vanguard for the public's pandemic resources, Bob Westbrooks is every bit as much a hero as those who fought the pandemic. And he has done the nation a tremendous service by translating his experience into compelling stories, lessons learned, and recommendations for the future. The public and policymakers should give equal attention to this important book.

–**Robert Shea**, CEO, GovNavigators, former Associate Director, U.S. Office of Management and Budget

LEFT HOLDING THE BAG

LEFT HOLDING THE BAG

A WATCHDOG'S ACCOUNT OF HOW WASHINGTON FUMBLED ITS COVID TEST

BOB WESTBROOKS

FORMER INSPECTOR GENERAL AND PANDEMIC WATCHDOG

GRACIE HOUSE

Left Holding the Bag

© 2023 Robert A. Westbrooks

All rights reserved. Printed in the United States of America.

ISBN paperback 979-8-9883953-0-0
ISBN hardcover 979-8-9883953-1-7
ISBN ebook 979-8-9883953-2-4

Published by Gracie House LLC

Contact the author at BobWestbrooks.com or on LinkedIn at *www.linkedin.com/in/bobwestbrooks*.

*To Tracy—my wife and my world—and to
our wonderful family;*

To the memory of those who lost their lives;

*To my friends in the oversight and law
enforcement communities, who battle fraud
day in and day out;*

*To those who courageously and patiently
serve in healthcare, and to other essential
workers at whatever station in life;*

*And finally to all those who may have
lost their health, lost a loved one, or lost
their way during the awful Pandemic of
2020–2023.*

CONTENTS

PART I

PART II

PART I

1

THE MOTHER OF ALL OVERSIGHT MISSIONS

*Facts are stubborn things; and whatever
may be our wishes, our inclinations, or
the dictates of our passion, they cannot
alter the state of facts and evidence.*
John Adams

I started a new job on a Monday in April 2020 and had the typical first-day jitters. Even after a twenty-six-year career in public service working for lots of bosses and in a variety of positions of increasing responsibility, I was filled with equal parts excitement and trepidation. Excitement for a new challenge; trepidation over the unknown. Only, that day, the feelings were a trillion times more intense.

The president of the United States had recently signed one of the largest financial rescue packages in US history to fight the COVID-19 pandemic, and I was starting my new job as the executive director of the new federal office responsible for conducting and coordinating independent oversight of the federal government's coronavirus response and $2 trillion in federal pandemic relief funds.

I was trying to wrap my head around a trillion. That's a lot of zeros. I was a lawyer, certified public accountant, criminal investigator, and a career watchdog; but I hadn't previously lived my day-to-day in the land of such large numbers. That first day I was working like most Americans who were able to—at home. I was working off of a fourteen-inch laptop screen in the spare bedroom, wondering the best time to squeeze in a grocery store run in the hope of securing one of the blessings of liberty—toilet paper—as the pandemic had forced a shutdown of the Washington, DC-area, left store shelves bare, and severely disrupted life as we knew it.

I would not be alone, and I would only play one part in a play with many pandemic oversight characters, but there would be no easing into this role and taking a few days to get the feel of things. By lunch time I was making calls to hire an attorney to join the team.

My inbox was immediately flooded with congratulatory messages and just as many or more consolatory messages on my appointment. The strained relationship between the White House and the community of inspectors general at that time was on the minds of a lot of people.

Although we had never met, House Speaker Nancy Pelosi released a statement later in the day wishing me well and bluntly warning: "The Trump Administration must not interfere with Executive Director Westbrooks' independence in his critical role leading the Pandemic Response Accountability Committee created in the CARES Act."

Senate Majority Leader Chuck Schumer released a statement on my appointment: "To hold this administration accountable, we need people who are fearless and fiercely independent from this president at the helm. Mr. Westbrooks appears to have the right background and a good reputation, and I am hopeful he will be the independent watchdog the moment calls for."

The majority leadership of the House Committee on Oversight also released a press statement: "As a former Inspector General, accountant, and auditor, Mr. Westbrooks will help the committee conduct strong oversight that is urgently needed. Americans across the political spectrum want the trillions of dollars being spent in response to the coronavirus crisis to be used effectively and efficiently—without waste, fraud, abuse, or profiteering."

I didn't receive any comparable public well wishes from members on the other side of the political aisle, which was not surprising. While there are some exceptions, generally politicians of all stripes typically only welcome rigorous independent oversight when it's directed at their opponents. That's just how it goes in Washington.

A week later, the nation's first pandemic fraud criminal charges were filed in federal court, courtesy of the FBI and federal prosecutors. This first pandemic fraud prosecution now seems almost quaint. Two Rhode Island men hatched their scheme to steal federal pandemic funds a mere ten days after Congress passed and President Trump signed the CARES Act authorizing, among other spending, an unprecedented $349 billion for forgivable government loans for small businesses. The men hatched this scheme before our oversight office was even open for business.

This was not the men's first rodeo. An informant tipped off a local police chief about a real estate fraud scheme the two were committing involving the sale of restaurants. And, by the way, the informant told police he had access to one of the men's Google email accounts and saw email exchanges between the two men discussing how they planned to dummy loan applications and supporting documents to obtain fraudulent loans from the new pandemic relief program run by the US Small Business Administration: the Paycheck Protection Program that came to be known as PPP.

The police chief called in the FBI, who called in an IRS special agent to help with the tax angle and a special agent from the Small Business Administration Office of Inspector General to help obtain the loan records. An informant with real-time access to evidence involving an ongoing crime is an agent's dream, but this can also be tricky. To avoid a messy future evidence suppression hearing, the agents exercised restraint and told the informant not to look at any more emails while they got a search warrant for the Google email records.

The two men submitted two fraudulent small business loan applications in the name of four non-existent businesses, claiming dozens of phantom employees. One of the men claimed his cell phone company had seven employees whom he laid off in March and he needed the money to pay their salaries. The other man submitted a loan application claiming dozens of employees at three restaurants he claimed to own, including a Rhode Island seafood restaurant. All lies.

For an agent, the next best thing to a confession is an undercover recording, and the latter is often a lot more fun, as you can imagine. An undercover FBI agent posing as a bank compliance officer placed a call to one of the men. The undercover agent got the man to repeat on tape his lies about the non-existent businesses and employees. With that, federal prosecutors in Rhode Island formally charged the two men with multiple fraud and conspiracy counts on May 5, 2020. These were the first pandemic fraud charges in the nation.

$

There's nothing like a crisis to test your mettle. A crisis will measure your capabilities and reveal your character. This is true of ordinary individuals and true of great nations. A crisis will either make you stronger or it will weaken you; it will either bring people together or tear them apart.

Beginning in 2020, the pandemic crisis put the US federal government to the test. I'm not talking about COVID test strips. The pandemic crisis tested our country's ability to

- Effectively communicate public health information to the American people in a clear, trusted, and unifying voice;
- Swiftly develop and implement safe, trusted, and minimally invasive public health countermeasures like social distancing policies and vaccines; and
- Quickly distribute targeted emergency aid, ensuring the money gets into the right hands.

The pandemic crisis tested the American people's ability to share common facts and unite for the common good, but that's mostly for another book.

For two and a half years—until my retirement as the pandemic emergency was winding down—I had a front row seat to this moment in American history. While my professional focus was primarily on whether federal pandemic funds were well spent and not lost to fraud or waste, all parts of our national COVID test were interconnected.

One could argue the national test ended in April 2023 when President Biden signed legislation ending the COVID-19 national emergency. That very week, *ABC News Health* published an article on how and why people are already forgetting their pandemic stories. For individuals this isn't necessarily a bad thing. We sometimes allow our memories to fade out of self-preservation to move on and avoid reliving a trauma. As a nation, however, it's critical that we do the exact opposite. We can't afford to forget our national pandemic story.

Tragically, we lost over one million Americans to the pandemic, among the highest number of deaths as a country and one of the higher mortality rates in the world. Many Americans died in a cold hospital room, connected to a ventilator, and alone. Survivors were often left unable to gather in remembrance.

Washington Post reporter Lena H. Sun, who covered the pandemic and lost her mother to COVID, later reflected on this time and poignantly wrote: "We were a nation awash in grief, an experience of loss that was, at once, personal and collective, an experience that forced us to find new ways to mourn—and to carry on."

For months on end, many Americans experienced a constant impending sense of doom as COVID case numbers rose and fell in waves across broad regions of the country. We witnessed the politicalization and polarization of public health. We saw disinformation weaponized to foment disharmony between family and friends and violence against strangers. We lost loved ones who needlessly died convinced COVID-19 was all a hoax.

In addition to the shocking loss of life, the pandemic will end up costing us—the American taxpayers—over $5 trillion. Our federal government spent more on pandemic relief, as a percentage of gross domestic product, than any other country in the world. The pandemic relief laws created and funded a slew of major new federal programs and funded quantum leap increases in other programs that were unprepared and ill-equipped for the task. Some parts of the federal system were overwhelmed, and in some cases federal agencies made big costly mistakes.

Washington doesn't have a rainy-day fund stashed in a shoebox in the closet somewhere. Every federal dollar spent during an emergency like a pandemic is put on the tab—your and your children's tab. It's added to the gross federal public debt—$31 trillion as of January 2023—and it's factored into future heated budget debates among lawmakers and citizens over which programs the nation can afford and who is more deserving of government assistance.

We lost *hundreds of billions* of pandemic relief dollars to fraud and waste—an unacceptable, unprecedented, and unfathomable amount in absolute and relative terms.

Federal and state computer systems didn't talk to each other, and even some computer systems within the same agency didn't talk. One social security number was used to file for unemployment insurance benefits in forty states (and was successful in getting benefits from twenty-nine states).

A fraudster who was successfully blocked from obtaining benefits in one agency program turned to another program in the same agency and struck gold.

Federal agency systems failed to check with the effective Do Not Pay list of ineligible payees run by the US Treasury before making payments; they failed to block pandemic relief claims from overseas; and they failed to detect when the same personal information (for example, name, address, social security number) was used repeatedly in the same program.

In the early months of the pandemic, federal watchdogs lacked an available data analytics function to quickly spot anomalies, patterns, and hidden links across government programs. Such a unit had been built following the 2009 economic crisis, but Congress allowed it to lapse. Valuable months would be lost rebuilding this critical counter-fraud capability.

During the pandemic emergency, federal investigators from multiple law enforcement agencies worked thousands of pandemic fraud investigations involving novice, experienced, and professional criminals. There would be fraud prosecutions of a former NFL player and a former US Olympic skater, a rapper and reality TV star, pastors and prisoners, police officers and politicians, college students and international fraudsters. The lure of easy money was even too much for the actor who played the Red Power Ranger in the 1990s TV series, who was indicted for his role in an alleged pandemic fraud scheme. The largest pandemic fraud prosecution as of April 2023 involved a forty-seven-person ring and $250 million.

In an unrelated investigation, the US Secret Service confirmed the investigation of members of a hacker group associated with the Chinese military who were linked to the loss of millions of dollars.

Pandemic fraud was pervasive, systemic, transnational, and industrial scale. Pandemic fraud was also just so conspicuous. In 2020, it seemed like every offender was using their newfound wealth to buy a Lamborghini. Buying a $200,000 Lambo for cash during a disruptive global pandemic wasn't proof of a crime, but it was what I would consider a potential lead. Agents and prosecutors had more than their hands full with the "Lamborghini cases," and federal law enforcement was soon overwhelmed.

The massive pandemic fraud crisis prompted Congress to later pass legislation extending the statute of limitations on pandemic prosecutions from five to ten years. Federal investigators, prosecutors, and auditors will be at this effort for years to come.

Accountability in Washington is scarce in normal times. That is not a new phenomenon, and increased political polarization has exacerbated matters. These were not normal times. With no pretense or apology, political leaders often reward those who have the fastest reflexes in pointing a finger and casting blame on the other side. Congress signed the federal pandemic relief check—or rather authorized the president to sign the check—and the American people were left holding the bag and shouldering the consequences to our fiscal and physical well-being.

If you were fortunate enough to survive the pandemic crisis with your health and wealth intact, you'd be tempted to grade Washington's response to the crisis on a curve and award an overall passing grade. That's understandable. We lived through so much history in three years that it's hard to remember the little things that should factor into such a grade, and it's easy to forget the details as we just want to get on with our lives.

The pandemic emergency spanned the Trump and Biden administrations, and the two presidents' radically different communication styles are reflected in the pages that follow. For some, President Trump's prolific tweeting about the pandemic, extemporaneous and hyperbolic style, and fondness for talk show interviews brought comfort. For others, these brought distress.

Regardless, the words and actions of both presidents are a matter of public record. According to the nonpartisan organization Pew Research Center, from the beginning, Democrats and Republicans would have sharply different views on whether the virus was a major threat to the health of the US population and have sharply different views on how presidents Trump and Biden handled the crisis.

From my seat, I believe Washington fumbled its COVID-19 test and, in many ways, failed the American people. There's plenty of blame to go around and no shortage of lessons for the next crisis. At this point, *who* did what is less important than recognizing *where* we fell short and *how* we're gonna fix it.

But to do that we have to first preserve our national pandemic story, reflect on how the pandemic evolved, and reflect on how Washington and the American public responded. It's not a pretty picture. Don't look away.

2

RELAX—EVERYTHING'S TOTALLY UNDER CONTROL
(JANUARY 2020)

Washington didn't have things "totally under control" and allowed misinformation to metastasize, which eroded public trust when we needed it most.

The mark of a skilled investigator is the ability to spot the out-of-the-ordinary, to weigh the import of a matter at a moment in time, neither underreacting nor overreacting, but rather giving the matter its due care. This comes more naturally to especially intuitive investigators, but for most it's a skill that's honed by experience until they possess the renowned detective's hunch.

Spotting the out-of-the-ordinary is exponentially more challenging when your job is to search for clues in the petabytes of data on the World Wide Web. On December 31, 2019, an investigator in China—who happened to be one of the 8,000+ public health experts around the globe who work in the United Nation's World Health Organization—had a hunch after coming across a media statement on the website of the Wuhan Municipal Health Commission. The commission's statement referred to cases of "viral pneumonia" in the city of Wuhan, the capital of Hubei Province with a population of 11 million.

At that point, the WHO may have been excused for missing the import of this web posting given that only about twenty-five people out of 11 million were reportedly ill, but the Chinese health officials undoubtedly viewed the news through the lens of the 2003 outbreak of severe acute respiratory syndrome, or SARS.

Around the same time, the WHO's Epidemic Intelligence from Open Sources (EIOS) platform also flagged a Chinese media report about the same cluster of cases. EIOS is a web-based system used by public health officials around the globe, and word spread fast about the Wuhan cluster.

Every day, EIOS gobbles up hundreds of thousands of open-source reports and articles to identify unusual information that machines and humans use to detect and assess emerging threats to public health. Once the Wuhan cluster was identified on EIOS, several health authorities from around the world immediately contacted the WHO seeking additional information.

Robert Redfield, MD, the director of the US Centers for Disease Control and Prevention (CDC), was contacted by his Chinese counterpart on December 31 and told about the cluster of "27 cases of unknown etiology." Dr. Redfield subsequently reported up the chain to Alex Azar, secretary of the US Department of Health and Human Services (HHS), who alerted the White House's National Security Council.

That's the public story of how our government first learned of the mysterious respiratory illness officially named by WHO originally as 2019 novel coronavirus and the virus itself that causes coronavirus as SARS-CoV-2 (severe acute respiratory syndrome coronavirus 2). We now refer to the illness simply as COVID-19. In the span of two years, the virus would cause the death of over one million Americans, cost the American taxpayer over $5 trillion, precipitate a public trust crisis involving historic levels of fraud, and be weaponized to foment disharmony among family and friends.

2020 was an awful year right from the start.

On New Year's Day 2020, WHO officials requested additional information from Chinese health authorities on the Wuhan cluster, and the WHO activated its incident management support team just to be safe. The next day, January 2, having not received a response, the WHO notified world public health officials through its Global Outbreak Alert and Response Network. By January 3, there were forty-five identified cases, and Chinese officials suspected these cases were connected to the Huanan Seafood Wholesale Market, a large seafood and live animal market, which suggested animal to human spread. Later, in 2023, a team of global scientists announced their research narrowing the culprit down to raccoon dogs, who interestingly enough are neither raccoons nor dogs, but are closer to foxes and raised for their fur.

Three years after the fact and with theories abound about whether COVID originated from a Chinese lab, President Biden would sign a bill with rare unanimous support from Congress to declassify intelligence on the origins of COVID-19.

An apt reflection on the cultural significance of social media, on January 4, 2020, the WHO notified the world about COVID-19 via Twitter with a tweet:

> #China has reported to WHO a cluster of #pneumonia cases—with no deaths—in Wuhan, Hubei Province. Investigations are underway to identify the cause of this illness.

Chinese media later reported the first-known COVID-19 death on January 11, a man who was a regular at the market. I didn't see the WHO tweet or read about the first death. Much of the news was dominated by the historic Trump impeachment trial in the US Senate.

On January 17, the CDC began screening air passengers at JFK International, Los Angeles International, and San Francisco International. At that time, public health officials were referring to the virus by the original clunky name 2019 novel coronavirus.

I recall seeing news reports about the first COVID case in the US, in Washington state, which was reported on January 21. I also recall trying to wrap my head around why the Chinese government would lock down the 11 million inhabitants of Wuhan on January 23 if there were only a handful of cases. That certainly seemed out of the ordinary.

President Trump was either trying to reassure the nation or downplaying the seriousness of the public health threat, depending on your political views, in a January 22 interview with CNBC.

"We have it totally under control. It's one person coming in from China, and we have it under control. It's going to be just fine," Trump said.

The following Monday, during our office's regular weekly stand-up meeting, I made a passing reference to my staff about the new "bird flu" from China. I closed the meeting with a halfhearted reminder for staff to wash their hands.

$

I'd been a federal employee since 1994 and rose through the ranks. At some point in my later career, when people would casually ask during social encounters what I did for a living, I would usually just leave it at, "I work for the federal government." If they followed-up, I'd say I was a manager. I was proud of what I did, and I wasn't trying to be mysterious or coy. It was just that most people didn't really understand what I did for a living even after I explained. It was just easier to say federal manager and move along.

To those who were interested and persisted, I would explain that I was the inspector general at a small federal agency with a staff of about twenty-five auditors and investigators. We conducted independent audits of government programs and conducted criminal investigations of people and companies who were suspected of defrauding the government.

I had joined public service after three years as a private practice attorney, then spent twenty years as a criminal investigator, broadened my skills to auditing, and climbed the management rungs until being appointed an inspector general.

The inspectors general were relatively obscure government officials to many Americans until the fall of 2019 when it was reported that a White House whistleblower filed a complaint with the inspector general of the intelligence community, Michael Atkinson. The whistleblower alleged that in a July 2019 phone call, President Trump pressured Ukraine's newly elected (and largely unknown at the time) President-elect Volodymyr Zelenskyy to investigate his political opponent Joe Biden and his son Hunter as a quid pro quo for security assistance. You may remember Trump's line: "I would like you to do us a favor, though—"

Atkinson shared the whistleblower complaint with congressional intelligence committees, as he was required by law to do. The president then fired Atkinson stating that he no longer had confidence in him. This led to the president's impeachment for which Trump was later acquitted by the US Senate.

Atkinson, a reserved and unassuming former federal prosecutor, was in the news through the fall and winter of 2019 and 2020, and his name was frequently uttered by political commentators on cable news shows. The term *I-G* was more widely used in conversation and the role of the independent watchdogs was becoming more commonly understood.

There are about seventy-five federal IGs who conduct independent investigations and audits and otherwise keep watch at federal departments, agencies, and other federal organizations. In theory, an IG can't be fired for reporting bad news.

Before the pandemic, I would often say during public remarks and at professional conference panels that I had the best job in the federal government. From 2015 until my appointment as executive director for the Pandemic Response Accountability Committee or PRAC (pronounced *prac* like *rack*) on April 27, 2020, I was the independent watchdog at a federal government corporation, the Pension Benefit Guaranty Corporation.

The PBGC is in many ways run more like a business than a stodgy federal bureaucracy and has been recognized as a "best place to work" for small agencies. The PBGC's mission is simple: protecting and preserving the private pensions of 35 million American workers whose company or union fell on hard times. Imagine your own parent or grandparent working at the manufacturing plant for forty years, which has since been shuttered, leaving them without means of support, even though they contributed from every paycheck to their pension fund.

I remember reading in the news a few years prior about the closure of the Bethlehem Steel plant in Baltimore. It was once the largest steel mill in the world employing 30,000. What happened to those union steel workers who earlier in their careers had bargained away wage increases for enhanced retirement benefits? The federal government through the PBGC helped make sure retirees at least got something for all their years of hard work. As IG, I found this mission most appealing. Many PBGC pensioners live paycheck to paycheck. A disruption of their monthly annuity checks because of a pandemic or otherwise would be immediately felt.

There are hundreds of federal programs like pension insurance that are the safety net for tens of millions of Americans—who also happen to be our family members, friends, and neighbors. Established safety net programs are used during a crisis to quickly distribute aid to Americans in need.

I first learned the meaning of public service earlier in my career at the US Postal Service. It's also where I honed my skills as an investigator and was first steeped in the notion of public trust.

Probably every American has a vague understanding that the mission of the US Postal Service is to deliver the mail and provide Americans with trusted, safe, and reliable mail service. In 1994, after I graduated from law school and practiced law for a few years, I became a US postal inspector. At the time, the US Postal Inspection Service was unique among federal law enforcement agencies. Postal inspectors conduct criminal investigations involving illegal use of the mail, and the same postal inspectors then were also responsible for conducting audits to improve the efficiency of the mail system.

I'll admit the image of a badge-carrying, gun-toting auditor/criminal investigator could be confusing and perhaps unsettling to some people. Long before the federal IGs were created by statute in 1978, the Postal Inspection Service recognized the utility of combining auditing and investigations.

The auditing experience taught me how to tighten agency procedures and systems—what auditors call internal control—to improve operations and prevent cheats from stealing from government programs. The investigator experience taught me how to pull threads and follow leads to bring people to justice if they are able to get their hands on public money (or US mail).

Some years into my federal law enforcement career, Congress created a separate Postal Service Office of Inspector General to which I later transferred. During my postal years, I saw firsthand how the federal government touched the lives of Americans every day. The Postal Service is too often the butt of jokes and fodder for complaints. Many Americans are dependent on the federal government through the Postal Service. For many of our nation's seniors and veterans in rural America, for example, mail-order pharmacies are a matter of necessity, not convenience.

Federal agencies like the Postal Service would later play a key role in the federal pandemic response. While postal inspectors investigated pandemic-related fraud, the Postal Service helped keep commerce flowing with home deliveries during the shutdown and later delivered free COVID-19 test kits to American households. The Postal Service was considered essential government, so it couldn't shut down and let their employees just work from home. Indeed, the postman's famous motto could now be modified to read: Neither *pandemic*, nor snow, nor rain, nor heat, nor gloom of night would stay these couriers from the swift completion of their appointed rounds.

IGs across government would also play a critical role in the federal pandemic response, independently policing trillions of dollars in federal relief spending and the federal pandemic response.

No country in the world has an oversight system quite like ours and thank God we have it. Money, power, and politics can lead people (inside and outside of government) to do incredibly stupid, selfish, or sinister things. But there are some quirks and nuances to the IG business that aren't intuitive.

Inspectors general don't run government programs and are prohibited by law from participating in agency operations. An IG is under the "general supervision" of the head of the agency, but an IG is not part of agency management. The IG reports directly to Congress. IGs can't order an agency to do anything; all an IG can do is make recommendations for corrective action that agency management is generally free to accept or not.

The IG mantra, embodied in the law and written on the hearts of everyone in the IG community is this: prevent and detect fraud, waste, and abuse. It's a challenge to stop fraud at the source, you understand, when you're required to stay independent of the management chain.

The IG concept in America predates the formation of the United States. George Washington borrowed the concept from the French for use in the continental army. The commander needed someone whom he trusted to act as his objective eyes and ears and to tell him how prepared his troops and materiel were for warfare. Over time, IGs were created for the army and navy and the "inspection" function was expanded to include investigations.

We Americans have a gift for improving on the ideas of others (baseball, hamburgers, and democracy come to mind by way of England, Germany, and Greece, respectively), and following Watergate, Congress improved on the IG idea and created offices of inspectors general for the large federal departments. Congress combined independent inspection authority with the authority to conduct audits of agency programs and operations with law enforcement authority to conduct investigations. To ensure independence and objectivity, the offices of inspectors general (OIG) were given the right to access agency records, to issue subpoenas for documents, and to administer oaths to witnesses.

Over the years, Congress added more and more IGs to provide oversight of departments, agencies, commissions, and government corporations. OIG special agents generally have the same arrest authority over federal crimes involving their agency programs that FBI special agents have over federal crimes generally. The FBI can't do it all.

Inspectors general do not formally enjoy a lifetime appointment like federal judges who "hold their office during good behavior," but an IG can only be fired or "removed" as the act is politely referred to in the law, by the president. And only then after the president sends a letter to Congress thirty days in advance of removal. Such a letter would be a big deal in Washington.

In the forty-plus-year history of federal civilian inspectors general prior to 2020, this has only happened once. President Obama removed an IG of a small government corporation, and it made national news. Unfortunately, that IG was investigating a city mayor who was a known Obama supporter. According to contemporaneous public accounts, though, the president's decision had the support of both the Democratic corporation board chair and the Republican vice chair and was based solely on complaints about the IG's erratic behavior.

Bottom line, IGs are truth-telling accountability partners who transcend politics, elections, and public opinion.

Now you understand why, when people asked me what I did for a living, it was sometimes just easier to say "federal manager" and move along.

$

Notwithstanding the president's reassuring comments about having the virus totally under control, pandemic response escalated quickly in the last days of January. On January 29, the president established the White House Coronavirus Task Force, headed by HHS Secretary Azar. The next day, the World Health Organization declared a "public health emergency of international concern due to the widespread transmission of the virus." This prompted the US State Department to issue a travel advisory urging citizens not to travel to China. On January 31, Secretary Azar declared a public health emergency, and President Trump banned foreign travelers from China from entering our country.

A disruptive global pandemic wasn't a black swan that suddenly landed in the Lincoln Memorial Reflecting Pool. It's been a topic of conversation and study in Washington for decades. I recall it being a risk concern when I was detailed to work on a US Senate subcommittee in 2001 and 2002.

President Obama's National Security Council had created a sixty-nine-page pandemic playbook that they left behind for the Trump team. The playbook, which is now publicly available online, is officially titled the "Playbook for Early Response to High-Consequence Emerging Infectious Disease Threats and Biological Incidents." It stressed the need for unified messaging and contained "decision-making rubrics" that would make any bureaucrat proud.

A few months before we heard of COVID-19, the Johns Hopkins University Center for Health Security, the World Economic Forum, and the Bill & Melinda Gates Foundation held a global pandemic exercise in New York City. This security planning event, with its enigmatic name, Event 201, brought together senior business, government, and public health leaders from around the world in a table-top simulation exercise to highlight unresolved policy and economic issues in pandemic response and to make recommendations to help the world better prepare.

Later in May 2020, when the country was feeling the full force of COVID, Trump would tell the media outside the Oval Office: "I inherited nothing. I inherited practically nothing from the previous administration, unfortunately" in the way of pandemic preparation.

Later that day from the White House briefing room, Press Secretary Kayleigh McEnany dismissively held up a copy of the playbook, with handwritten notes scribbled on the cover and held together with a small black binder clip. She compared it to two black three-ring binders she held up for the press corps.

"Some have erroneously suggested that the Trump administration threw out the pandemic response playbook left by the Obama-Biden administration," McEnany said. "What the critics fail to note, however, is that this thin packet of paper was replaced by two detailed, robust pandemic response reports commissioned by the Trump administration."

Just as we were facing this burgeoning public health crisis, our nation was seeing a growing parallel crisis of public trust. The social media echo chamber, which amplify and weaponize misinformation and conspiracy theories, was turning its focus to science and public health officials. Public trust in government is low in normal times, and we were becoming as polarized as perhaps ever since the Civil War.

Public health was being politicized, and it was recognizable immediately. In fact, at the end of January, Facebook, now Meta, announced that it was taking significant action to prevent the spread of public health misinformation that was infecting its platforms. The social media giant announced that it would immediately start to remove "content with false claims or conspiracy theories that have been flagged by leading global health organizations and local health authorities that could cause harm to people who believe them." The Facebook announcement explained:

> We are doing this as an extension of our existing policies to remove content that could cause physical harm. We're focusing on claims that

are designed to discourage treatment or taking appropriate precautions. This includes claims related to false cures or prevention methods—like *drinking bleach* cures the coronavirus—or claims that create confusion about health resources that are available. We will also block or restrict hashtags used to spread misinformation on Instagram, and are conducting proactive sweeps to find and remove as much of this content as we can. (emphasis added)

Drinking bleach? Some Americans' distrust of government officials, including career public health officials, was already to the point where people were taking online medical advice from unknown strangers and drinking bleach to prevent getting the coronavirus.

Russia, China, and other adversaries were flooding the US and Europe with dangerous disinformation, including suggestions like drinking bleach to cure COVID. These bad actors would later use the same channels to undermine the public's faith in the efficacy of face masks and the safety of vaccines, according to the FBI, the US Department of Defense, and the intelligence agencies of some of our European allies.

One of the recommendations from the November 2019 Event 201 global pandemic exercise was this: Governments and the private sector should assign *a greater priority to developing methods to combat mis- and disinformation prior to the next pandemic response.* Rather than combat it, some political leaders did just the opposite. Knowingly or unwittingly, they gave aid and comfort to foreign enemies and domestic trolls by amplifying their messages.

The month of January 2020 closed with the Italian prime minister confirming the first two coronavirus cases in Italy. The *Washington Post* selected for one of its images of the week a picture of a masked and surging crowd outside a Philippines medical facility attempting to buy masks, after police raided the facility for hoarding and overpricing masks. Public fear was growing.

One of our sons, who recently graduated from college with his degree in nursing, got a job offer to work in the emergency room at a nearby hospital. He would start in mid-March. He would be our second hospital nurse in the family.

3

MIXED MESSAGES FROM WASHINGTON
(FEBRUARY 2020)

Mixed messages from Washington leave Americans worrying whether COVID-19 will be a "very bad cold" or cause a global economic meltdown—and whether they should cancel their scheduled cruise. The coronavirus gets an official name, and wearing face masks becomes political.

During his February 4, 2020, State of the Union address, President Trump briefly mentioned the coronavirus about halfway through his speech. He noted that the administration was coordinating with the Chinese government and would take all necessary steps to safeguard our citizens from this threat.

House Speaker Nancy Pelosi was dressed in white along with other Democratic congresswomen to commemorate the 100-year anniversary of the passage of the Nineteenth Amendment, which gave women the right to vote and to express support for an equal rights amendment.

At the conclusion of the president's address, Speaker Pelosi rose to her feet as custom, and while standing next to an applauding Vice President Mike Pence on the dais, she dramatically tore in half her copy of the president's State of the Union address. Depending on your views, it was a supremely disrespectful act or a boss move. The move unquestionably symbolized how divided we were at a time when the COVID crisis was about to engulf the nation.

I kicked off the next week at work leading a large meeting with our new outside auditors, a Big Four accounting firm. One of an inspector general's typical responsibilities is to oversee the annual audit of the agency's financial statements. In 2020, we changed auditors after awarding the audit contract to a different public accounting firm. This was our first group meeting, and the firm brought a large group of auditors to meet our team.

In conjunction with the annual financial statement audit, the auditors also look at what are called "improper payments," or government payments that should not have been paid or were paid in the wrong amount. This can happen for many reasons, including fraud or administrative error.

Federal agencies are generally required to include in their annual report the percentage of payments they believe were improper. In 2019, before the pandemic, the federal government estimated that it made $175 billion in improper payments across all federal programs. That's an important number to keep in mind.

In addition to generally supervising the annual agency financial statement audit, inspectors general are fundamentally in the business of *payment integrity* to help ensure the agency is paying the correct amounts to the right people, *program integrity* to help ensure federal programs are working the way they are supposed to work and outsiders aren't stealing federal money, and *personnel integrity* to help ensure senior leadership, federal employees, contractors, and grantees are obeying the law and acting in the government's best interests and holding them accountable when necessary.

At 6:00 p.m. on Monday of the first week of February, I got an out-of-the-ordinary phone call from my head of investigations regarding an employee integrity matter. He called to let me know that he and his FBI special agent partner just got a confession from one of our investigative subjects. This subject happened to be our agency's head of contracting.

This guy, who I'll call Jim, oversaw $350 million a year in Pension Benefit Guaranty Corporation contracting. This was a big case and would likely be major news. I had a vague recollection of only one other case of this magnitude happening in the federal government in my career and that was several years ago. While Office of Inspector General (OIG) special agents and FBI special agents regularly catch federal contracting officials engaging in various misdeeds, including some big dollar cases, rarely does it involve someone who was the head of contracting for the agency.

We had received a confidential complaint about Jim a year prior, alleging that he had possibly steered a contract to a college friend. We were covertly working the investigation with the FBI and a federal prosecutor. We had hit a dead end in the search for evidence, but by February the team had enough information to confront Jim. They showed up at his home unannounced, ringing his doorbell one evening after work for a voluntary interview.

It was over. Jim was caught off guard, and like many in his predicament, he was relieved to finally unburden himself and admit what he had done. As Jim admitted to the agents, he helped a company get a government contract by tailoring the contract requirements to the company and giving them nonpublic information and pricing guidance. The contract was for $500,000, but Jim later modified it to $3.3 million. For all his misdeeds, Jim received $48,000 in cash, silver coins, ammunition, and a rifle scope.

In federal white-collar investigations, agents typically don't immediately arrest the subject on the spot. That only happens in TV shows that need to wrap up loose ends by the end of the episode. Federal prosecutors often prefer to take their time and methodically prepare their case. These kinds of criminal subjects often receive a target letter from the US Attorney's Office, strongly suggesting that they retain a lawyer and contact the prosecutors to arrange a meeting to review the evidence and discuss a possible guilty plea.

As it turned out, Jim's court case would ultimately be delayed due to the pandemic. Federal courts were shut down for months for all but violent crimes and other emergencies to reduce exposure. This affected hundreds of criminal prosecutions around the country that were in the pipeline. The pandemic also meant that federal investigators suddenly had to find new ways to work white-collar investigations, maintaining social distancing where possible. By the time federal district courts reopened, they were flooded with new pandemic-related fraud cases. Federal investigators were deluged with pandemic fraud complaints to investigate in addition to the routine Jim-type cases.

Jim pled guilty in May 2020 and was later sentenced to a period of home detention followed by supervised probation—both proceedings done via Zoom. At that point, we were all still under home detention, so it wasn't much of a penalty. I have to believe the lenient sentence given by the judge was likely due to COVID cases spiking in our nation's prisons, where social distancing isn't feasible.

I know the issue of prisoner health and safety during COVID was top of mind for Justice Department inspector general Michael Horowitz, who had his staff conduct a nationwide survey in April to determine how federal inmates and Bureau of Prison staff were being protected. His office would later create a website dashboard so loved ones of inmates and the public could monitor the number of COVID cases, deaths, and vaccination rates in our nation's federal prisons. This dashboard was a fine example of what we would later brand and promote as agile oversight.

With the pandemic raging, Jim's case barely registered in the local news. In a bizarre twist, the federal contractor who bribed Jim was not only convicted of conspiracy to commit bribery of a public official, but also subsequently charged with fraud after misusing pandemic loan funds to pay his defense attorney.

$

On February 11, from the World Health Organization's head-quarters in Geneva, Switzerland, the WHO director-general announced that the coronavirus had a new official name: COVID-19.

"Having a name matters to prevent the use of other names that can be inaccurate or stigmatizing," the WHO director-general said. "It also gives us a standard format to use for any future coronavirus outbreaks."

During a television interview with Geraldo Rivera that night, President Trump said, "In our country, we only have, basically, twelve cases and most of those people are recovering and some cases fully recovered. So it's actually less."

The next day I flew to Tallahassee to speak at a fraud conference and share our experiences in protecting pensioners from identity fraud and detecting retirement account takeovers. The pandemic would later spawn a secondary epidemic: identity fraud involving public benefits.

My eighty-three-year-old mother, who more closely followed current events, nagged me before the trip that I really should think about wearing a face mask on the plane. I'll admit to searching for masks on Amazon before shrugging off the idea as too extreme and continuing with my uneventful trip.

At the conference I shared some lessons learned from our investigations and audits that found a few contractors working in the agency's customer service office who were stealing pensioners' personal information. Our office helped the agency tighten up its practices to reduce this risk that agency insiders could cause harm. We made a couple of arrests. Our auditors recommended that the agency strengthen pre-employment background checks on contractors, limit the computer files they could access, and secure paper printouts that contained pensioners' personal information and shred them when no longer needed.

When I returned from my trip, I called Mom and defiantly reported back that of all the people I saw from DC's Reagan National Airport to the Tallahassee airport and back, I saw exactly one person wearing a mask.

News reporting in February 2020 on the potential health and economic impact of COVID-19 was all over the place. One CNN report quoted a professor of pathology at the University of Hong Kong who predicted that "this is just going to be like SARS and the world is going to get basically a very bad cold for about five months." While another CNN report warned that "things are looking to be much different with the coronavirus. The global economy remains fragile and an extended outbreak could tip the current aging business cycle into a global recession, right when US markets are seeing some of their highest valuations in history."

One headline asked, "Is the coronavirus peaking? Investors are hopeful," noting that the S&P 500 climbed .9 percent. Another headline declared, "The coronavirus is already hurting the world economy. Here's why it could get really scary."

The world economy was different from the one that existed during the 2003 SARS outbreak. Much of the world now was dependent on Chinese manufacturing (think iPhones and auto parts), and the coronavirus was already causing supply chain disruptions that would soon be felt across the world. If parts of the country shut down like Wuhan, then Americans would not be traveling on airplanes, staying in city hotels, attending conferences, or eating in restaurants they found on Yelp.

Cruise ships became a focus of attention. One February 2020 CNN headline is especially cringy with the benefit of hindsight: "Why it's still OK to take a cruise amid the coronavirus outbreak." The article quoted an infectious disease and travel medicine specialist at the University of Washington School of Medicine who said, "I think there's extremely low risk of getting novel coronavirus on a cruise ship." The next day, *Time* magazine ran a story on the *Diamond Princess* cruise ship under the headline: "This Cruise Ship Has the Highest COVID-19 Infection Rate in the World."

On February 24, the Trump administration's budget director sent a letter to Congress requesting $1.25 billion in emergency funding acknowledging "additional Federal resources are necessary to take steps to prepare for a potential worsening of the situation in the United States."

Masks became political by the end of February 2020. Perplexing messaging from the government didn't help matters. On February 27, the CDC tweeted:

> CDC does not currently recommend the use of facemasks to help prevent novel #coronavirus. Take everyday preventive actions, like staying home when you are sick and washing hands with soap and water, to help slow the spread of respiratory illness.

The US Surgeon General took a different tone with a tweet he later deleted:

> Seriously people—STOP BUYING MASKS! They are NOT effective in preventing general public from catching #Coronavirus, but if healthcare providers can't get them to care for sick patients, it puts them and our communities at risk!

By the end of February, though, at least one federal health official was trying to cut through the noise and was using dire language typically reserved on the East Coast for hurricane warnings. In a CDC briefing, Nancy Messonnier, MD, who served as the incident manager for the federal COVID-19 response, told Americans to brace for impact of COVID-19.

In stark language Dr. Messonnier warned, "Disruption to everyday life may be severe . . . Schools might have to close, conferences could be canceled, businesses might make employees work from home." She had told her own children, she said, to prepare for "significant disruption to our lives."

As we closed out February, there were still no cases reported where I lived in Montgomery County, Maryland, and our county health officer reported that the risk to the general public remained low.

4

DON'T PANIC, BUT WE'LL NEED TO SHUT DOWN THE COUNTRY
(MARCH 2020)

A panicked nation looks to the White House for reassurance after grocery stores run out of basic necessities, the NBA suspends its season, and Tom Hanks tests positive for COVID. The president declares a national state of emergency and orders a 15 Days to Slow the Spread shutdown. Governors are left scrambling for ventilators, Domino's Pizza launches contactless delivery, and Congress authorizes the largest emergency aid package in US history.

In the opening days of March, Congress authorized over $8 billion for emergency COVID-19 spending, more than six times the administration's request. All Senators, Republicans and Democrats, voted in favor of the legislation except for Kentucky Senator Rand Paul. In a speech on the Senate floor, Senator Paul said, "I think we should not let fear or urgency cause us to lose our minds and cause us to act in an irresponsible fashion." On the House of Representatives side of the Capitol, Representative Matt Gaetz tweeted out a picture of himself wearing a gas mask, which he wore on the House floor as he cast his vote on the legislation. The image went viral.

At the office, my comments to staff about COVID-19 were developing a hardening edge, reflecting the increasing seriousness of the situation. Things started hitting close to home, at least for me, on the weekend of March 7 and 8.

Over that weekend, the media reported that the Italian government was considering a lockdown of Lombardy and other northern provinces to combat the virus, New York was reporting eighty-nine cases, and public health officials reported one of the first DC-area–related cases. The DC-area case involved an individual who attended the widely attended Conservative Political Action Conference at the Gaylord Resort at the National Harbor in Maryland.

Then the first case involving a DC-area resident was confirmed. A rector at Christ Church Georgetown was hospitalized and tested positive for coronavirus. Hundreds who attended services at the church were asked to self-quarantine for two weeks. I saw all this on the cable news chyrons against the background of footage from Lombardy. Masked uniformed police stopping citizens and panicked and masked travelers racing through train stations hoping to catch a train to outrun the virus and the shutdown.

March 11, 2020, in fact, may well mark the date the foreign virus became an American reality.

Many of us looked past news reports of the first US case on January 21, the first US death on February 29, the *Diamond Princess* cruise ship being quarantined in the Port of Yokohama, Japan, and even the lockdown of the Lombardy region of Italy. But it was on Wednesday, March 11, that COVID-19 hit home. ESPN and NPR called it "The Day that Changed Everything." At the time, there were six known COVID deaths in the US.

Early in the afternoon, after the mayor of San Francisco banned gatherings over 1,000 people in the city, the NBA Golden State Warriors announced the decision to play their scheduled March 12 game against the Brooklyn Nets without fans in attendance. Later that day, Tom Hanks posted a purposefully unglamorous and unfiltered picture of himself and his wife, Rita Wilson, from Australia. "Hello folks. @ ritawilson and I want to thank everyone here Down Under who are taking such good care of us. We have Covid-19 and are in isolation so we do not spread it to anyone else . . . Remember, despite all the current events, there is no crying in baseball. Hanx." The post was liked by 3 million.

That night, in Oklahoma City, the NBA's Thunder were set to tip off against the Utah Jazz. After warm-ups and as the game was about to start, the two coaches met the referees at half court to announce they were canceling the game. Jazz center Rudy Gobert had tested positive, and the crowd was sent home. Within the hour, the NBA announced they were suspending the 2020–2021 season.

"The NBA is suspending game play following the conclusion of [Wednesday's] schedule of games until further notice," the league said in a statement. "The NBA will use this hiatus to determine next steps for moving forward in regard to the coronavirus pandemic."

On the same day, the World Health Organization declared COVID-19 a global pandemic. In his accompanying remarks, the WHO director-general said, "We have never before seen a pandemic sparked by a coronavirus. This is the first pandemic caused by a coronavirus. And we have never before seen a pandemic that can be controlled, at the same time. WHO has been in full response mode since we were notified of the first cases. And we have called every day for countries to take urgent and aggressive action. We have rung the alarm bell loud and clear."

At 5:30 p.m. that Wednesday evening, I emailed our staff to announce that our physical office would be closed on Thursday with mandatory telework so we could test our COVID preparedness and response plan. Events escalated quickly in the DC-Maryland-Virginia region on Thursday, and after the Maryland governor announced steps to protect the health of Marylanders like shutting restaurants and bars, I sent an emergency notification to all staff ordering full-time telework for all staff beginning on March 13 and until further notice.

This was the day that changed work life perhaps forever.

On March 12, Montgomery County, Maryland, which had reported its first COVID case on March 4, announced the closure of libraries, parks, and recreation centers. County employees were ordered to telework beginning on March 16. Our local public school system announced that schools would be closed from March 16 to March 27. Hard-copy school materials would be made available, and the school system had set up food pickup sites for those dependent on free and reduced priced meals.

That first COVID case in our county was diagnosed at the hospital where our daughter worked as a nurse. Within a few weeks COVID testing tents would be set up outside the emergency room of her hospital, and we worried every shift whether her unit had enough personal protective equipment we all came to know as PPE to keep her safe.

Meanwhile, it was business as usual at the New York MTA, which runs the city's subway and buses. The MTA even had a little fun acknowledging the misinformation on social media. The MTA tweeted that they were running regular weekday service: "If that changes, WE will let you know. And it won't be a screenshot of a random text forwarded to you from your cousin."

Not all our staff were welcoming of mandatory remote work. While all appreciated the efforts to keep them safe, some were apprehensive about telework not being a choice but a mandate, and whether their home had an appropriate quiet place to conduct business. Some staff—like millions of parents across the nation—had school-age kids at home and were wondering how they could work from their dining room table. For some, the true extroverts, the inability to socialize in person with colleagues was disquieting.

On Friday, March 13, President Trump declared a national emergency. Earlier in the day he had tweeted his thanks to the cruise industry for voluntarily suspending operations, and the president commented on the cruise and travel industries in his press conference.

"I can tell you it's an industry that was very badly impacted by what's going on with the virus, and it's a great industry, it's a very important industry," Trump said. "And we will be helping them and we will be helping the airline industry if we have to, assuming we have to."

That weekend was chaos.

In Midland, Texas, a Burmese father was shopping at a Sam's Club with two children, ages six and two. A twenty-one-year-old man followed the family into the store. The man picked up a serrated steak knife and bent the blade so it was resting across his knuckles facing out. He then punched the father in the face, cutting him with the knife blade. He fled the store only to return a few moments later. This time the man picked up an eight-inch knife and went after the two children who were seated in the shopping cart. He cut the six-year-old millimeters from the boy's right eye; the cut wrapped around to the back of the child's skull.

"Get out of America!" he yelled as he was pinned down. The man told police officers that the father and his kids were Chinese and were responsible for spreading COVID. He was later sentenced to twenty-five years imprisonment for the brutal and senseless attack.

The president's senior advisers were on the Sunday talk shows. On *Fox News Sunday*, Treasury Secretary Steven Mnuchin said the administration would be working with Congress on a "significant but not huge" coronavirus aid package. They would focus on small businesses with under 500 employees and hard-hit segments like the cruise, airline, and hotel industries. Larry Kudlow, director of the White House National Economic Council, was on *Face the Nation* where he stressed that the bill would be "helping families and middle income and blue-collar type folks."

From both a personal and professional perspective, it felt like we were preparing for a hurricane to make landfall. On Sunday, March 15, I wrote in my daybook:

> It's Sunday night and the calm before the
> storm. NYC public schools canceled classes
> and St. Patty's parades and bars are closed.
> News is breaking almost by the hour. CDC is

recommending no groups of 50 and preventing contact with vulnerable populations. We are 100% telework and there is talk among Fauci and others that we may be facing a 2-month shutdown. Are we ready? . . . As long as the supermarkets and pharmacies stay open we're good. The Fed announced today a cut in interest rates to zero and a $700 billion [quantitative easing program]. These actions are being matched by other central banks . . . clearly concerned about a financial meltdown. Images on the news of long lines at gun shops . . .

One of our middle sons had started his new job that Monday morning as a nurse at a county hospital. He would begin his nursing career in emergency department medicine just as the pandemic hit our region. He was a pandemic ED nurse.

At my work, Monday came, and our staff connected for our regularly scheduled Monday stand-up meeting via Skype from our homes. It was awkward, but we were connected. We were all experiencing this shutdown together, and I was relieved that we prepared to hunker down together for the storm. And just like snow-related government shutdowns in Washington, I wanted to make sure that the work continued apace. First order of business: we needed to find our rhythm. I was pleased that despite the upheaval in the nation and our work environment, our team managed to issue an audit report by the end of the week. Remote work would have no effect on our productivity.

Ventilators became a political football. On a conference call with a group of governors, President Trump told the governors that they should not wait for the federal government.

"Respirators, ventilators, all of the equipment—try getting it yourselves," Trump told the governors during the conference call. "We will be backing you, but try getting it yourselves. Point of sales, much better, much more direct if you can get it yourself." This turned into acrimonious snipping between the president and the Democratic governors of New York and Michigan.

Later that day, March 16, President Trump and the White House Coronavirus Task Force issued new guidelines branded as "15 Days to Slow the Spread." The guidance urged Americans to work from home whenever possible, to avoid restaurants and bars, and avoid discretionary travel to places like shopping malls or for social visits. It wasn't technically a national shutdown, but it was close.

The Dow Jones responded with the largest point drop in history.

On Tuesday, March 17, the Administration proposed a $1 trillion stimulus bill. Treasury Secretary Mnuchin warned Congress that the unemployment rate could reach 20 percent if Congress didn't act. The unemployment rate at the height of the Great Depression was 24.9 percent.

"Americans need cash now," Secretary Mnuchin said during a White House press briefing. "I mean now in the next two weeks."

President Trump ordered the US Navy hospital ship USNS *Comfort* to New York to serve as a temporary overflow hospital for the anticipated surge in cases. The USNS *Mercy* was dispatched to Los Angeles.

Restaurants across America either shut down or pivoted to a new delivery model called curbside pickup. Even Domino's Pizza pivoted to protect their drivers and sales revenue. Beginning on March 17, Domino's switched to "zero contact delivery," which later became contactless delivery. In other words, the Domino's driver would ring your doorbell and leave the pizza on your front steps. We occasionally ordered Domino's through the pandemic years, and we had one driver who consistently announced his delivery by banging on the door like a Deputy US Marshal serving a fugitive warrant. We always gave a nice tip, so it wasn't that.

On Thursday, March 19, California's Democratic Governor Gavin Newsom took the extraordinary step of issuing a statewide shelter-in-place order. He would be the first governor to do so, but Republican Governor of Ohio Mike DeWine would follow suit a few days later. In the weeks that followed, forty-three governors issued orders directing residents to stay at home and nonessential businesses to close. Minimum-wage grocery store workers, like the kid from the neighborhood who works as a part-time cashier, were suddenly considered "essential workers."

On Saturday, March 21, senior adviser to the president, Jared Kushner, met with a bipartisan group of Silicon Valley entrepreneurs, business executives, and venture capitalists in the White House Situation Room. The meeting was convened to discuss the need for medical equipment and supplies. According to a later *Vanity Fair* report based on first-person accounts from more than one attendee, some in the group were stunned with what they heard.

According to these witnesses, Kushner told the group, "Cuomo didn't pound the phones hard enough to get PPE for his state . . . His people are going to suffer and that's their problem." Kushner explained, "The federal government is not going to lead this response. It's up to the states to figure out what they want to do," and "Free markets will solve this. That is not the role of government."

In my experience, this is exactly the role of the federal government in the time of crisis. I have yet to see a disaster strike a community, district, or state where the political leaders of the area affected did not universally expect the federal government to take a dominant role and help its citizens. This is true whether you're talking about tornadoes in Kansas, hurricanes in Florida, or train derailments in Ohio.

It was not clear initially how long the federal government would be working from home or whether there would be more strict restrictions. On Sunday night, March 22, President Trump tweeted in all caps:

> WE CANNOT LET THE CURE BE WORSE THAN THE PROBLEM ITSELF. AT THE END OF THE 15 DAY PERIOD, WE WILL MAKE A DECISION AS TO WHICH WAY WE WANT TO GO!

I was stunned enough by a Representative Liz Cheney tweet later on Tuesday, March 24, that I took a screenshot.

> There will be no normally functioning economy, if our hospitals are overwhelmed and thousands of Americans of all ages, including doctors and nurses, lay dying because we have failed to do what is necessary to stop the virus.

The "no normally functioning economy" sounded dire, but as a father of two hospital nurses, I found the dark "lay dying" comment more personally distressing.

Things were starting to look grim in places like New York, especially in nursing homes. Based on news reports, New Jersey and Florida seemed right behind. We worried about my father-in-law, a retired police officer and former Marine and Vietnam vet who now lives out his days in the veterans' home in southern Maryland. Alzheimer's had robbed him of his swagger.

Before the pandemic, we'd stop at Dunkin' Donuts on the way to visit him and pick up a chocolate-covered donut and his favorite coffee: large with cream and three sugars. Even in his current condition, that former beat cop had a wicked sweet tooth and could down some coffee. Pandemic visitor restrictions put a pause to that for him and the millions of Americans in our nation's nursing homes.

In the best of times, the American public health system is challenged to provide adequate and equitable care and treatment for our citizens. The pandemic would soon lay bare the many gaps in our nation's healthcare system. It would disproportionately impact our most vulnerable family and friends, especially the elderly in assisted living facilities.

A later audit by the Health and Human Services Office of Inspector General found that a large percentage of nursing homes (twenty-three of the twenty-four in their sample) were not complying with federal requirements for COVID infection prevention and control. A separate audit from that office would be bluntly titled: "COVID-19 Had a Devastating Impact on Medicare Beneficiaries in Nursing Homes During 2020."

Hard-hit states like New York and Connecticut were still scrambling for personal protective equipment and ventilators. On March 26, the president called in to the *Hannity* show and told the host, "I don't believe you need 40,000 or 30,000 ventilators," disputing the claims of state officials. "You know, you go into major hospitals sometimes they'll have two ventilators, and now all of a sudden they're saying, 'Can we order 30,000 ventilators?'"

The president went on to explain the challenges with manufacturing ventilators.

"When you talk about ventilators, that's sort of like buying a car," he said. "It's very expensive. It's a very intricate piece of equipment. The good ones are very, very expensive."

Just how chaotic, desperate, and uncertain things were hit me later that night, as I lay in bed in the quiet of the night recalling my trip earlier that day to the grocery store.

On March 26, the day before the $2 trillion CARES Act was signed into law, while the news was reporting a possible 20 percent unemployment rate, I went to the Weis Markets grocery in town to pick up a few things. First, I surveyed the stockpile of supplies that had temporarily taken over our living room. My wife had been preparing us for the past couple of weeks, with regular grocery runs yielding just a few more bags of diapers and wipes for the grandsons; and tuna, peanut butter, coffee pods, and toilet paper for the rest of us. She would have made FEMA proud, threading the needle between prepared citizen and irrational hoarder. But I had a foreboding that COVID-19 would significantly affect our lives in the weeks to come and went to the store to pick up some extras.

As I was making my way into the store, I noticed new tape on the floor, marking every six feet for social distancing. As I wheeled my cart around, I was stopped cold, in the face of empty shelves that stretched from the checkout to the back of the store. My eyes widened as my mind registered that never in my fifty-plus years as an American had I faced such a lack of basic necessities. It took my breath away.

I've seen plenty of bare shelves before snowstorms and hurricanes, but this was different. "All eggs, limit 1," read one sign hanging on an empty shelf. I then saw a familiar face, a longtime casual friend who worked at the store. We were both wearing face masks. Mine was royal blue, fashioned out of an impossibly thick cotton weave, and handsewn by some woman in Ohio who took to selling masks on Etsy to capitalize on the Amazon backorder. I leaned in to my friend and asked in a conspiratorial tone when they expected the delivery trucks. Her body stiffened straight as she held up her hands, "Six feet please!"

The next morning, I awoke early to be at Walmart, the paragon of global supply chain management, when it opened at 7:00 a.m.

"It runs out within twenty minutes after it hits the shelves," the associate ruefully said to me as I stared at empty shelves, "and even we don't know when the trucks are coming or what they're bringing us."

I apparently was not alone on March 27, 2020, sensing the chaos, frenzy, and dread.

Later that day, President Trump signed into law one of the largest emergency aid packages in US history. The 300+ page piece of legislation was called the Coronavirus Aid, Relief, and Economic Security Act, or CARES Act, and it passed by voice vote in the House and unanimously in the Senate. The bill—which had a legislative gestation period of about seven days from introduction to passage—authorized about $2 trillion in pandemic relief spending.

The CARES Act included some independent oversight and accountability mechanisms to protect tax dollars from fraud and waste. The act created the Pandemic Response Accountability Committee, a new congressional oversight commission, and a new special inspector general for pandemic recovery with a confusing and overly broad name to oversee a specific pot of pandemic relief money for banks and lenders.

In a signing statement separately accompanying the bill, President Trump ominously wrote that he would not allow the new special inspector general for pandemic recovery, insisted upon by Democratic lawmakers, to issue pandemic oversight reports to Congress "without presidential supervision."

What I found interesting (and I was not alone in this observation) was that the president only mentioned the new special inspector general for pandemic recovery and not the Pandemic Response Accountability Committee. Some thought this may have just been an oversight by the White House and that the president intended to limit both oversight offices. Within a week, President Trump announced his intention to nominate Brian Miller to the special IG position.

Miller was a former IG who at the time of this nomination was serving as special assistant to the president and senior associate counsel in the Office of White House Counsel. I knew him from his previous role as IG at the General Services Administration, and he did good work.

In 2012, for example, his office was responsible for one of the most viral pictures in the history of government waste investigations. The picture was of a shirtless senior GSA official luxuriating in a Las Vegas resort hot tub with a glass of red wine. These were the perks for arranging lavish and wasteful government conferences in Las Vegas. For months, the picture was all over Capitol Hill and the national news. The official eventually pled guilty to lying to investigators, and the OIG investigation changed the rules on federal government conferences.

Given his current role, though, you can imagine how Miller's nomination was received by opponents on Capitol Hill. In any event, at that moment in time, the president's signing statement and his intention to nominate Miller as special IG for pandemic recovery meant nothing to me. I was occupied and content with running my small office and keeping our home stocked with groceries and necessary provisions.

The ink wasn't even dry on the CARES Act before a fifty-year-old California mother and her son—who happened to be incarcerated for murder and on death row in San Quentin State Prison—saw an opportunity to make a fast buck. In what may have been one of the first pandemic fraud schemes in the nation, the mother and son conspired in March to file bogus claims for the $1,200 Economic Impact Payments, or CARES Act stimulus checks, that the Internal Revenue Service was sending to all eligible individuals.

According to charging documents, in March, the son texted his mom the personal information of fellow prisoners, and the mom used this information to file fraudulent claims. In April, the son coordinated with an unknown individual to email a spreadsheet containing the personal identities of over 9,000 individuals. Between May and June, the mom filed over 100 claims for stimulus checks on the IRS's online portal.

On March 29, President Trump announced Project Air-bridge, to be led by his son-in-law and adviser, Jared Kushner. For weeks, states had been bidding against each other and the federal government for personal protective equipment, driving up prices. There was not enough to go around, and the *US News & World Report* called the situation a "global jungle" for PPE.

Through FEMA, the federal government would pay the expedited shipping costs incurred by six US companies to fly in personal protective equipment they purchased from China. In exchange, these companies were supposed to sell 50 percent of the PPE to prioritized healthcare facilities in designated COVID hot spots. Project Airbridge promised to cut shipping time from up to forty days by sea to around three days by air. The first flight from Shanghai to New York brought 80 tons of PPE.

The next day, Maryland Republican Governor Larry Hogan, who also served as chairman of the National Governors Association, shut down our state.

I was startled at 3:04 p.m. when the governor's emergency public safety alert was pushed to my phone.

"This is a deadly public health crisis—we are no longer asking or suggesting that Marylanders stay home, we are directing them to do so," said Governor Hogan. "No Maryland resident should be leaving their home unless it is for an essential job or for an essential reason such as obtaining food or medicine, seeking urgent medical attention, or for other necessary purposes."

The month of March ended with breaking news about a COVID outbreak on the aircraft carrier USS *Theodore Roosevelt*, which was on deployment in the Pacific Ocean. The ship's captain sent an email up the chain of command after 100 sailors tested positive. The captain's email warned that social distancing was not possible, and he requested that all nonessential sailors be evacuated. The request was denied and the email was leaked to the press.

Captain Crozier was later relieved of command, and the news showed the video of his sailors swarming him and chanting as he disembarked the carrier for the last time: "Cap-tain, Cro-zier! Cap-tain, Cro-zier!"

The invisible COVID-19 was everywhere and impacting everything and soon we were literally at each other's throats.

PART II

5

"THE ROUGHEST TWO OR THREE WEEKS WE'VE EVER HAD IN OUR COUNTRY"
(EARLY APRIL 2020)

The watchdogs begin to bark, alerting Washington and the American people to trouble. The president warns Americans to brace for "one of the roughest two or three weeks we've ever had in our country." The Small Business Administration starts disbursing small business pandemic loans seven days after passage of the CARES Act and quickly blows through $349 billion. The job market craters, and a new independent office, the Pandemic Response Accountability Committee, begins coordinating pandemic oversight across government.

very night at exactly 7:00 p.m., New York City residents across all five boroughs would open their windows and clap to salute healthcare workers who risked their lives, many of whom were working without sufficient personal protective equipment. Beyoncé, Lady Gaga, and other celebrities came together for a globally broadcast event, *One World: Together at Home*. Co-host Stephen Colbert told the global audience they weren't asking for donations. This event was to pay tribute to healthcare workers and other essential workers who were putting their lives on the line. The Rolling Stones played virtually from four socially distant and separate locations.

As of April 1, about 1,000 Americans had lost their lives to COVID-19. By the end of the month, this number would grow to over 66,000. Deborah Birx, MD, the White House coronavirus coordinator, briefed the American people on the latest models. The best-case scenario showed that the US might experience as many as 240,000 deaths. If we didn't take preventive measures, the models projected we could lose up to 2 million Americans. President Trump warned us to brace for a "hell of a bad two weeks . . . This is going to be one of the roughest two or three weeks we've ever had in our country."

The northeast region was particularly hard hit, especially New York where city morgues and funeral homes ran out of space for the dead awaiting burial or cremation. New York City police officers found a U-Haul truck outside a Brooklyn funeral home with dozens of bodies stacked inside.

New York Governor Andrew Cuomo was holding daily press conferences, which were televised nationally. Cuomo offered a calm and reassuring voice. The governor was in charge, and he had the right people at the table with just the right amount of content on PowerPoint slides behind him to emphasize key points.

When the governor's little brother, Chris Cuomo of *CNN News*, got sick with COVID-19, the governor had him on via Zoom and the two playfully bantered and carried on for viewers. Even though the New York information was of little immediate relevance to me as a Marylander, I tuned in to watch for clues and frankly because the press conferences offered some alternative to the sometimes-unpredictable White House briefings.

Governor Cuomo would go on to win an International Emmy for these pressers, but it would be stripped from him soon after following his sexual harassment scandal and resignation. It also later came to light that his administration underreported the COVID-19–related deaths of 4,100 New York nursing home residents. A top Cuomo aide was recorded saying that the Cuomo administration had intentionally withheld the death data out of concern that the Trump administration would use it against Cuomo.

The outside world was upside down with the fog of the pandemic and misinformation, but I was getting adjusted to working from home. Telework was no longer an occasional break from the office that was accompanied by the slight feeling of guilt for working in solitude. I no longer had to endure the one-and-a-half to two-hour drive to DC each way. For me, like many Americans, the office was no longer a geographic place.

I was growing comfortable. I filled the extra time reading and thinking and exercising. The flexibilities of full-time remote work would now allow me to focus on work-life balance. At the same time, I was compelled one quiet Saturday morning to do something that never seemed remotely necessary. I gathered and organized all my important papers including life insurance and survivor benefits, and I created a memo for my wife listing these benefits along with my end-of-life and funeral instructions just in case something should happen.

In those early days of the shutdown, I scheduled daily 9:00 a.m. video calls for all staff. On the Monday after the CARES Act was passed, I gave our staff a brief update on the legislation and noted how this would likely have a significant impact on several other OIGs. I jokingly said something along the lines of "Thank God we're not affected because I don't want to have anything to do with that hot mess."

The primary purpose of these calls, though, was not to convey substantive information. I felt more than anything we needed to stay connected as a team and a community as we navigated through the pandemic and the transition to remote work. Our people needed to see and know that we were all going through this crisis together. I viewed these calls as a group well-being, or welfare, check. In a matter of days, I noticed that staff were logging in earlier just to catch up with each other and otherwise socialize.

While the work of our office was not initially affected by the CARES Act, the inspector general community immediately got down to business with the Pandemic Response Account-ability Committee. The committee would quickly come to be known as the PRAC, as Washington loves its bureaucratic acronyms. Glenn Fine, acting inspector general at the Defense Department, was named chair, and the group formed several committees to plan its work.

Meanwhile, some of my fellow inspector general watch-dogs began barking immediately, warning the administration, Congress, and the American public. Hannibal "Mike" Ware, the inspector general of the US Small Business Administration, and his team were the first to sound the alarm. Within a week of the law's passage, they issued a report on stimulus loan fraud risks and lessons learned from their audits in previous disasters. He urged SBA management to closely review the supporting documentation for these loans to prevent fraud.

Jobs market data were starting to come in and were no longer just dire predictions. On average, prior to the pandemic about 250,000 workers per week file for unemployment benefits. On April 4, new claims reached a record 6 million in one week, for a 14.7 percent unemployment rate. A total of over 10 million Americans were out of work.

On April 6, Health and Human Services acting inspector general Christi Grimm and her team issued a report, a pulse survey conducted by her office between March 23 and 27, with hospital administrators from 323 hospitals across forty-six states, the District of Columbia, and Puerto Rico. Among the key takeaways of this survey: Hospitals were facing significant challenges testing and caring for COVID-positive patients while keeping staff safe, personal protective equipment and durable equipment like respirators were in short supply, and health facility capacity across the nation was strained.

This report immediately caught my attention. I was not the only one.

As an inspector general, I was in awe that Grimm's team could plan and complete this work and issue a public report within such a short period of time. As a father of two hospital nurses, I was grateful that the issue of protective equipment shortages and medical staff safety was being brought to the White House and public's attention.

Although I had only known Grimm a short while, I knew her to be one of the most competent oversight professionals in the community. She worked her way up through the ranks, and she exuded positivity and passion for healthcare oversight. That night during the White House Coronavirus Task Force briefing, President Trump was asked about the report. He responded by criticizing her findings as "wrong" and "just her opinion" and insinuated her views were politically motivated by asking who appointed her.

The next day, the president tweeted:

> Why didn't the I.G., who spent 8 years with the Obama Administration (Did she Report on the failed H1N1 Swine Flu debacle where 17,000 people died?), want to talk to the Admirals, Generals, V.P. & others in charge, before doing her report. Another Fake Dossier!

To be blunt, it was among the most personal, nonsensical, and factually incorrect public remarks a US president has ever uttered about an IG in the forty-year history of federal inspectors general.

An inspector general's duty is to objectively report the facts, good or bad, and Grimm was only temporarily acting in the position a few short months. She had been with that office since 1999, though, providing effective independent oversight for both Republican and Democratic administrations. She was highly qualified to be nominated by the president and confirmed by the Senate to serve in the role permanently. Nominations are unquestionably within the president's discretion, however, and now this nomination was most assuredly out of the question. The pulse survey report and the president's response sealed Grimm's fate, at least for the time being.

Other federal offices were going through the same issues as our office at the Pension Benefit Guaranty Corporation in pivoting to remote work, and so the Council of Inspectors General on Integrity and Efficiency invited a couple of inspectors general including myself to be panelists for a webinar titled "Creating a New Virtual Work Culture." One of my fellow panelists was SBA inspector general Mike Ware.

Mike Ware is one of the hardest-working and dedicated watchdogs in the business. He's a role model and a friend. Prior to becoming an inspector general, and before Ware was appointed SBA inspector general, I served as deputy inspector general at the SBA, running the day-to-day operations. At some level, I could relate to what he was going through in terms of his increasing pandemic oversight responsibilities.

The SBA helps small businesses get loans and government contracts and provides them financial relief after disasters. One of the projects I was associated with during my time at SBA was the High-Risk Loan Review program.

This program reviewed SBA-backed small business loans made by banks where the borrower stopped making payments and the bank sought the reimbursement guarantee from SBA. These loans are called 7(a) loans for the section of the Small Business Act that authorizes these loans. SBA OIG auditors would periodically examine a block of loans to determine whether the banks who approved these loans had failed to do due diligence when they approved the loans. If so, the SBA could refuse to pay the guarantee and the bank would be on the hook.

When the government is paying fees to banks for giving out government-backed loans, there needs to be some way to keep banks honest. Otherwise, unscrupulous bankers may look the other way and rubber-stamp government-guaranteed loan applications. By the time I left, we saved the SBA millions of dollars. Mike Ware continued this High-Risk Loan Review program after he arrived at SBA and developed other programs to prevent and detect loan fraud.

Ware and his team would eventually be responsible for independently overseeing more than $1 trillion in pandemic--related small business loans and grants—one of the largest pandemic oversight portfolios in the federal government, with a combined staff of a little over 100 auditors and investigators.

There were reasons why Congress and the White House were so focused on aiding small business during the pandemic—and why the SBA administrator is a member of the president's cabinet.

Small business is the backbone of the US economy. They employ almost half of all private-sector employees. The majority of businesses in the country are small businesses. The economy was at the precipice in spring 2020, and many small businesses it seemed were falling off the cliff.

One of the signature components of the CARES Act was a new program called the Paycheck Protection Program, or PPP. It's usually referred to with the redundant "program" to avoid having to call it what would have been an otherwise unfortunate name, the PP program. The PPP program provided emergency financial assistance to millions of Americans employed by small businesses, generally defined as having 500 or fewer employees. In the CARES Act, Congress initially authorized $349 billion in these loans that the small businesses would not have to pay back if they used the funds to continue to pay their employees.

Given the time it takes to stand up a new program, Congress decided to repurpose the 7(a) loan program and permit SBA-approved lenders to distribute the aid. Lenders began approving loans seven days after the CARES Act was enacted, and the program ran out of money on April 16. In just fourteen days, the SBA approved 1.6 million loans totaling $349 billion.

Former NFL quarterback Tom Brady scored. His sports nutrition company, TB12, Inc., received a $960,855 PPP loan issued by Cambridge Savings Bank. Tennis legend and entrepreneur Serena Williams opted not to apply for a PPP loan. "Other companies need it way more than us," she later told *Fast Company* magazine. She pivoted her clothing company, S by Serena, and repurposed in-stock fabric to make face masks. I was told by someone in my social circle that local financial advisers were calling small business clients in my community telling them they were fools if they didn't apply for this program.

Many small businesses, especially those without established strong relationships with their banker, were left out in the cold and were locked out of the Paycheck Protection Program. This disproportionately affected minority-owned businesses. The SBA inspector general's office would later issue a flash report calling attention to the fact that the SBA failed to prioritize borrowers in underserved markets as required under the law and failed to collect demographic information making it impossible for the agency to determine loan volume to the intended prioritized markets. Flash reports to management and Congress are one way that IGs report potential management and funding problems that require immediate attention.

To be sure, Congress was asking lenders to take on risk with the Paycheck Protection Program and many lenders incurred additional costs in modifying their IT systems. At the same time, these lenders received billions in fees coupled with special protections in the CARES Act.

You'll recall the SBA inspector general's prepandemic, High-Risk Loan Review program I just mentioned saved the taxpayers millions of dollars. This is the program that examined loans where the lender had failed to do due diligence when they approved the loan. In those cases, the SBA could deny the government guarantee and the lender would be responsible for their poor underwriting. Congress included in the CARES Act a special "hold-harmless" provision essentially protecting lenders from accountability for making bad PPP loans.

In the initial program rules, called the interim final rule, SBA was clear about their expectations of lenders: "The lender does not need to conduct *any* verification if the borrower submits documentation supporting its request for loan forgiveness and attests that it has accurately verified the payments for eligible costs. The Administrator will *hold harmless* any lender that relies on such borrower documents and attestation from a borrower." (emphasis added)

The $349 billion Paycheck Protection Program would be run on the honor system.

To be fair, lenders may or may not have enthusiastically participated in the program absent this language. We'll never know.

The United Kingdom had a similar pandemic relief program called the Bounce-Back Loan Scheme. A key difference between the US and the UK programs was that in the UK the banks had to put up their own money first. In the US, lenders were allowed to play the game with taxpayer dollars—the classic moral hazard.

There was another bug in the Paycheck Protection Program.

Because of the pandemic, all but federal first responders and essential workers were working from home. This included workers at the Internal Revenue Service, and the IRS had temporarily closed all Taxpayer Assistance Centers. At a same time, the IRS was tasked under the CARES Act with a seemingly impossible task: immediately sending out Economic Impact Payments to taxpayers, as the law specified "as rapidly as possible."

By May, the IRS had sent out over 150 million payments totaling over $260 billion. Implementation of the stimulus checks was one of Washington's wins during the Trump administration. But this left the IRS with few staff or the bandwidth for other tasks that it sometimes is asked by agencies to do. One of these tasks is their Income Verification Express Service to obtain tax return transcripts. In the normal course of business, the SBA and its lenders rely upon the IRS as a critical mechanism to verify information. IRS suspended this service due to the pandemic.

To prevent delays with PPP loan approval, Congress included language in the CARES Act that SBA "shall not require an applicant to submit a tax return or a tax return transcript." In other words, SBA could not cross-check a loan application against the most credible data on income and expenses in the government's possession: prior tax records filed under penalty of perjury.

The Small Business Administration, on their own accord, made a change to their loan approval rules. Before the pandemic, any SBA loan applications from a member of Congress or business entity in which they have a 10 percent or more interest had to be approved by the SBA's Standards of Conduct Committee. In April, the SBA authorized a blanket approval for these loans.

At least twelve members of Congress, from both parties, received millions in forgivable pandemic small business loans for their or their immediate relatives' businesses. My point is not that these loans were per se improper. It is that blanket approval for members of Congress with little transparency further erodes public trust in government.

$

As I settled into my new home-work routine, I experimented with an old pastime. Before I started my workday, I'd periodically enjoy watching an inning or two of professional baseball from Taiwan. The 2020 Major League Baseball season had been postponed in March, and I saw this website trending on Twitter and gave it a try. With the time difference, these games were broadcast in the mornings on Eleven Sports with English-speaking commentators, and I tuned in to watch the Rakuten Monkeys. Instead of playing to an empty stadium, Rakuten filled their stands with cardboard cut-outs and robot mannequin fans along with live, masked cheerleaders. These folks were making the most of this.

The shelter-in-place, though, was cramping the style of our college-age son. From his bedroom fifteen feet away, he would bombard me with a relentless torrent of texts begging to be allowed out of the house. At one point I just responded with a screenshot of a news story of the Maryland State Police arresting twenty-eight people for violating the governor's executive stay-at-home order.

On one early April afternoon, I was walking off lunch with my wife and son on the path near our home. Midway through the walk, as I was reflecting on how I was making the most of the situation, I received a cell phone call from a number I didn't recognize. I normally don't answer these calls, but for some reason I did on this day.

On the other end was an inspector general colleague whom I had gotten to know while I was chair of the inspectors general professional development committee. Paul Martin was the affable inspector general at NASA whose defining feature is an irreverent sense of humor that he skillfully uses to defuse tense situations, sometimes to the collective cringe of other meeting participants.

After exchanging pleasantries, Martin asked if I'd consider the position of executive director of the PRAC.

I initially chuckled to myself thinking about how I recently told my staff that Congress had passed this massive piece of pandemic legislation, the CARES Act, and, thank God, we as an office were not affected, which was great because I wanted nothing to do with that hot mess. I politely told him I'd think about it before we ended the call and I continued on my way.

"Who was that?" my wife asked.

"Paul. The IG at NASA. He wanted to know if I was interested in a new job. 'No thanks. I'm good.'"

6

"SO YOU'RE THE STUPID SON OF A BITCH THEY GOT TO TAKE THE JOB"
(LATE APRIL 2020)

The Pandemic Response Accountability Committee is expected to pick up where the 2009–2015 Recovery Accountability and Transparency Board left off, but the PRAC is forced to rebuild crisis oversight from scratch, during a national emergency, and with an administration that didn't welcome oversight. Confounding public health information from Washington raises alarms.

My initial reluctance to the offer of leading the Pandemic Response Accountability Committee staff office was partly due to events that had happened earlier in April. I was also comfortable in my current position, and a global pandemic is a terrible time to change jobs.

A few days prior to the call from Paul Martin, the Council of Inspectors General scheduled a 2:30 p.m. conference call to discuss the recent firing of IG Michael Atkinson by President Trump. We never got to that discussion item though. The night before our meeting, at the president's press conference, was when he criticized Grimm over the pulse survey report on personal protective equipment affecting hospitals' supplies.

Moreover, in the morning before our afternoon conference call, President Trump made an out-of-the-ordinary and complicated personnel move that directly affected the PRAC.

Immediately after the CARES Act was signed into law, the Council of Inspectors General named Glenn Fine to serve as chair of the PRAC. Fine was and is one of the most respected people to ever serve in the federal oversight community. He made his bones previously serving for eleven years as the inspector general for the US Department of Justice. That is one of the most challenging and high-profile IG jobs, serving as the independent watchdog for the FBI among other DOJ agencies.

Prior to the pandemic, Fine had come out of retirement and was serving as the deputy inspector general for the Department of Defense (and acting IG after the previous Defense IG had retired). In the final months of the Obama administration, Fine was nominated by the president to serve as inspector general for the Defense Department, but the Senate failed to vote on this nomination before President Trump took office.

President Trump removed Fine from his acting role and named the inspector general of the Environmental Protection Agency to concurrently serve as acting IG of the Defense Department, effective immediately, to take Fine's place. Most people knew what that meant and the motive behind the move. The move meant that Fine was no longer eligible to serve as PRAC chair. This took place ten days after the PRAC was created as the independent pandemic oversight office and before it even started any pandemic oversight work.

It was a shocking and unexpected move, but not out of character for the president considering his comments at a March 23 press conference when the CARES Act was still in discussion. At that press conference, the president was asked about the apparent lack of independent oversight in the original draft CARES legislation.

"I'll be the oversight," Trump said.

That comment raised eyebrows and hackles on both sides of the aisle. The very next day at the White House coronavirus daily briefing, Larry Kudlow acknowledged there would be independent oversight after all. Referencing some of the emergency pandemic aid, Kudlow said, "That fund, by the way, will be overseen by an oversight board and an inspector general. It will be completely transparent."

Senator Gary Peters and Representative Carolyn Maloney went to work to hold the administration to its word.

The PRAC was not a novel concept. Congressional staffers had dusted off a copy of the American Recovery and Reinvestment Act of 2009, the fiscal stimulus bill that provided nearly $800 billion to end the Great Recession triggered by the subprime mortgage crisis. Staffers had cut and pasted language from the Recovery Act to the draft CARES Act bill to create a new oversight mechanism to ensure any pandemic oversight would be independent from the administration.

The House draft originally named this organization the Coronavirus Accountability and Transparency Committee, which someone short-handed to the CAT Committee. Clever, but the name was perhaps too cute for some and the CATC didn't roll off the tongue. The Senate draft originally called it the Coronavirus Stimulus Oversight Board, but CSOB didn't work either and someone came up with the Pandemic Response Accountability Committee. The Senate's proposed name, the PRAC, won out.

The draft language was vetted through the inspector general community, and the initial response from some IGs was that a new oversight office wasn't necessary. Wiser heads prevailed and the inspector general community responded to Capitol Hill with some suggested modifications to the draft to bring it up-to-date.

There was no question that this new oversight body was to be, in the words of one congressional staffer, "strongly modeled" after the Recovery Accountability and Transparency Board created in the Recovery Act of 2009.

That office, affectionately called the RAT Board by some, was made up of inspectors general overseeing Recovery Act money. (That unfortunate acronym likely explains the failed CAT Committee suggestion.) The inspectors general hated the name and preferred to call itself the Recovery Board. President Obama had named Department of Interior inspector general Earl Devaney to serve as chair of the Recovery Board. During the Recovery Act bill signing, President Obama tasked his vice president, Joe Biden, with overseeing the $800 billion in Recovery funding.

"As part of his duty," President Obama said, "Joe will keep an eye on how precious tax dollars are being spent. To you, he's Mr. Vice President, but around the White House, we call him the sheriff."

During the board's existence from 2009 to 2015, Vice President Biden worked closely with the Recovery Board, and according to most observers this high-level collaboration resulted in improvements in the public visibility of federal spending data and acted to keep fraud to relatively low levels.

There are, though, some significant differences between the Recovery Board legislation in the Recovery Act and the PRAC legislation in the CARES Act. The PRAC would have an inspector general to serve as chair but would also have a full-time executive director to supervise and coordinate PRAC functions and staff.

By law, the executive director had to have experience auditing and managing oversight of large organizations and expenditures. The statute inexplicably capped the pay at a rate less than many federal senior executive service positions. The position didn't require formal Senate confirmation but did require the consultation of congressional leadership— namely, the minority leader and Speaker of the House and the majority and minority leaders of the Senate. That's one of the reasons my appointment was the subject of tweets by Pelosi and Schumer on my first day on the job.

This was the position I was being asked to play: the middleman between the full-time professional staff and the PRAC chair, vice chair, and the nineteen other inspectors general who were members of the committee and effectively its board of directors.

My job would be to iron out any wrinkles and smooth any lumps across government and make sure oversight and law enforcement agencies had the data and investigators they needed to conduct pandemic oversight. I would facilitate "coordinated, comprehensive oversight" across government. I would sift through mountain ranges of data, connect the dots, and draw attention to pandemic oversight matters of concern.

Even though I had immediately dismissed any interest in the executive director position, when I got back online after finishing my post-lunch walk, I pulled up the CARES Act and read through the PRAC sections. I would not be bored. This was big.

I had a call a few days later with Paul Martin and Department of Justice inspector general Michael Horowitz, who had quietly assumed the role of acting PRAC chair in the wake of Fine's removal. They eventually offered me the position.

All things considered, this was the worst possible time to change jobs and leave a job that I was very good at doing. This was technically a step down from my current role as inspector general. I would be trading in a job with almost complete autonomy, no direct boss, and a three-member board of directors, for a job with far less autonomy, two direct bosses, and twenty-one IGs on my board of directors. I was going from big fish in a little pond to middle fish in the middle of the ocean.

Then there was the fact that we were operating under a stay-at-home order, and it did not escape me that there are no how-to books on setting up an office in a global pandemic. And the kicker was that I would be taking a pay cut because of an unreasonably low salary cap that Congress wrote in the CARES Act—no one has yet satisfactorily explained the rationale on that inscrutable stroke of the pen.

On the other hand, in the pro column, the public service calling and massive challenge nagged at me. I read and reread the statute. If you stare at something long enough, things become clearer.

This was the mother of all oversight missions, and who is really prepared to create a new office to oversee over $2 trillion in emergency federal spending during a global pandemic, I told myself.

In one of the most sublime conversations of my then thirty-two-year marriage, my wife walked into my home office as I sat silently in my chair contemplating the opportunity. I gave her my list of pros and cons, knowing this position would exact a toll on both of us. She walked out nodding in acknowledgment. A few minutes later she walked back in and in a subdued but clear voice said, "Hey, I think you should take the job. I believe in you," before walking back out. And that was it.

The week before I was to start as executive director, I witnessed one of the most unforgettable press conferences in presidential history. It was during the April 23 White House Coronavirus Task Force briefing that President Trump brought up the medicinal value of bleach, the issue that Facebook had previously warned us about.

"We tested bleach," the president said from the podium. "I can tell you that bleach will kill the virus in five minutes."

Looking at his coronavirus response coordinator Deborah Birx who was seated along the wall of the press room, with her head resting on her hand staring into the abyss, the president mused,

> So, supposing we hit the body with a tremendous—whether it's ultraviolet or just very powerful light—and I think you said that that hasn't been checked, but you're going to test it. And that I said, supposing you brought the light inside the body, which you can do either through the skin or in some other way, and I think you said you're going to test that, too. It

sounds interesting. And then I see the disinfectant, where it knocks it out in a minute. One minute. And is there a way we can do something like that, by injection inside or almost a cleaning. Because you see it gets in the lungs, and it does a tremendous number on the lungs. So it would be interesting to check that.

Words have consequences, especially words uttered by a president from the White House briefing room podium. The president's extemporaneous comments immediately raised alarms prompting the maker of Lysol to issue a warning to consumers not to inject or drink their products and prompting public health officials across the globe to issue public safety warnings against drinking bleach.

On April 24, Congress authorized another $321 billion to replenish the Paycheck Protection Program, which had run out of money. Funding for this one pandemic program was now edging up to the total amount of the Recovery Act spending.

My blast off, or appointment day, was scheduled for April 27.

As an inspector general, I had been scrupulously nonpartisan. I worked just as hard to keep my board chair informed whether it was Labor Secretary Tom Perez (Obama appointee), Alex Acosta (Trump appointee), or Eugene Scalia (Trump appointee). I got on equally well with their political appointed senior leaders, regardless of party. This approach would be even more important in my new role, especially in this climate.

My appointment was announced at a 10:00 a.m. virtual meeting of the members of PRAC, followed by a press release. I was "reporting for duty" I told the PRAC members, and I looked forward to working with them individually and collectively on the mother of all oversight missions. I knew them all, some very well. Now I would be working for them, supporting their offices.

In my daybook on my first day on the job, I jotted down two initial thoughts I had for the PRAC: agile oversight and listening sessions. Over time these two ideas, with the significant input of others, would evolve and morph and become two signature accomplishments of the PRAC.

Beginning my first morning, my to-do list exploded, and I tried to compartmentalize tasks into now, next, and later actions. My now tasks included reaching out to key partners and stakeholders, and I needed to next start designing the organization. I reached out to schedule introductory calls with senior officials from the White House's Office of Management and Budget (OMB) and the congressional watchdog Government Accountability Office (GAO).

These were desperate, or at least urgent, times so I started by identifying what resources we could borrow immediately from friends and allies. There's no instruction manual with something like this. My gut was telling me that I'd need to beg, borrow, and deal my way to the solution.

Shakespeare famously wrote, "The first thing we do is, let's kill all the lawyers." As a lawyer myself—and as a federal executive who's worked frustratingly close with lawyers—I can tell you the Bard had a point, but the first thing we needed to do was hire an experienced lawyer to navigate through the bureaucracy and enable all that begging, borrowing, and dealing.

By lunchtime, I sent an email to line up a lawyer from another OIG whom I could borrow on a long-term reimbursable basis and who could handle all the odds and ends that come with standing up a new organization. We also needed an IT person so we could actually get work done, given that we were 100 percent remote.

On the same day my appointment was announced, the PRAC also launched our federal spending website. You can't oversee federal spending if you can't see who's getting the money and what they're using it for. In government speak, this is called transparency.

The Treasury Department operates a website called USASpending.gov to show the American public how their tax dollars are being spent. Congress tasked the PRAC with maintaining a similar public website focused on pandemic spending, and we were given thirty days by law to do it. On the same day I was appointed executive director, the PRAC launched the website pandemic.oversight.gov. The website since dropped the dot to PandemicOversight.gov.

The PRAC's website was also intended to be strongly modeled after the Recovery Board's website. In the law, this meant that federal agencies would be required to publicly report their pandemic obligations (that is, firm commitments to spend federal money) and expenditures (which would be federal money that has been paid out).

For states, counties, and others who received federal pandemic relief money, the CARES Act set up a reporting process almost identical to the Recovery Act. Every quarter, recipients would be required to report the amount of federal pandemic funds they had spent, who they passed federal funds to, the specific name and description of the projects or activities the money went to, and the estimated number of jobs created or retained as a result of the federal funding.

The PRAC, however, can't order federal agencies or recipients of federal funds to do anything. It would take the full support of the administration to make all that public spending reporting happen. This one desire of Congress in the CARES Act—recipient spending reporting across all federal programs to ensure timely, complete, and accurate reporting of federal pandemic spending—would unfortunately never come to fruition. And it wasn't for wont of the PRAC trying.

Thirty days is not a lot of time to build a website, and operating under a shelter-in-place order presented some complications. The PRAC met its statutory deadline. On launch day, the 1.0 version of the website had some agency pandemic spending plans and a graphic donut showing the percentages of how the money was being spent by broad categories such as emergency lending, small business, individuals, healthcare providers, and others. This simple donut graphic proved to be a tedious and time-consuming task, tracing appropriations in the 300+ page legislation to specific federal programs. Getting the website up in thirty days was a virtual barn raising led by Postal Service IG Tammy Whitcomb and her dedicated team at USPS OIG.

I began Day Two with a courtesy call to former Recovery Board chair and Interior inspector general Earl Devaney. Days before my appointment, a well-known and respected former White House OMB official wrote an opinion piece on how in building the PRAC, the IGs needed to replicate the successes of the Recovery Board. It was clear, the Recovery Board would be the filter that we would be judged by.

Devaney was enjoying his retirement from the balcony of his Fort Lauderdale condo when he answered my call. I had met him before and of course knew him by reputation. As Interior IG, Devaney led some of the most significant public corruption investigations since Watergate. But he didn't know me prior to my appointment.

When I gave my name, Devaney just laughed and said, "So you're the stupid son of a bitch they got to take the job."

We laughed and he then graciously shared his experiences with the Recovery Board and gave me advice on next steps.

I already knew he was a legend in the oversight community, and it was clear to me why after this call.

He told me that the Recovery Board was so successful because he had the ear and support of the White House, particularly the vice president, and that meant that agencies took him seriously. Devaney and Vice President Biden met regularly on the Recovery Act and everyone in government knew it. Devaney was fiercely independent and blunt, but he also recognized the reality that it takes two to do the oversight tango.

Regarding pandemic spending, Devaney told me bluntly, "Look, the money's already out. The notion that you're gonna be able to prevent fraud—," I could almost hear him shaking his head through the phone.

The media were already reporting on the Small Business Administration blowing through the initial $349 billion in Paycheck Protection Program funding. Devaney also knew that only about 30 percent, or around $260 billion, of the Recovery Act's $800 billion was in the form of grants, contracts, or loans. The rest was in tax benefits and entitlements, which his team didn't focus on. There were also significant differences in the velocity of spending. It took about eighteen months for the federal government to spend about 70 percent of the Recovery Act's $260 billion. In other words, the Recovery Board had a much longer runway than the PRAC would have.

Expectations for the PRAC were high. Nobody's more so than the expectations I had for myself. In my daybook I wrote, "Don't fumble the moment."

Tuesday of week one was my fifty-fourth birthday, but there was little time for any celebration. I broke for a quick dinner with my family. I got back online after wolfing down a slice of birthday cake to finish some mandatory IT security training and worked into the evening.

While I was back at my laptop—as if to underscore Devaney's point on the pandemic funds being already out the door—a businessman from Encino, California, was busy defrauding. On April 28, I would later learn he submitted six fraudulent PPP loan applications to Bank of America and eight fraudulent PPP loan applications to Wells Fargo. Along with some additional fraudulent applications he later submitted, he sought a total of $27 million on behalf of eight fake companies claiming over 100 employees. All lies. He would later be convicted and sentenced to eleven years in prison.

I wouldn't be alone on this journey, and I wasn't technically PRAC employee number 1. That distinction goes to Kathy Tighe, a former federal executive who was asked to come out of retirement. Tighe was the former inspector general of the Education Department and the former chair of the Recovery Board after Devaney retired. Tighe was one of the first people called after the CARES Act passed, and she was immediately brought on as senior adviser.

Kathy Tighe was a role model for me. A few years earlier, she and I were on an event panel together speaking about risk management and oversight challenges. She was at the end of her career as inspector general at a large cabinet department, and I was a recently appointed IG at a small federal corporation.

A lawyer by training, Tighe is a fundamentally kindhearted person who goes out of her way to encourage others. She encouraged me early in my career and it was humbling now having her effectively working for me. She was gracious about it, and she is responsible for much of the PRAC's early successes.

On Thursday, April 30, we sent an email to all forty inspectors general whose agencies received pandemic funding asking them to identify their agency's top pandemic challenges. One of our first projects would be to set the stage and identify the top risks or challenges from across government.

Beginning this first week, I started a close working relationship with the PRAC chair Michael Horowitz and vice chair Paul Martin. For months, we would end every day with a tag-up call, until we reduced the frequency to three times a week and eventually twice a week. Michael Horowitz has a rare combination of stamina, smarts, and savvy. He and Paul Martin provided board-level direction and guidance every step of the journey. As chair, Horowitz was the public face of the Pandemic Response Accountability Committee, while I worked behind the scenes.

A diverging of two Americas was on full display on April 30. During the day, armed and angry demonstrators in Lansing, Michigan, stormed the state capitol protesting Governor Gretchen Whitmer's stay-at-home order. President Trump later tweeted support for the protesters:

> These are very good people, but they are
> angry. They want their lives back again, safely!
> See them, talk to them, make a deal.

That night, my wife and I put our phones down long enough to watch Amy Poehler and Nick Offerman as they reunited with castmates for *A Parks and Recreation Special*, one of our favorite shows from the good old days before the pandemic. The special was to benefit some charity, and the premise cleverly involved Leslie Knope and her Pawnee friends working a phone tree on a video call to make sure everyone was socially distant and safe at home. The liberal Leslie Knope and the conservative Ron Swanson coming together during this moment of crisis in America could only exist—it seemed—on a fictional television sitcom.

7

WASHINGTON HAS LITTLE APPETITE FOR INDEPENDENT OVERSIGHT

(MAY 2020)

Mayhem and disorder in America pull the nation further apart. Widespread unemployment insurance fraud pops up on the radar. The pandemic inspectors general get to work making sense of federal pandemic spending data and making it visible to the American public, while Washington displays little appetite for accountability or providing a unifying message to the nation. The president fires another inspector general watchdog.

The Statue of Liberty stands in the Upper New York Bay peering down toward the South Brooklyn Marine Terminal. In May 2020, the terminal was filled with rows of refrigeration trucks parked neatly and storing ninety bodies apiece. New York City had lost 20,000 to COVID in two months.

By the beginning of May, over 68,000 Americans had lost their lives to COVID-19. We ended the month with about 107,000 deaths. While we crossed the grim 100,000 death milestone, thankfully there were signs that the COVID wave was starting to recede.

Aside from the pandemic, May was a month of mayhem and social disorder. Shocking videos of armed protesters taking over the Michigan state capitol over pandemic restrictions were all over the news on May 1. One news picture went viral. It was an image of an enraged white protester with a buzz cut and long beard baring his fangs and screaming in the face of a police officer, who was wearing a COVID mask but nothing resembling riot gear. The officer seemed to be just taking it and was otherwise demonstrating remarkable restraint.

We ended the month with the murder of George Floyd in Minneapolis at the hands of a police officer and in front of bystander police officers and witnesses. Protests erupted in cities across America. There were peaceful protesters and protesters who looted and set buildings ablaze. Black Lives Matter went viral in May 2020. In the twenty-two-day period following Floyd's murder, there would be over 850 demonstrations in over 300 counties with an estimated 750,000 protesters.

Governor Hogan issued orders allowing Maryland counties to use local COVID data and make their own decisions about when to relax restrictions, and he broadened the list of statewide "permitted outdoor activities." Walking or running on the park paths was deemed an acceptable outdoor exercise activity. Playgrounds, however, were still closed to limit children's exposure, and the one near my home sat vacant for weeks encircled with orange vinyl construction barrier fencing to keep children away.

At the PRAC, we were laser-focused on the frenzied federal pandemic response spending and with getting timely and complete data from the administration to make available on our website and to analyze for fraud and waste, all while building the team.

On May 1, Friday of my first full week, I started what would become a great working relationship with one of the teams who would play an outsized role and ultimately have a major impact in pandemic oversight: Treasury Office of Inspector General (OIG), led by its acting inspector general, Rich Delmar, and its head of audit, Debbie Harker.

The Treasury OIG was given extraordinary responsibilities in the CARES Act. The Treasury Department would be administering massive new pandemic relief programs involving hundreds of billions of dollars. The Treasury OIG was given responsibility to monitor this spending and recoup it when it had been misspent—not a typical inspector general function.

Treasury Department leadership, with the support of the White House, were initially contesting the inspector general's authority under the CARES Act and contesting whether the Treasury Department even had to publicly account for the hundreds of billions of taxpayer dollars.

Working with the Treasury OIG team, we drafted an email for PRAC chair Michael Horowitz to send to the White House. We were deeply concerned from the beginning that the administration did not have the reporting mechanisms in place to publicly account for billions of pandemic response dollars and lacked the desire to create new ones. Our chief concern was that the only government-wide pandemic spending guidance that had been issued was simply insufficient.

Meanwhile federal agencies were shoveling out cash. Lots of it.

Shortly after the CARES Act was passed, the White House, through the Office of Management and Budget (OMB), issued guidance to federal agencies on how to publicly report spending of the $2 trillion. To the dismay of the oversight community, this OMB guidance didn't require agencies to report the specific information that Congress specified in the law to help ensure the American public could see exactly who was receiving federal funds, exactly what they were using it for, and how many jobs were being retained or created from this stimulus money.

There was, for example, no way to trace federal money from Treasury's $150 billion Coronavirus Relief Fund to a grant recipient like the Montgomery County, Maryland, government down to one of the county's many subrecipients. There was no way for the Congress, the PRAC, or the American taxpayer to tell whether federal pandemic relief money was used to buy personal protective equipment or going into the pocket of a corrupt local official. Transparency is at the heart of accountability.

To make matters worse, the little financial reporting the White House was requiring of agencies would not take effect until July 2020. Federal agencies were instructed to use existing reporting systems, which flow from agency financial systems to Treasury's public website USASpending.gov. This reporting is normally done quarterly. In a small concession, OMB required agencies to increase the reporting frequency from quarterly to monthly. OMB also required agencies to tag pandemic spending with a special code and tag COVID-related contracts with a specific code in the federal procurement system. In terms of guidance, such oversight would be too little, and it would arrive too late.

"Time is of the essence, and the Administration is committed to the rapid delivery of these funds to the COVID-19 relief and response efforts," the acting OMB director wrote in the issuing memo. There was one sentence in the guidance that I found encouraging. OMB promised that additional guidance providing further details would be forthcoming. Unfortunately, that additional guidance never came.

The oversight community was not consulted on the OMB memo, and this would have been especially appropriate since the memo included some language that attempted to sink the work of the inspectors general and the PRAC. The memo stated that the independent watchdogs are to "work closely with OMB and agencies . . . to *coordinate* COVID-19–related oversight efforts, *leverage* available technology to *minimize burden* and *duplicate efforts*, and *re-prioritize* lower priority audit work to allow agencies and OIGs to better support higher priority COVID-19 work." (emphasis added)

This language may seem reasonable on its face, but to those knowledgeable about government oversight, it blatantly crossed the line. Inspectors general are nothing if not independent. Independence is a bedrock principle, and if we followed this language to the letter, it would have impeded the independence of our oversight. The overall tone of the memorandum, issued after the president fired Atkinson and Fine, was not lost on me. We just ignored the offending language and went about our business, letting the chips fall where they may.

Inspectors general couldn't wait until July to get eyes on CARES Act spending. If agencies weren't transparent with the American people about their pandemic activities and the OMB-directed government-wide reporting would be too late, inspectors general would take matters into their own hands. Mark Greenblatt, a dynamic force and the inspector general at the US Department of Interior issued a flash report on May 5, summarizing how Interior was spending its pandemic relief funds.

The law called for the PRAC to serve as liaison to OMB and Treasury, but we soon discovered that we had wildly different views of the fundamentals of oversight. OMB could not yet support video conference calls, so we were left with phone bridge calls with multiple participants. Early conference calls with OMB, inspector general officials, and the PRAC were heated with little agreement on basic facts and the nature of independent oversight.

One senior official insisted that I worked for the administration, and that the PRAC should prioritize inspector general pandemic audit work to what the administration believed to be most important. Call me cynical, but even the most enlightened and self-reflective administration does not welcome independent oversight with open arms. Independent oversight doesn't work like that.

OMB's initial pandemic leadership and guidance was in stark contrast to its efforts following the 2009 financial crisis.

One day after the Recovery Act was signed into law in 2009, OMB issued a sixty-two-page memo, titled M-09-10 in bureaucratese, containing initial Recovery Act implementing guidance. Key components of this initial guidance were organized around agencies being required to prepare and issue spending plans and public reporting of spending information.

Seven months later, OMB updated that 2009 guidance ordering agencies and recipients of federal funds to report details on spending to a new reporting and data collection system built by the Recovery Board. The system was called

Federalreporting.gov, and it wasn't a perfect system. It was a heavy lift for some public servants and recipients, but it provided much needed visibility into how billions of federal tax dollars were being spent.

As for pandemic spending, OMB sent out a data call to federal agencies in May asking agencies to identify the names and corresponding identifying number (called Federal Assistance Listing) of the programs being used to spend pandemic relief money. The inspector general community was separately working with their agencies to identify what funding they received in the pandemic relief laws so the watchdogs could oversee this money.

Astonishingly, both OMB and the oversight community had to resort to a manual data call to pull these data together. For those unfamiliar with this phrase, a manual data call is Latin for, "We don't know. Do you?" In other words, OMB and the IGs were sending emails to the agencies asking them to self-report which codes were being used to track pandemic relief spending.

Nobody in the federal government had a clear view into where all the federal pandemic money was going.

On May 1, the same day as our first communication to OMB about serious deficiencies in CARES Act public reporting of federal spending, the president signed an executive order giving Agriculture Secretary Sonny Purdue the authority to invoke the Defense Production Act to force our nation's meat-processing facilities to remain open during the pandemic.

The CDC was reporting high rates of infections and deaths at 115 meat and poultry processing plants in nineteen states. The hard-working men and women who were keeping food on our tables often worked in conditions that made social distancing a near impossibility.

Around this time, I first heard about the Trump administration's efforts to expedite vaccine development, through a public-private partnership called Operation Warp Speed. This effort would support multiple COVID-19 vaccine candidates from different pharmaceutical companies with funding and expedited approval processes.

Any glimmer of optimism I had with the news of Operation Warp Speed was quashed that Friday night when the president announced that he had nominated a Justice Department lawyer to be the inspector general of the Department of Health and Human Services and would be sending his name to the US Senate for confirmation. The nominee had been a federal prosecutor for about four years, a position that typically involves no role in supervising or managing employees and certainly no role in overseeing audits or audit teams. And that point wasn't lost on observers.

The Health and Human Services inspector general's office is one of the largest federal oversight offices with approximately 1,600 staff. They are responsible for oversight of the massive Medicare and Medicaid programs, which are a significant percentage of the federal budget. In addition to investigating healthcare fraud, HHS OIG issues over 200 audit and evaluation reports each year. To many, it was obvious that the acting inspector general was being punished for the sin of reporting the bad news in April about hospital supplies and readiness.

The White House statement announcing what's called "the intention to nominate," got a lot of press, but the White House never even bothered to follow through with the required paperwork to the Senate for the actual nomination and that individual never served in the role.

Washington, during this time, had little appetite for independent oversight. IGs would get calls from reporters or hear rumors from others that they were next to be fired. The thought crossed my mind more than once that Horowitz may be receiving the "Friday evening" phone call from the White House. One longtime inspector general retired during this time and in doing so felt compelled to issue a press release making clear: "This decision has been long in the works and is for entirely personal reasons. I have not been told or asked to resign."

Much of my time as executive director was spent attending video meetings, reading everything I could get my hands on describing agency programs and trying to determine exactly what skill sets we needed to hire for.

The PRAC was not alone, of course, in the mission of pandemic oversight. Oversight is a team sport, and other individuals, organizations, and groups were busy trying to fill in the gaps.

A colleague who works for a private-sector firm that does dark web intelligence for law enforcement sent me a report showing what was already popping up on the dark web. There were how-to tutorials on pages like "Covid 19 Scampage" along with plenty of stolen personal information for sale.

An attorney at the Justice Department took the initiative to bring federal investigators together to form an informal pandemic fraud working group. Agents from all the major federal law enforcement agencies were on these regular conference calls where important investigative information was shared. It was on one of these calls that I first learned about the scope and nature of unemployment insurance fraud schemes that began in Washington state and spread throughout the country.

The US Secret Service, we were told, had uncovered a massive, large-scale fraud involving an international fraud ring and was warning law enforcement and the states. Seven states had already been targeted, and the Secret Service said in a subsequent law enforcement bulletin: "It is extremely likely every state is vulnerable to this scheme and will be targeted if they have not been already."

According to the Secret Service, this ring was believed to involve hundreds, if not thousands, of mules with potential losses in the "hundreds of millions." A money mule is someone recruited by a criminal to move money acquired through criminal activity. Some mules do so knowingly, and others are unaware they are participating in the crime.

This level of fraud was the direct result of another significant gap in the pandemic relief laws.

Self-employed workers were allowed to use an honor system to "prove" (or self-certify) their lost wages to claim pandemic unemployment benefits. Fraudsters immediately recognized this flaw and flooded the state unemployment systems, using stolen personal information that was widely available from prior large data breaches and inexpensive to purchase on the dark web.

The Labor inspector general's office issued an alert memo to the Labor Department in May urging the agency to work with Congress to close this loophole on self-certification. This was the first of many warnings issued by this office.

I met with good government groups like the Project on Government Oversight (POGO), which is a nonprofit, nonpartisan independent watchdog. They similarly expressed concerns about the lack of transparency in federal pandemic spending data and were demanding action. I also met with a group representing state auditors and heard their concerns about insufficient federal guidance from OMB.

On May 11, two weeks into my new role, I delivered my first remarks at a webinar event hosted by an association of government financial and accounting managers. I commented on the extraordinary times we were all living through, which as of that day was responsible for the deaths of 79,000 Americans. I mentioned the first Paycheck Protection Program fraud case in Rhode Island, and I talked about the agile oversight work we were already seeing from the OIGs. I held up the SBA stimulus loan lessons learned report, the Health and Human Services pulse survey on hospital supplies and readiness, the Labor risk alert on unemployment insurance fraud, and the Interior flash report on pandemic spending.

I also mentioned a report from Department of Veterans Affairs inspector general Mike Missal and his team who examined the readiness of VA healthcare facilities like the veterans' home where my father-in-law resided. In 2020, his facility was the site of one of the largest and deadliest COVID outbreaks in the state and among one of the largest in the nation. COVID would take the lives of over sixty-six residents and one staff member.

I found time to put together a written PRAC stand-up plan, after getting advice and counsel from Tighe and others. This plan started with dissecting the two CARES Act sections that pertained to the PRAC and identifying the specific "shalls" and "mays" in the statute. In other words, I was identifying what exactly Congress was expecting us to do and what Congress was giving us permission to do, if we used our discretion.

To find our rhythm and demonstrate progress, I set thirty-day sprint periods with deliverables and set a goal of having the organization fully operational by our six-month mark, September 27.

Friday night, May 15, about two weeks into my new job, brought another shocking announcement out of the White House. The president announced that he was firing State Department inspector general Steve Linick. I had previously served alongside Linick on the federal inspectors general executive council. I knew him to be a polished, charismatic lawyer and watchdog who didn't shy away from tackling tough issues.

There is an old quote of dubious authorship that says: to avoid criticism, do nothing, say nothing, be nothing. Secretary of State Mike Pompeo asked President Trump to fire Linick, complaining that his work was "undermining" the department's mission. Only a few years before Linick had been criticized after reporting on allegations involving Secretary Hillary Clinton's use of a private email server. Linick was a dedicated public servant and diligent fact finder who faced criticism from both Democrats and Republicans and deserved better.

$

In our region, our favorite restaurant in town was permitted to reopen for curbside service in May. Social distancing and the two-month shutdown was taking a toll on the restaurant industry. We took advantage of weekly comfort food from our favorite restaurant while being able to support a local small business. We consciously increased our business hoping they could hold on. I found their BBQ chicken salad held up well enough in a plastic carryout container and hit the spot. The workers were always so genuinely appreciative of our business. The restaurant survived the lean pandemic months in part, I would later learn, by availing themselves of a $112,500 forgivable Paycheck Protection Program loan.

To celebrate Governor Hogan lifting the Maryland stay-at-home order, we took a family day trip one Saturday to Cumberland to visit our oldest son. We spent the afternoon doing "permitted outdoor activities," or the things you sometimes never get around to doing. We explored the city of Cumberland on foot, walked the Knobley Tunnel Trail to the C&O towpath, and visited the historic train station. We later visited my mom and sat on her ground-floor condo patio wearing face masks and talking through her screen door.

Local news showed massive crowds on the Ocean City, Maryland, boardwalk over Memorial Day weekend. I was disappointed we had already canceled our beach vacation rental for August but confident we made the right call. My Memorial Day Monday was uneventful, but a thousand miles to the west, a match was struck.

Shortly after 8:00 p.m. on Monday, May 25, Minneapolis police officers responded to a call about a possible counterfeit $20 bill being used at a corner grocery. They encountered a Black man, later identified as George Floyd, and a struggle ensued. While Floyd was handcuffed and face down on the ground, Officer Derek Chauvin presses his knee into Floyd's neck for about nine minutes, as Floyd cried out multiple times, "I can't breathe." Bystanders pleaded with the officers and recorded the whole takedown on their cell phones.

Floyd was later pronounced dead at the hospital, and the cell videos went viral. Protesters around the country took to the streets to demand justice.

After protesters torched a Minneapolis police station, President Trump responded on Twitter with tweets like "when the looting starts, the shooting starts," and a separate one in which the president said, "I can't stand back & watch this happen to a great American City, Minneapolis. A total lack of leadership. Either the very weak Radical Left Mayor, Jacob Frey, get his act together and bring the City under control, or I will send in the National Guard & get the job done right—"

Twitter took the unprecedented action of slapping a warning label on the president's tweets, which read, "this Tweet violated the Twitter Rules about glorifying violence. However, Twitter has determined that it may be in the public's interest for the Tweet to remain accessible."

In Oakland, a federal police officer guarding the federal courthouse was shot and killed by an unknown suspect initially believed to be Antifa, a radical left-wing group. We later learned the murderer was a US Air Force sergeant with ties to the right-wing extremist group known as boogaloo.

$

On Friday, May 29, the last workday of the month, the PRAC officially issued a solicitation for our federal pandemic response website contract. It took twelve volunteers from the federal inspector general community and twenty versions, but in only twenty-five days we were now able to solicit bids to hire a vendor to update and maintain a robust transparency website and help us manage and analyze pandemic data. Later that day in unrelated news, President Trump announced that the United States would be pulling out of the World Health Organization.

It's hard to think strategically when you're staring at fires. I needed the quiet of a Saturday morning to think through how to move forward, particularly with one of the ideas I had on day one: agile oversight.

I had written a chapter for a book about risk management and inspectors general a year or so before the pandemic hit and wrote about agile oversight. I found the concept fascinating. It's an idea that started years before in the world of software development as an alternative to the traditional way to build IT systems.

The basic premise with agile development is to work together with your customer to deliver early and continuous pieces of the whole and iterate improvements over short periods of time called sprints. Continuous communication is intended to avoid getting to the end of a long project to discover you're delivering something that is of no use. An IG pandemic oversight audit that would take eighteen months to complete would not be as helpful as more near real-time insights.

Private-sector auditors have adopted the agile approach, but the concept had not caught on with federal inspectors general. One main reason was that our reports by law are required to be made public. Even under the best of circumstances with seemingly irrefutable evidence, inspector general oversight reports are sometimes harshly criticized by hypersensitive federal officials and sometimes dismissed as being just plain wrong. Our reports have to be bullet-proof, and the agile approach increases the risk of making a mistake or being incomplete.

At the same time, inspectors general have a unique point of view regarding risk intelligence that needs to be shared with agency management, the administration, Congress, and the American public. This risk intelligence needs to be shared as quickly as possible, while there is time for management to make course corrections, even if the intelligence is less than complete. This also means that watchdogs need to share the risk intelligence in a way that can be easily understood. Federal managers should be able to quickly grasp: the "what," the "so what," and the "now what."

I was inspired by the pandemic oversight work we had seen already from my colleagues at the Small Business Administration, Department of Health and Human Services,

Department of Labor, and Department of Veterans Affairs. I spent May 30 creating a proof of concept for an agile oversight playbook. I wanted us to spread the message to other auditors and watchdogs, federal and state, that a national crisis like the pandemic requires that we deliver insights now to policymakers. Time was of the essence with pandemic oversight. Insights now, or #InsightsNow, became one of our battle cries—and synonymous with agile oversight.

With significant input from others, I also ended May with some clarity on the vision for the staff office of the PRAC. This vision guided us through the next year or so as we hired more and more staff and ultimately grew to fifty-plus full-time staff, along with fifteen data scientists we embedded within inspector general offices. Baked into our vision were notions of public trust and good government—and significantly—we would be an intentionally designed remote team. I thought of it as a distributed workforce in a virtual workspace.

I had to convince some others that an intentionally designed, fully remote organization could work in the federal government. Leaning into the shutdown and openly embracing remote work meant we could hire the best talent regardless of their zip code. With mission in mind, we didn't try to replicate an office; we built to an imagined future state. It was a leap of faith, but this allowed us to assemble a team of the best and the brightest.

This strategy significantly widened the talent pool. We found no shortage of professionals outside the DC metro area with top-flight credentials and a passion for public service. We hired talented people who were unable to move to DC (especially during a pandemic). We hired talented people from traditionally excluded populations like military spouses with families on the move. Recruitment and retention aside, the PRAC's remote work environment attracted professionals who better represent America's communities.

The PRAC would at one time have staff in the DC-area and in five time zones, in communities large and small throughout the US and one territory. It was a team of professionals from various social backgrounds and with varied lived experiences, which allowed us to conceptualize issues with fresh and local perspectives.

Also baked into our staff vision was the desire to leave a legacy for the next crew who would have to oversee emergency spending. The COVID-19 pandemic may be a once-in-a-hundred-year event, but we knew it wouldn't be the last crisis in our lifetimes to require a massive federal response.

8

ANOTHER CRISIS COMPETES WITH THE PANDEMIC FOR THE NATION'S ATTENTION
(SUMMER 2020)

The second COVID wave hits with public acts of incivility and protests, and fraud goes viral. The Treasury Department resists calls to make pandemic spending data public, as the PRAC goes about the business of building a leading-edge remote team and developing workarounds.

For me, the initial shock of the pandemic crisis was beginning to fade by the summer. News was no longer breaking on an hourly basis. My sense of time expanded and was beginning to return to normal. I could think in terms of seasons again and not days and months. As exigencies waned, government agencies should have also expanded their field of vision.

Unfortunately, Washington remained operating largely in pandemic "response" mode and failed to shift gears. Agencies should have begun transitioning to recovery mode and significantly increasing their antifraud activities, but I saw little evidence of that occurring, except when they were pushed by their IGs. For its part, I found Congress largely distracted, disengaged, or disinterested in fulfilling its important congressional oversight role. There were some exceptions, but too few to cut through the noise or make a difference.

On June 1, the Treasury Department electronically deposited $984.15 into our family checking account. This was our first stimulus check as the public called it, or Economic Impact Payment as it was called in the CARES Act. For the Internal Revenue Service, it was a tax relief credit. In other words, the IRS was giving you back (in advance), some of the taxes you owed for 2020.

The theory behind the stimulus checks was that you would go out and spend the extra money and keep the economy from tanking. I don't pretend to be an economist. I do know that while we as a family could always use the extra money, the pandemic did not affect our personal finances. Additional rounds of stimulus checks would continue under the Biden administration. From my personal perspective, these payments were not based on need and were, therefore, government waste. Not in every instance, of course. Millions of Americans needed the extra funds. But I also knew some did not.

A Stanford University economist studied the economic impact of what was ultimately three rounds of stimulus payments under the Trump and Biden administrations and concluded that while these payments—totally over $800 billion—had "a big impact on personal disposable income" they "led to little to no increase in consumption and thus did not stimulate the economy."

It was summertime and just when we thought it was safe to rip off the face mask and get back in the water, a second COVID wave hit the country. Florida was especially hard hit. In July, federal prosecutors charged a Miami father and his three adult sons for peddling a bleach-based fake "miracle" cure for COVID.

President Trump urged Americans to mask up to protect themselves and others.

"We're asking everybody that, when you are not able to socially distance, wear a mask," he said from the White House. "Whether you like the mask or not, they have an impact, they have an effect, and we need everything we can get." The president later tweeted, "We are United in our effort to defeat the Invisible China Virus, and many people say that it is Patriotic to wear a face mask when you can't socially distance. There's nobody more Patriotic than me, your favorite President."

Despite Florida being a COVID hot spot, Governor Ron DeSantis rejected calls for a statewide mask mandate.

"I believe you can catch more flies with honey," DeSantis said.

I can't say whether this approach encouraged more voluntary mask wearing, but the sentiments expressed by some government officials seemed to embolden rude and sometimes criminal conduct from anti-maskers.

A couple of videos from this time went viral on Twitter. A maskless Florida man raged in a Costco screaming, "Get back!" while he rushed toward the store manager. An older woman in the Midwest was filmed deliberately coughing on a grocery store worker. A California woman at a Trader Joe's refused to wear a mask, and when the store manager politely told her about the store mask policy, she proceeded to throw a fit.

"My doctor says—!" she raged.

I unfortunately personally witnessed an act of incivility in my hometown. I needed a haircut badly, so I made an appointment with my barber shortly after Montgomery County allowed barbershops to reopen with restrictions. My barbershop is operated by three Vietnamese American immigrants, and during my appointment I watched a woman berate Kim for cutting the woman's fidgety young son's hair too short. The mom complained. She complained loudly. She complained loudly over and over.

"Okay, sorry," Kim said repeatedly. Kim told the mom that she wouldn't have to pay, but that didn't stop the haranguing. Then the little boy started in. There was something in the way the woman talked down to Kim and the way the boy derisively said "she" in talking about Kim. I had no doubt that I was witnessing anti-Asian hate. It was relentless. The woman wouldn't leave.

President Trump had recently spoken at a youth rally in Arizona about COVID, repeating the phrase "kung flu." This divisive term was all over social media again. It wasn't funny, and it likely emboldened some people to act on their darkest impulses and fears.

I intervened and de-escalated the situation in the barbershop and thankfully the mom left dragging her little monster with her. I could tell by her reaction that Kim was no stranger to racial animosity. It was a feeling I have never experienced. My first pandemic haircut left me equal parts sad and mad.

Anti-Asian hate spiked across America during the pandemic. According to the Anti-Asian Hate Crime Report (2021), hate crimes against Asian Americans increased by 145 percent in the sixteen largest cities in the US in 2020 compared with numbers from 2019. According to one research paper, hate crime against Asian Americans surged when the blaming labels including "kung flu" or "Chinese virus" were used publicly.

The US Commission on Civil Rights—an independent, bipartisan, and fact-finding federal agency—sent a letter to US senators in May with their concerns and recommendations to address anti-Asian racism and hate crimes. Early in the year, the FBI had warned local law enforcement to expect a surge in anti-Asian hate crimes.

The White House began phasing out Project Airbridge in June. Under this public-private arrangement, FEMA spent over $200 million to transport about one billion personal protection items that had been purchased in China by six US medical supply distributors. The companies were supposed to provide 50 percent of these items to designated COVID hot spots.

The inspector general's office for the Department of Homeland Security later reported on the program. Auditors essentially found that Project Airbridge was a dud. Medical supply distributors had ample domestic inventories on hand, it turned out, and they only ended up providing 35 percent of supplies to the designated facilities instead of the agreed-upon 50 percent.

The inspector general attributed Project Airbridge's unnecessary air shipments of medical supplies to the pressure

FEMA faced to get supplies distributed quickly and the *limited understanding* of commercial supply and demand. FEMA was given one week from idea to implementation. Limited understanding is the polite way of saying that those leading Project Airbridge, including presidential adviser Jared Kushner, had little idea what they were doing. Career professionals at FEMA may bear some responsibility, but certainly not all.

Just as the second COVID wave hit, protests over racial injustice, police brutality, and George Floyd's murder continued to spread to cities across the nation in the summer of 2020. A *New York Times* article from July labeled Black Lives Matter one of the largest movements in US history, estimating that up to 26 million people may have participated in demonstrations.

Public health researchers would later determine that these large-scale gatherings had no impact on COVID rates, but numerous scholars and authors have written about how the two issues converged. Common ground between conservatives and progressives was shrinking as divisions grew wider. Some progressives who tended to be more agreeable toward social distancing measures decided that social justice was more important. Some conservatives who resented social distancing measures were now calling out what they viewed as hypocrisy by progressives.

The sociological significance of the convergence of the pandemic with the protests is beyond the scope of this book. All I knew was that none of this helped us unite for the common good during the pandemic, and Washington and the nation were now juggling two national crises.

In August, the city of Kenosha, Wisconsin, was seized by riots and protests following another police shooting. The county declared a state of emergency and the Wisconsin

National Guard was deployed. Kyle Rittenhouse, a seventeen-year-old with an AR-15 from Antioch, Illinois, traveled to the city to voluntarily patrol. He fatally shot two protesters and wounded another. In a phone interview with a *Washington Post* reporter after his arrest, Rittenhouse said he used the $1,200 he received in pandemic unemployment benefits to buy the gun. A jury would later acquit Rittenhouse of murder charges.

My top priorities in June were recruiting our senior leadership team and establishing the right work culture. Molding the right culture up front is a lot easier than trying to reshape it after it has formed calluses. But it still takes a clear intention, a lot of work, and a little bit of luck.

I was reviewing scores of résumés and conducting interview after interview to hire key staff. We were building a team and often hiring people I only met over video calls. We were a lean government start-up, and we acted like one by using the hiring flexibilities Congress gave us. These authorities included being able to set salaries up to a ceiling, to directly hire people without having to go through the normal federal hiring processes, which can take months, and to hire federal retirees without it affecting their pensions.

I was looking for people who believed in the vision and shared our values of public service. I was trying hard to avoid the temptation of "any warm body will do."

Every hire was a gamble that the person would be day-one ready and would fit in culturally with other team members and our many partners. It was about finding the right person at the right time in their career, and every new hire changed the team chemistry. I discovered that some people are just unable to tolerate ambiguity and uncertainty. Some people can survive through it. We needed people who would thrive in this environment. At the same time, I was juggling, and I had too many balls in the air—building, leading, and often doing the work.

Aside from staffing, one of the balls I was juggling was our first virtual listening forum, which we held on June 3.

The CARES Act gave us special authority to conduct public hearings. I can't specifically speak to how much thought went into granting us this authority, but I can tell you it was a provision in the Recovery Act legislation and was used sparingly. My guess is nobody bothered to take the provision out of the CARES Act draft when they cut and pasted the language from the Recovery Act.

Regardless, in a hyper-partisan political environment, congressional hearings may not be the most suitable venue to determine objective facts. The PRAC could use this hearing authority to shine a spotlight on experts and key witnesses, and we did.

During this time, congressional committees were holding their hearings virtually, so we decided to follow suit. We suspected, correctly as it turned out, that we could attract more prominent witnesses and reach larger audiences with virtual forums.

With minimal staff at the time, I was calling and emailing to line up our potential witnesses and the technical support team needed to host a virtual event. For our first forum, our witnesses included Ashish Jha, MD, MPH, then a global health expert at Harvard who would go on to become the White House COVID-19 Response Coordinator.

In his statement before the committee, Dr. Jha was clear: "There is only one path that allows us to keep our economy open and prevent hundreds of thousands of additional deaths: a robust testing, tracing, and isolation strategy. Of course, such a strategy needs to be paired with ongoing modest social distancing and universal mask wearing, which are critical to keeping the virus under control."

The president of the American Nurses Association spoke on the continued scarcity of personal protective equipment, which was requiring some nurses to decontaminate and reuse N95 masks, the respirator type of highly protective face mask. He also talked about the mental health impact of the pandemic.

The head of the National Association of State Auditors, Comptrollers and Treasurers talked about the urgent need for better financial reporting guidance from Washington so the states could account for the massive spending. A representative from the American Legion expressed concern about the limitations of telehealth for some of our nation's veterans.

The forum was live streamed on YouTube and reached a couple of thousand viewers.

At that point, nobody in the federal government had a clear and unobstructed view into where $2.6 trillion in federal coronavirus relief funding was going, who was getting it, and what it was being spent on.

The congressional watchdog Government Accountability Office (GAO) was required under the CARES Act to issue bimonthly spending reports starting in June. In its initial report, GAO called out "the absence of comprehensive data" and laid responsibility squarely at the feet of the White House. GAO specifically faulted the Office of Management and Budget (OMB) guidance that gave agencies until July to report COVID-19–related spending.

We repeatedly raised our concerns with the administration about the lack of timely and comprehensive guidance for federal agencies and recipients. It wasn't just the PRAC and GAO, though, who were frustrated. We also heard from state officials through the National Governors Association. State officials told us that regardless of what OMB said in its initial guidance, it would be the states receiving federal pandemic funding who would later be held accountable and publicly criticized for not following the rules. They wanted and needed federal guidance now on how to spend and report on these federal funds.

In early June, we learned that Treasury Secretary Mnuchin told members of Congress that the administration would not be releasing the names of Paycheck Protection Program borrowers. This was a serious blow to federal spending transparency over what had by then grown to $670 billion in taxpayer dollars. The news was met with immediate howling from the PRAC, the press, public interest groups, and some members of Congress.

Michael Horowitz and I took the rare step of sending a letter, signed as PRAC chair and executive director, to congressional leadership on June 11. I called a senior Treasury official on Saturday in advance and gave him a read-out on the letter. We weren't going to share a copy in advance. This was a heads-up call. We weren't inviting edits to the letter or soliciting comments. We just wanted to play fair and tell the administration in advance that this letter was coming. Most inspectors general prefer to operate from a position of "no surprises."

We were officially, publicly and in writing, bringing to Congress's attention our significant concerns about the serious deficiencies in the financial reporting of pandemic-related spending. It wasn't just that the reporting would not happen until July. Even with the delay, the reporting by agencies would not include all the data required to be reported under the CARES Act, and there was a dispute with Treasury and OMB over whether significant programs involving billions of dollars were even subject to public reporting.

Mistakes sometimes happen when new laws are drafted. This is especially true when a large, complicated bill is cobbled together and passed in a matter of days, without time for the members of Congress to read, let alone understand, what they are voting on.

The 300+ page CARES Act was so large that it was divided into two parts: Division A and Division B. Unfortunately, the PRAC and the inspectors general were referenced in one division of the act, while the other division contained major programs including, among others, the Paycheck Protection Program ($670 billion); the Emergency Economic Stabilization Fund ($454 billion) for banks; and the Coronavirus Relief Fund for payments to states, tribal governments, and local government ($150 billion).

When a bill this size gets introduced and passed in seven days, the following are the kinds of ambiguities that pop up. Did Congress intend for the PRAC and the inspectors general to have jurisdiction over all pandemic relief funding in both divisions of the legislation or just those programs listed within their same division?

With the Treasury Department questioning whether the inspectors general and PRAC had jurisdiction over all programs in both divisions of the CARES Act, we started getting questions from congressional staff for our opinion on how they could fix what became known as the Division A issue. It would take new legislation to fix the problem.

In the meantime, we had a mandate in the law to post federal spending data on our public website, and by necessity we began to develop workarounds to fill in the gaps. Workarounds became a "secret" to our success.

We couldn't initially post USASpending.gov federal spending data from the primary federal government spending website because there was no way to segregate pandemic spending from general federal spending. Those data would not be available until at least July.

In the short term, we grabbed federal COVID-19–related contracting data from the Federal Procurement Data System and posted those data on our website in June, along with a Track the Money tool, which allowed users to search contract spending by state and county. Users could also download the complete data set to conduct their own analysis and sort by category of the goods or services purchased.

Meanwhile, news organizations and public interest groups had filed a Freedom of Information Act lawsuit, and the Justice Department was resisting efforts in court to force Treasury and the SBA to publicly release Paycheck Protection Program data. The public, the Congress, and the media were demanding to know who got PPP loans and how much they got. The Justice Department maintained that releasing the small business borrower names would also divulge confidential payroll information that could be deduced from the amount of the loan.

Bowing to pressure, Secretary Mnuchin partially reversed course in a June letter to lawmakers, and the administration agreed to provide relevant congressional committees with nonpublic loan level data "with the understanding that nonpublic personally identifiable and commercially sensitive business information will be treated as confidential."

The administration then took the position that they would publicly release only partial PPP data. For small business loans under $150,000, they would redact the borrower's name. For loans over $150,000, they would not report the exact loan amount. This, too, was unacceptable from our perspective because it would mean the public would not have full transparency on 89 percent of PPP loans and 50 percent of the total federal dollars spent. We'd have to pry the Paycheck Protection Program data out of their cold hands—which we ultimately did in early November thanks in part to the help of a lawsuit by the media.

We issued our first PRAC pandemic oversight report in June. We had surveyed the inspectors general and summarized the top pandemic challenges facing the federal government. The first challenge, unsurprisingly, was the lack of financial management of pandemic-related funding. Our concern about the public reporting of pandemic-related spending and the significant amount of money federal agencies may lose to fraud and waste as the result of improper payments was front of mind and a consistent theme.

In an emergency, you take all the help you can get from family and friends, and with this report, we got help from the team at the NASA Office of Inspector General who did a lot of the heavy lifting producing this first report, under the leadership of their inspector general and our PRAC vice chair, Paul Martin. NASA didn't receive much in the way of federal pandemic relief, but Martin volunteered to serve as PRAC vice chair, and he and his team were key PRAC contributors at every turn.

In July, Treasury OIG negotiated a compromise with the Treasury Department regarding the $150 billion Coronavirus Relief Fund that supported state, local, and tribal governments. Treasury Department attorneys ultimately conceded that the Treasury OIG and the PRAC had jurisdiction over this program, and the department agreed to work with Treasury OIG to provide transparency on this spending.

The Treasury OIG and the PRAC seized the initiative and made sure there would be public reporting on this $150 billion pot of money by creating a new web reporting portal for state and local governments that received Coronavirus Relief Funds. In the absence of action by OMB, Treasury OIG itself established guidance on how, when, and what data to report. They were only able to do so because of quirky language in the CARES Act giving them expanded authorities. This would ultimately be one of the most consequential workarounds in the PRAC's history.

We had multiple conversations with OMB leadership about the need for a government-wide recipient reporting portal to identify all pandemic spending. We were told that existing systems simply could not be modified to take on this task, and it would be eighteen months at the earliest to build a new system.

Some OMB career staff looked for win-wins with us. In August, at our urging OMB issued a Controller Alert to agency chief financial officers. This alert provided guidance to help strengthen the quality of the descriptions of projects where the federal pandemic dollars were being used. It was a small victory.

At the end of July, we received from the Treasury Department the first COVID-coded emergency spending data from USASpending.gov—6.5 million rows of data—and we relaunched our website using these data and coupling it with visual displays and mapping. These data don't tell the whole story of pandemic spending due to various known gaps, so we continued developing workarounds and pressing agencies for additional data for both the website and our analytics mission.

Meanwhile, to improve our PandemicOversight.gov website, we had a surreal and auspicious video call with the team at USAFacts.org, a nonprofit public interest group dedicated to shedding light on federal spending. It also happens to be the brainchild of former Microsoft cofounder and CEO Steve Ballmer.

Ballmer himself participated in the call. He was the center square on the video call as he shared with our small staff things to consider in website design and his experiences with the limitations of federal spending data. While Ballmer was the star, joining us on the call was a slightly disheveled young man dressed casually in a T-shirt. He was a young USAFacts.org staffer, and he explained how he came up with workarounds to gather COVID-positive test results and deaths at the state and local level because federal data were not reliable. He was ingenious, persistent, and agile, and just the kind of person we wanted on our team.

After the call, Paul Martin and I had the same reaction. How can we use our hiring flexibilities to hire people like that? I emailed Ballmer's representative to ask how we could recruit similar talent to join our team. She told me to forget about traditional government job postings. The way to reach college students and recent graduates was through the Handshake app. And that kid on the call? He was from Ballmer's graduate class at Stanford.

This interaction with Ballmer and his team was the inspiration for what became the PRAC's Data Science Fellows program. We would use our legal authority and resources to hire bright, recently graduated data scientists. We would place them in the offices of inspectors general free of charge to that office. The fellow could work remotely from anywhere in the country.

To provide opportunities and promote diversity and inclusion, we would recruit from university programs across the country, not just from elite schools on the coasts. This program would provide a pathway to public service for those who wanted to continue their federal career, and it became a valuable talent pipeline for OIGs.

$

It was clear by this time that we were facing a historic level of fraud.

Massive COVID-related fraud schemes were being uncovered and reported in the news, and we were seeing only the tip of the fraud iceberg. The massive pandemic relief spending programs provided a large attack surface and were irresistible targets for fraudsters.

In 2019, the federal government, through the Department of Labor, gave the states about $27 billion annually for unemployment insurance, which are state-administered programs partially funded by federal tax dollars. In response to the pandemic, the federal government would spend over $872 billion in federal unemployment insurance funding in the CARES Act and other related emergency spending bills, a 32x increase.

Pandemic relief legislation provided additional weekly benefits, a $300 or $600 per week kicker, and created a new temporary program called the Pandemic Unemployment Assistance (PUA) program for self-employed, gig workers, and others who would not typically qualify for state unemployment benefits. Normally, states would have historical wage records from employers they can use to verify whether someone is eligible for unemployment insurance. With the workers who were now eligible for unemployment insurance benefits under the PUA program, there were no prior employment records to check. Applicants would be able to file for unemployment benefits and self-certify as to their previous income.

On July 15, Maryland Governor Hogan announced the state had exposed a $500 million unemployment insurance fraud scheme involving 47,000 applications.

"The state of Maryland has uncovered a massive, sophisticated criminal enterprise involving widespread identity theft and coordinated fraudulent unemployment insurance claims in Maryland," Hogan said during a news conference. The scheme included fraudulent claims filed in the names of Governor Hogan, his lieutenant governor, and several members of the governor's cabinet.

Criminal charges in the Maryland case would never be filed (as of June 2023 at least), which unfortunately turned out to be the norm in cases involving transnational criminals who attacked our programs. The relative anonymity of the internet and weak extradition authorities in some nations meant many international fraudsters were often beyond the reach of the long arm of the law—for now. Rest assured, federal investigators and prosecutors are busy working some of these cases, but they are undeniably more complex and time consuming.

Department of Labor OIG special agents are responsible for preventing and detecting unemployment insurance fraud and frequently work with the FBI, the US Secret Service, and state investigators. Before the pandemic, they averaged about 100 unemployment insurance fraud investigations a year. In the first six months of the pandemic, they had opened 2,500 investigations. By March 31, 2021, that number would grow to 15,000.

In June 2020, Labor OIG special agents, in collaboration with Oklahoma officials, prevented nearly $15 million in fraudulent unemployment insurance claims. The OIG analyzed the digital fingerprint of applicants and identified nearly 3,800 fraudulent claims before they were paid out, including 1,300 filed from a range of internet protocol addresses located in London.

In July, the FBI issued a press release, "FBI sees spike in fraudulent unemployment insurance claims filed using stolen identities." The FBI attributed the stolen personally identifying information to online purchases of stolen personal information, previous data breaches, computer intrusions, cold-calling victims while using impersonation scams, email phishing schemes, physical theft of data from individuals or third parties, and from public websites and social media accounts.

Most Americans would be shocked to learn how much of their personal information is available for sale on the dark web. The low price that this information fetches reflects just how available it is.

One of the largest data breaches occurred in 2017 and involved the credit bureau Equifax. Investigators traced the theft to China, and the Justice Department ultimately charged four Chinese military-backed hackers. These hackers were part of a team known to intelligence and law enforcement officials as APT 41.

To give you an idea of the serious risk these hackers pose to private- and public-sector computer systems, APT stands for Advanced Persistent Threat. Hacking is their full-time job, they're good at it, and their team works in shifts. The Equifax breach is the largest known hack of personal information involving state-sponsored actors. These hackers harvested the names, dates of births, social security numbers, and other personal data of 145 million Americans. In December 2022, the Secret Service publicly acknowledged that these same hackers stole at least $20 million in pandemic funds from the federal government and over a dozen states. The total amount is likely much higher.

"It would be crazy to think this group didn't target all fifty states," Secret Service agent Roy Dotson told reporters. Dotson played a distinguished role serving as the Secret Service national pandemic fraud recovery coordinator. The Secret Service later publicly confirmed more than 1,000 ongoing investigations involving transnational and domestic criminals defrauding pandemic programs and characterized APT 41 as "a notable player."

That is just one hack. Government agencies, companies, and organizations are attacked every day. As a result, your name, social security number, address, and date of birth can be purchased on the dark web for less than the price of a Chipotle burrito.

In addition to the pandemic unemployment insurance program and the Paycheck Protection Program, we were seeing large-scale fraud in another SBA program: the Economic Injury Disaster Loan program. In Washington, this program is routinely referred to as the EIDL program. To save you from yet another acronym, allow me to refer to these as disaster loans.

Through this disaster loan program, SBA provides low-interest loans to small businesses, nonprofits, farms, and other organizations. The president declared COVID-19 a disaster, and this declaration authorized SBA to provide disaster loans to eligible entities. In addition, the CARES Act provided billions for a new related small business disaster program: emergency advance grants. Grants don't have to be paid back.

By July 31, the SBA had received 14 million disaster loan applications, and approved over 3 million applications for around $170 billion. Additionally, SBA disbursed nearly 6 million emergency advance grants, totaling $20 billion. Within all the pandemic relief legislation, Congress provided SBA more disaster loan funding than all the years combined since the SBA was created in 1953.

Just like with the pandemic unemployment insurance program, the self-certification language in the CARES Act's small business loan programs resulted in massive fraud.

The disaster loan program is run by SBA itself, unlike the Paycheck Protection Program, which used approved lenders. SBA could approve a loan based on the applicant self-certifying the business's start date, type of business, annual gross revenues, and cost of goods sold. In other words, the SBA would take a loan applicant's word for it. While there was some automated checking of data, these loans would largely be approved based on an honor system.

Disaster loan fraud scams soon went viral. An SBA customer service representative who later spoke to reporters on the condition of anonymity said, "I've never seen anything like it. I don't think they had any processes in place. They just sent the money out."

The level of fraud being reported in the disaster program prompted SBA inspector general Mike Ware and his team to issue a report in July raising "serious concerns" of fraud. Mike's team had received complaints from nearly 440 financial institutions ranging from small, local credit unions to major national institutions. Their concerns included accounts established using stolen identities and schemes on social media where organized fraud rings were recruiting and convincing people to provide their personal information.

One way to tell if an agency is taking its watchdog seriously is by flipping toward the back of an audit report and reading what is labeled "Management's Comments." This is a section required by professional auditing standards to get management's views. In response to the July inspector general report raising "serious concerns," SBA downplayed the watchdog's concerns and boasted of the "robust set of internal controls," which they said, "contrary to the OIG's assertions, . . . have in fact saved taxpayers billions of dollars." SBA was not yet taking the fraud issue seriously enough.

$$\text{\textcircled{\$}}$$

At home, we were doing our family grocery shopping largely via Instacart. The masked delivery person would pick the groceries off the shelves based on our online order and drop off bags on our porch. It was contactless delivery with a distant wave of acknowledgment and thanks while the driver was backing out of our driveway. We had a routine of staging the shopping bags on the counter before wiping down the individual packages with disinfectant wipes. Home grocery delivery services were available before the pandemic, but the prolonged crisis would take that business to the next level.

Our college-aged son was excited to begin his college experience at Towson University in August, having transferred there from community college. He secured on-campus housing and moved in the week before school started. He started making friends and having fun. Both he and the university were overly optimistic though. The university's anticipated return to normalcy for the fall 2020 semester was abruptly but predictably suspended on August 26, when Towson canceled in-person classes and closed the campus. Too many students had tested positive. It would be another semester of remote learning.

The pandemic was not through with us yet.

9

WHO ARE THESE PEOPLE? SCAMS AND IDENTITY FRAUD
(FALL 2020)

Inspector general watchdogs develop new approaches to address the sprawling pandemic fraud crisis, the White House hosts a super-spreader event, and the president gets COVID and is hospitalized. Governors impose restrictions on interstate travel, and the FBI thwarts a plot to kidnap a governor over her COVID countermeasures.

A Labor Day 2020 Twitter post, from an account dedicated as an apolitical memorial for healthcare workers who died from COVID-19, tallied the losses:

> Over 1100 healthcare workers have died of covid in the US. Working in a nursing home is now America's deadliest job. Some still don't have adequate PPE.

The Health and Human Services Office of the Inspector General released a report on nursing homes later in the fall. More than 67,000 nursing home residents had died of COVID-19–related illnesses, representing almost 30 percent of all COVID-19 deaths in the US at the time.

The Pandemic Response Accountability Committee's six-month anniversary was on September 27, and that was the date I had set in the stand-up plan to have all our key leaders and major components in place. Everything was going according to plan, even if we were still working through some of the finer details of how we would use federal pandemic spending data and analytics to fight fraud. I would remind myself and the team that we were moving forward, with the required urgency, in a swift and deliberate manner.

According to reports, state unemployment insurance systems were being overwhelmed with new applications. Kansas received 12 million phone calls to its customer service line in April 2020. Louisiana experienced a 3,500 percent increase in claims between January and April 2020. Claims in Ohio increased 1,300 percent between January and April 2020.

As states tried to address the fraud they were experiencing, they sometimes flagged legitimate applicants as false positives delaying benefits. This happened to someone in my social circle. It took weeks before their application was approved. News stories would report on people who filed for unemployment insurance only to discover that someone had already filed a claim in their name. In September, the Colorado labor department reported that more than 75 percent of claims for the federal unemployment assistance program for self-employed workers and independent contractors since July were determined to be fraudulent. In one two-week period, the state received 50,000 fraudulent claims.

Several states began using digital identity verification services of private vendors, which requires a selfie or photo ID to verify the person is who they say they are. This digital identity is validated by comparing it with other records from the credit bureaus, departments of motor vehicles, and cell phone providers.

When state unemployment insurance agencies began using computer selfies and algorithms to verify that the face on the screen (who took the selfie) matches the picture on the driver's license, fraudsters turned to 3-D printed masks.

Fraudsters filed multiple claims for benefits using a common email "dotting" method to avoid detection. Gmail and some other email services don't recognize periods in the part of the email address before the @ sign. Move the period around and some government computer systems would think it's different people, while Google will deliver all the emails to the same email account.

In response to fraud experiences across the states, the Justice Department and its law enforcement partners established the National Unemployment Insurance Fraud Task Force, a multi-agency task force supported by analytical and intelligence support from DOJ's International Organized Crime Intelligence and Operations Center (IOC-2). We hired an investigative analyst and detailed her to work at IOC-2 to support this mission.

In the SBA's disaster loan program, "account change" was one common early fraud technique. Scammers would apply for loans and get approved using someone's stolen identity, including their bank account information. SBA would verify all this information on a first pass in approving the loan. Once the loan was approved but before disbursement of the money, the scammer would log into the SBA's web portal and change the bank account to one under their control. SBA didn't re-verify the new bank account after any changes.

In October, the SBA OIG reported that the SBA paid over $13 billion in potentially fraudulent disaster loans to bank accounts that differed from the original bank accounts listed on applications and approximately $58 billion in potentially fraudulent loans to applicants using the same internet address, the same email address, the same street address, or the same bank accounts. According to many, the SBA wasn't exercising sufficient oversight of their disaster loan contractor, or their PPP lenders, and neither the agency nor its partners were nimble enough to quickly respond to emerging fraud trends.

Once again, the SBA gave no indication that the agency was taking pandemic fraud seriously enough, at least according to how they reacted to the warnings from their inspector general. The Management Comments section of this report complains that the watchdog "grossly overstates the risk of fraud."

Banks are required to file suspicious activity reports with the Financial Crimes Enforcement Network, or FinCEN. By October, banks had filed 20,000 reports related to disaster loans.

Fraudsters were one or more steps ahead of the federal agencies trying to prevent fraud. As soon as SBA or a state labor department made a change to tighten controls, that information was posted on the dark web.

New fraud variants were popping up regularly on the dark web, including tutorials to defeat fraud controls. I first toured the dark web hellscape a few years back in a law enforcement training class. I knew vaguely that there was a part of the internet that is considered the seedy part of town that's off the beaten track. At that training class, though, the undercover cyber investigator showed us exactly where people go to shop and order whatever drug, kink, immoral, or sadist act they're in the market for. The dark web is online content that traditional web browsers can't find.

The underlying technology was originally developed by the US Navy Research Laboratory to protect the identities of intelligence agents as they exchange information online. As you can imagine, content on the dark web has only grown over time and now attracts those who want to conceal their identity for nefarious reasons. Law enforcement and fraud analysts conduct surveillance on these sites to find out about the latest fraud trends, but it's challenging to keep up.

Another fraud variant we were seeing was the fake farm disaster loan scheme. Fraudsters would use stolen identities to file multiple small-dollar disaster loan applications claiming to be farmers. It didn't matter what address they used: urban apartment, townhouse, or suburban tract home. SBA didn't check whether the address was a bona fide farm. Identity fraud victims would first learn about the fraud when they received a monthly bill notification from SBA reminding them to make their monthly loan payment. There were clusters of these cases all over the country: Rhode Island, Florida, North Dakota, Maine, and even Alaska.

Later this season the SBA inspector general and its external independent auditor issued its annual financial statement audit. The SBA's financial books were an irreconcilable mess, especially regarding reporting on the Paycheck Protection Program and the disaster loan program. The external auditor, one of the Big Four accounting firms, had to disclaim the audit opinion because of the number of accounting deficiencies and weaknesses. Once again, SBA disagreed with most of the findings of the independent auditor.

In response to the hair-raising, eye-watering, and jaw-dropping level of fraud, we needed new thinking. I thought of this as let's think differently, together.

The CARES Act doesn't even mention the PRAC doing data analytics, but it was clear that Congress expected us to pick up where the Recovery Board left off. Even before I got this job, I read the opinion piece in *The Hill* from a former senior level Recovery Act–era official. Its headline, "Fighting fraud in the CARES Act—Rebuild the ROC."

One of the great accomplishments of our predecessor, the Recovery Board, had been its fraud data analytics function they called the Rock. In 2010, the Recovery Operations Center (ROC) was a state-of-the-art data analytics center that found fraud indicators across federal spending data sets and sent fraud referrals to OIG investigators. It was the first cloud-based federal IT system of its kind, and the Recovery Board won awards for its efforts. As revolutionary as the ROC was, times had changed, and we needed to move beyond the realm of lore.

I also knew from talking with the inspectors general that unlike the Recovery Act days, the problem they were facing now was not finding fraud in the data. With the pandemic, some offices, especially at the SBA and the Labor Department, were drowning in fraud complaints, and their own data analytics offices were effectively using agency data to find even more fraud.

According to a September 2020 survey by TransUnion, on average 10 percent of Americans had reported being the victims of identity theft relating to government programs since the beginning of the pandemic. Fraud, particularly identity fraud, was rampant. The SBA Office of Inspector General was inundated with fraud complaints from citizens and financial institutions. Prior to the pandemic, they had three employees to triage about 700 hotline complaints a year. In the early months of the pandemic, they were deluged with 6,000 complaints per week.

The inspectors general needed immediate help, so analog solutions would have to do in the short term. To support the SBA OIG, we reached out to the other offices in the oversight community and asked for volunteers who could pitch in and go through these fraud hotline complaints. We arranged for ten oversight professionals from around the community to manually input hotline complaints into the SBA OIG investigative case management system.

Our data scientists built a hotline risk scoring model that could identify the highest risk complaints to help thin the haystack of fraud complaints so SBA investigators could find the needles. This would be the first of several technology projects we would pursue in the name of pandemic oversight.

While we were deciding on a recipe for success and gathering the right ingredients, we also knew that we needed to find a quick and easy win. For that, we looked to one area that was largely within our control: data sharing among the offices of the inspectors general.

A few years before the pandemic, Congress gave inspectors general special legal authority to match one agency data set against another. Ordinarily, to protect a citizen's privacy against big brother, the law requires two agencies to have a written agreement with certain restrictions in place before sharing data. In 2016, Congress exempted inspectors general from this requirement, but this legal authority was not being used as liberally as many hoped.

We put together a data sharing working group in July to bring the community together to focus on using the existing legal authority to share data among the offices of inspectors general to find fraud. This group was getting busy in the fall sharing ideas and approaches on how to match data across government programs.

Meanwhile, we were still looking for workarounds to get more public federal spending data to post on our website.

In early September we relaunched our website with a new address: PandemicOversight.gov. We mapped federal spending data to the location, or place of performance, to show where the money was being spent. We made it easier for the public to file fraud complaints. We posted our analysis of what was then four coronavirus response bills showing the large spending buckets. We also added pandemic oversight reports, so the public and policymakers could read more about what inspectors general were finding in their audits and investigations. Later in September we added federal spending data from Treasury's $150 billion Coronavirus Relief Fund program.

In November we finally obtained the complete Paycheck Protection Program data from the SBA. With the Freedom of Information Act lawsuit still pending in federal court, we thought it prudent to wait for the judge's ruling before we decided what PPP data we would publicly post on our website. We used the data for nonpublic investigative purposes and shared it with OIGs and other law enforcement agencies.

This would be another key distinction between the PRAC and the Recovery Act–era's ROC. If one of our partners had the capability to do their own analytics, we would act as a data broker and provide them with the entire data set. Many OIGs asked for complete program data sets to do analysis themselves, and we also shared the data with the FBI and Justice Department components. This took a heavy burden from the shoulders of the beleaguered desk officer at the SBA OIG who had been inundated with requests for law enforcement assistance from day one. Sharing data was another one of our "secrets" to success.

The Paycheck Protection Program data availability issue was resolved for good in November when a federal judge rejected the SBA's argument in the Freedom of Information Act lawsuit and ordered the public release of the loan data. We would now post data on our website for the public to see and search for those who received PPP loans.

One of the benefits of public transparency is that it supports the work of other important oversight players, like good government groups and the media. One issue, for example, that was identified with Paycheck Protection Program data involved the role of financial technology or FinTech lenders (think online lenders).

In part to reach underserved communities, the SBA authorized FinTech firms to participate in the Paycheck Protection Program. While FinTechs did serve this purpose, there were also questions about how well FinTechs scrutinized loan applications to detect fraud. Thanks to publicly available federal data, public interest organizations, the media, and academic researchers were able to research the role of FinTech firms in the facilitation of fraud. In my judgment, these nongovernmental sources conducted exceptional pandemic oversight for the benefit of the American people.

Researchers at one university later found that PPP loans processed by FinTech lenders were generally more likely to be accompanied by suspicious indicators than loans processed by traditional banks and credit unions, although the top three established FinTechs had particularly low rates of indicators of potential fraud.

In November, we released a study we commissioned from MITRE, the independent, federally funded research and development center. We asked MITRE to examine data gaps that impact transparency in federal pandemic relief spending at the program level. This report independently confirmed what we suspected: there was insufficient information describing the purpose of federal spending awards; there were no project level data to show how federally funded projects were progressing; there was no subrecipient information; and there was no information about how many jobs were created or retained as a result of federal spending.

The MITRE report also pointed out the level of effort that was required during the Recovery Act days to ensure robust public reporting from recipients of federal stimulus funds. It's not an easy task. That effort required extensive training, a call center, and outreach to individual state and local government recipients, all of which required significant time and money. Congress overlooked all this when drafting the CARES Act.

Additionally, the Recovery Act–era reporting structure was better suited for "shovel ready" projects, which are visible to the public, who can see their tax dollars at work with their very own eyes. For example, a citizen may be peeved enough with a stalled road construction project in their town that they look up on the federal government spending website and see that the project is reporting 100 percent completion with zero funds remaining on the project. This would raise a red flag and may indicate fraud, waste, or abuse.

During this season we issued our agile oversight toolkit, a seminal product that helped change the way that watchdogs think and talk about part of their oversight work. We produced this toolkit for federal, state, and local auditors as guidance on how to provide independent and objective insights during public emergencies. This is among the PRAC projects that I am most proud of, and it took a team from the community of inspectors general to put the toolkit together and build support for its use. The pandemic required new thinking to come alongside traditional audit work.

Agile just didn't mean fast. Speed was important, of course, but with agile oversight we meant innovative, iterative, and customer focused. It meant being comfortable working with partial or incomplete information. We issued the toolkit with explanations of how professional auditing standards applied, and we provided examples from different offices to inspire creativity. The term *agile oversight* entered the lexicon of OIGs and federal and state auditors.

One of the most consequential events in the fall of 2020, for people on both sides of the political spectrum, was the death of Supreme Court Justice Ruth Bader Ginsburg on September 18. Progressives mourned the loss of a champion, and conservatives celebrated the opportunity to remake the Supreme Court. A Supreme Court confirmation hearing was yet another event that distracted political leadership.

The president waited eight days after Justice Ginsburg's death and then nominated Amy Coney Barrett to fill the vacancy. The White House planned a convocation in the Rose Garden to announce the nomination. At least 200 people attended the event. A dozen attendees later tested positive for COVID-19, causing some to call it a super-spreader event.

The White House decided to forgo contact tracing. With so many White House staff and visitors who live in DC and adjacent counties, local health officials were concerned. They were concerned enough that DC and nine neighboring jurisdictions issued a joint health advisory asking individuals who visited the White House in the prior two weeks to get tested and contact their local health departments. The White House was a COVID-19 hot spot in late September 2020.

On October 2, the White House announced that President Trump and the First Lady had tested positive for COVID, along with several White House staff. One of the few official photos of President Trump wearing a mask is of him walking to the Marine One helicopter for transport to Walter Reed Medical Center in Bethesda, Maryland, where he stayed for treatment. Worried and masked White House staff huddled on the White House drive. When the president returned to the White House after three days in the hospital, he walked up the South Lawn stairs to enter the balcony. He stopped for a photo op, took off his mask, and saluted.

The White House later posted a video where the president thanked the Walter Reed staff and said that during his three-night stay he had "learned so much about coronavirus . . . One thing that's for certain—don't let it dominate you. Don't be afraid of it. You're going to beat it." The president said, "We have the best medical equipment. We have the best medicines. All developed recently. And you're going to beat it."

This pandemic wave spiked in the Midwest, and Wisconsin was especially hard hit. Political and legal challenges exacerbated the situation. The state supreme court had struck down Wisconsin Governor Tony Evers's "Safer at Home" order. The Republican-controlled state legislature filed a motion in court to support a legal filing challenging the governor's mask mandate within hours of President Trump announcing he had tested positive. A professor of epidemiology at UW–Milwaukee's Zilber School of Public Health was interviewed by the media at the time.

"In no other state are government officials and public health officials so disempowered to just take control of a public health crisis," the professor said. "It's really stunning what's happening here."

Meanwhile in Michigan, the FBI arrested thirteen members of the Wolverine Watchmen who allegedly plotted to kidnap Governor Whitmer from her home in part because of her COVID countermeasures.

State governors began placing restrictions on interstate travel. In Pennsylvania, the governor announced out-of-state visitors would be required to self-quarantine for fourteen days or present a negative test within three days before arrival. In New York, Governor Cuomo issued similar restrictions on out-of-state visitors to his state. In November, Maryland set a record for highest single-day number of new cases with 2,910 reported.

Alabama Governor Kay Ivey announced that the statewide mask mandate and stay-at-home order would be extended until January. "These are some of the darkest days since COVID-19 became a part of our daily conversations," Ivey told reporters, referring to record-breaking hospitalization numbers the state recorded in December. "The facts are indisputable. Our cases continue to rise. We have more Alabamians diagnosed with COVID-19 than ever before."

The COVID death toll in the US had reached 200,000 on September 24, and this grim milestone was recognized on the National Mall with a display of small American flags representing the 200,000 lives lost. This number would grow to 350,000 during the fall of 2020.

$

In our community, movie theaters were still shuttered by order of the county executive. Theaters would not open until March 2021, and only then at 25 percent capacity. Some theaters and theater chains did not survive. Regal Cinemas ultimately filed for bankruptcy and closed dozens of theaters around the nation. Our favorite community theater was not one of the lucky ones.

In fall 2020, though, in a throwback to a simpler time, someone had the great idea of opening a pop-up drive-in movie theater at the Frederick County Maryland fairgrounds. It was a bit of Yankee ingenuity in the Free State. Food trucks were parked along the perimeter, and the movie was projected on a big screen while the audio was broadcast through the radio. My wife and I spent a cool fall evening sitting in lawn chairs, eating corn dogs and nachos from the opened tailgate of my truck, and watching the quintessential drive-in movie, *American Graffiti*, as the sun set behind the screen and beyond the Blue Ridge Mountains. We forgot about the pandemic for a few hours.

That fall I experienced two other life events that were seriously affected by the pandemic.

The first was taking our youngest son for his driver's test. The Maryland Motor Vehicle Administration was allowing tests again by appointment only, but both driver and examiner had to wear a mask in the car. After my son passed, I memorialized the occasion with the traditional picture in the parking lot of the new driver smiling and holding up his license. I took one picture masked and one unmasked.

Then there was the upcoming election. I have not missed voting in an election since I became of age. I didn't relish the thought of waiting in line for hours packed next to strangers. But we weren't going to lose our voice because of COVID, so for the first time we decided to vote early to avoid the crowds. My wife and I went to our nearby county recreation center one day around noon to cast our votes. To our great surprise, a huge line snaked out the door and into the parking lot. We were all masked and maintaining social distancing as we exercised what some call a privilege and others call a fundamental right.

Going into the presidential election, the polls were close. Biden canceled his campaign rallies due to the pandemic, while President Trump was holding his rallies with mask requirements. In Texas, a band of flag-waving Trump supporters surrounded the Biden campaign bus on the highway and blockaded it with their pickup trucks in a stunt portending the conflicts that would follow the election.

In late November, following the election of Joe Biden, Treasury Secretary Mnuchin announced he was returning $455 billion of unspent CARES Act emergency lending funds back to Treasury's General Fund. According to Mnuchin, the funds had not been needed. To critics, the action was to move the funds beyond the reach of the incoming president. As with many things in Washington, the truth probably was somewhere in the middle.

10

A SHOT OF HOPE AND ANOTHER COMPETING NATIONAL CRISIS
(WINTER 2020–2021)

Violence continues and vaccines arrive. New York cancels New Year's Eve. We debut the Pandemic Analytics Center of Excellence and PRAC Fraud Task Force to better share resources across government. Congress is preoccupied with other matters after protesters storm the US Capitol, and the president is impeached and acquitted again. New OMB leadership engages on pandemic oversight.

Following the election of Joe Biden, members of the far-right group Proud Boys clashed with counter protesters in downtown Washington on December 12. On December 21, armed protesters in Oregon broke windows and stormed the state capitol to protest COVID-19 restrictions.

December also brought some encouraging news. Congress finally fixed some of the problems in the CARES Act. President Trump signed into law the Consolidated Appropriations Act of 2021. Buried in this bipartisan spending bill were provisions clarifying the Division A issue (PRAC and the inspectors general had jurisdiction over all pandemic spending), removing the CARES Act language that prohibited the Small Business Administration from requesting IRS tax records before approving disaster loans, and adding a documentation requirement to substantiate pandemic unemployment insurance claims.

In this regard, Congress had paid attention to the oversight community and the many staff-level briefings over the past several months from the PRAC and the inspectors general at Labor and SBA had paid off.

In other important pandemic news, the FDA issued its first emergency use authorization for a vaccine developed by Pfizer for individuals sixteen years of age and older. Rapid vaccine development would be one of the clear Washington wins under the Trump administration.

The first round of vaccines arrived in Montgomery County later in the month. Vaccines would first be distributed to frontline healthcare workers and staff and residents in nursing homes. The next group to get the vaccine, the 1Bs, would be essential workers and those over the age of seventy-five. Mom signed up for email alerts and visited the county vaccine information website every day. She had no hesitancy. She wanted the vaccine as soon as she could get it.

We launched our Pandemic Analytics Center of Excellence (PACE) in December. We held multiple listening sessions with the inspector general community to hear what they needed in terms of data analytics—and to discern what services they could use but just didn't know it yet.

One thing was loud and clear. The inspectors general had more fraud complaints than they could handle. At this stage, the PACE would just be adding to their burden if our only service was to generate more fraud complaints, many of which may be false positives, which is sometimes the case when you are working with limited information. We wanted to create a network of networks of people who knew where the data were sitting in various agencies and a plan for how to get the data and how to use the data.

The PACE name was a carryover from my prior job as inspector general. Witnessing emerging cyber-fraud and technology like robotic process automation being adopted by federal agencies, I thought how in the world could watchdogs provide oversight if we were always playing catch-up? I started saying that it was not enough for watchdogs to just keep up with government's use of data and adoption of emerging technology; we needed to set the pace. With the pandemic, it would not be enough to just try to keep up with fraudsters. As technologists, we need to be a step ahead.

The PACE would build on the legacy of the data analytics of the 2009–2015 Recovery Operations Center (ROC), while recognizing the changing times. We would expand beyond the business of generating fraud referrals and dive into developing technology-enabled solutions to the problems facing watchdogs, like cross-program data matching, hotline risk scoring models, and robot process automation.

We had an $80 million budget at the time, and we were contacted regularly by vendors claiming their data analytic tool or service was exactly what we needed to fight pandemic fraud.

The PACE was built using a center of excellence model to recognize the great data analytics work that was occurring in the offices of inspectors general. Since the Recovery Act–era, many offices built their own data analytics capabilities, and it would be waste of tax dollars to duplicate what they were already doing. We could never catch up with an OIG like Health and Human Services or the Department of Labor. They had significant head starts with talented PhD data scientists on staff and had made major technological investments over the past several years.

We would mind the gap by conducting data analytics and visualizations to do tasks like identifying people who received federal funds from more than one program. We called those multi-dippers. We would provide investigative support to OIGs like dark web and social media open-source intelligence to identify hidden relationships. We would share leading practices by sponsoring learning events and webinars. We would share tools and services such as open-source computer code that could be used to associate and link similar information in a data set. For example, we'd write and share code that would link the records "John Smith" with "J. Smith" and "John A. Smith" as possibly the same individual.

For those OIGs who had robust data analytics capabilities, we would serve as a data broker and provide them complete data sets like the nonpublic Paycheck Protection Program and the disaster loan program data. Many OIGs would use these data to discover federal workers in their own agencies who committed fraud.

With the official launch of the PACE, we also began recruiting for our Data Science Fellows program.

$

As a proper ending to 2020, New York City canceled the Times Square New Year's Eve ball drop, disappointing the millions who tune in to watch the crystal ball hail the new year and the million people who attend in person. With the third COVID wave peaking, January 2021 was the cruelest month in terms of cases, deaths, and hospitalizations. In January the daily death rate was over 3,300, and there were 130,000 daily hospitalizations compared to 73,000 during the summer 2020 second wave.

I kicked off the 2021 new year with a new desk and a new resolution.

I had resolved that in 2021 I would correct one bad micro habit that was driving me crazy. By this stage of the PRAC, my days were largely filled with video meeting after meeting. I had to pivot quickly from one subject to the next, often with little to no break. I didn't want to keep an open mic all day in my home office, especially with a busy household. At least in our organization, at this stage of the pandemic and remote work, when someone started talking while on mute, it elicited an extreme reaction from the rest of the participants on the call. Some would nearly jump out of their chairs and practically yell at you: "You're on mute!"

For my 2021 New Year's resolution I was determined to remedy this, so I began keeping tic marks in my daybook for the number of times I was called out that day for being on mute. "Bob, you're on mute!" was a YOM. I told staff on the first workday of the new year about this resolution as a public accountability measure. In the first weeks of 2021, I averaged two to three YOMS a day, and sometimes I gave myself a .5 if I caught myself before being admonished. By February, I had largely corrected this remote work bad habit and no longer had to keep track.

The biggest event that winter—and among the most significant events in US history—occurred on Wednesday, January 6, 2021.

I had a full calendar that day and was tied up midday on a webinar with New York and New Jersey state auditors. I had a call-back interview with a job candidate, and we released a video on our agile oversight toolkit.

At 1:49 p.m., DC police declared a riot after rioters stormed the US Capitol. I was on the video call with the New York and New Jersey officials when my wife burst into my office short of breath.

"Have you seen the news? You have to turn on the news!" she said.

By the time it was over, five people were dead and at least fifty-six police officers and five civilians were injured. Supporters of President Trump had stormed the United States Capitol, forcing Congress to evacuate. Some were calling for Vice President Pence to be hanged before his Secret Service detail was able to get him to safety with minutes to spare.

Other images from the day burned into memory include Missouri Senator Josh Hawley holding a raised fist of support to the protesters before running away to safety; US Capitol Police Officer Eugene Goodman, confronting a mob and redirecting them away from the Senate chamber with his COVID mask pulled down in the chaos; and the horned helmet and shirtless QAnon Shaman ransacking the Senate chamber and sitting in the chair of the president of the Senate.

After order was restored, Congress reconvened and around 3:00 a.m. on January 7 formally certified Joe Biden as the next president of the United States.

It wasn't just progressives or Democrats who were outraged. On the Senate floor, Senate Majority Leader Mitch McConnell condemned the actions of the rioters saying, "The mob was fed lies. They were provoked by the president and other powerful people." A month later he would tell reporters during his weekly news conference, "We all were here. We saw what happened. It was a violent insurrection for the purpose of trying to prevent the peaceful transfer of power after a legitimately certified election, from one administration to the next. That's what it was."

A year later, on the one-year anniversary of the event, Senator Lindsey Graham issued a press release saying, "I still cannot believe that a mob was able to take over the United States Capitol during such a pivotal moment—certifying a presidential election. It would have been so easy for terrorists to boot strap onto this protest and wreak even further destruction on the US Capitol. Regardless of the reason for the assault on the Capitol, to lose control in such a fashion twenty years after 9/11 is stunning. Those who defiled the Capitol on January 6 are being prosecuted, as they should be. I have consistently condemned the attack and have urged that those involved be prosecuted to the fullest extent of the law. I hold the same views as those who attacked the federal courthouse in Portland, Oregon, and committed other acts of violence throughout our nation."

Capitol rioters were subsequently identified and arrested one by one.

The Senate voted by unanimous consent to award Officer Eugene Goodman the Congressional Gold Medal for his bravery that day.

Donald Trump was impeached a second time for his actions, or lack thereof, in the riot. He became the first US president to be impeached for a second time. He was acquitted by the US Senate four days later, in a 57–43 vote. Senate Democrats and Independents were joined by seven Republicans in voting for conviction, but they were ten votes short of the required two-thirds majority for conviction.

This was yet another crisis that engulfed the nation and divided us along ideological grounds. There simply wasn't enough oxygen in Washington for vigorous congressional pandemic oversight. One administration was on the way out the door while the next was confronted with multiple crises and a new one knocking at the door: a stalled economy.

The first congressional hearing on pandemic oversight where PRAC chair Michael Horowitz was invited to testify was not held until March 25, 2021, a year after the largest stimulus package in US history had been passed.

$

In one of his first acts after inauguration, President Biden had the US rejoin the World Health Organization.

In January 2021, we issued our first joint pandemic oversight report. The report tells one small part of the federal pandemic response story.

Under the leadership of the Health and Human Services inspector general, the six OIGs who have oversight of federal healthcare programs came together to look at how these programs administered and paid for COVID-19 testing for the millions of Americans who receive benefits under these programs.

We concluded that the federal government was not currently designed for massive public health efforts. Aside from identifying opportunities to save taxpayer money, we found that federal programs didn't do targeted COVID testing based on risk, even though we knew that some demographic groups were disproportionately affected by COVID-19. Our findings echoed what the Government Accountability Office had been warning Congress. We needed a national COVID testing strategy.

January also brought to a head a rare internecine squabble between two inspector general members of the PRAC. This is a wonky and small (but important) part of the national pandemic oversight story.

In the CARES Act, Congress created a new inspector general called the special inspector general for pandemic recovery (SIGPR). The position was created as a direct result of President Trump's comment, "I'll be the oversight," while the CARES Act was being considered. The designation "special" signals that the position is for a specific program or group of programs and for a limited time. Unfortunately, this name was overly broad and caused confusion. SIGPR was not *the* pandemic inspector general but was a *member* of the PRAC with jurisdiction over a specific pot of money.

Unfortunately, this specific pot of money was largely the pot of money that Secretary Mnuchin had given back to the Treasury general fund in late November 2020. SIGPR took an expansive view of their jurisdiction beyond the specific pot—an interpretation that overlapped their jurisdiction with the Treasury OIG. This put the two offices at odds.

The Treasury OIG sought a favorable legal opinion from the Government Accountability Office, while SIGPR requested a legal opinion from the Justice Department. The Justice Department concluded that SIGPR's jurisdiction was limited to the specific pot of money. SIGPR would spend the next two-plus years pleading with Congress for more jurisdiction and money.

In January, the SBA OIG reported that it had collaborated with the Treasury Department's Do Not Pay service and identified approximately $3.6 billion in potentially fraudulent Paycheck Protection Program loans. The report urged the SBA to use Do Not Pay. The OIG auditors had briefed SBA on their preliminary findings five months before, in August 2020. SBA's management's response to this audit that "efforts were underway" struck the OIG as too little, too late.

In February we hosted a virtual listening forum to get the perspectives of small business owners. We heard about the problems many small businesses, especially minority-owned small businesses, had in accessing lenders and understanding government filing requirements.

Our outreach and engagement directorate, or comms team, would organize several virtual listening forums over the next two years bringing together experts on a range of topics. The comms team also refined our PRAC public voice. Our products, what our comms director would sometimes call "collateral," looked quite different from what inspectors general typically put out. We would regularly get kudos for our more informal and visual style that was readable and serious.

We were also occasionally quirky when the circumstances allowed. Our social media person, for example, would tweet our message coupled with popular memes that she'd sometimes have to explain to me before I could sign off on them. I knew we were on the right path when someone replied to one of our early tweets with a comment to the effect: "I don't know who took over the PRAC account, but more please."

We also issued an update to our top pandemic challenges report. Based on the data quality issues and fraud we were seeing, we added a few new challenges: preventing fraud against government programs, protecting the public against pandemic-related fraud, and data transparency and completeness.

In early February, the Department of Defense OIG released its evaluation of the Navy's response to COVID-19 onboard Navy warships like the USS *Theodore Roosevelt*. The auditors found that the Navy generally had in place policies, plans, and procedures to mitigate the spread of COVID in the fleet; however, regarding the *Roosevelt* and one other ship that experienced outbreaks, leadership mistakes were made.

On February 8, I received an email introduction and request to meet Deidre Harrison, the new White House Office of Management and Budget acting deputy controller. She would be my counterpart. This call was the beginning of a great working relationship with one of the smartest and most dedicated public servants I have had the privilege to work with.

Harrison is no shrinking violet, and on video calls I would sometimes have to discreetly lower the volume to prevent my laptop speakers from getting blown out. Five foot four at best, she is gifted with the smarts to go toe-to-toe with anyone in government on just about any issue. She would later be joined by Jodie Morse, an OMB attorney, whom I found to be an energetic, problem-solver-type lawyer who knew the law and was able to grasp nuanced policy implications and interagency politics.

We had different roles and different bosses and always maintained our independence. It was a symbiotic, mutually beneficial relationship, which engendered trust and candor. This is how oversight is supposed to work.

The three of us would consult, confer, and commiserate on many matters over the next year. I'm sure they literally didn't work 24/7, but I sometimes wondered from their many after-hours emails and calls. The taxpayer got their money's worth and then some from those two.

Our new thinking and new approaches to combating pandemic fraud didn't stop with the Pandemic Analytics Center of Excellence and our new collaborative engagement with OMB.

During this season, we finalized plans for a PRAC fraud task force after meetings and listening to the OIGs. Our emphasis would be to complement and not compete with the other offices. We wouldn't be using our funding to hire an army of special agents, which would put us in direct competition with the offices of inspectors general, who were also in the market for trained and certified federal investigators to address their burgeoning workload.

We also concluded that the traditional law enforcement task force model would not be a viable option. We couldn't expect an inspector general for an agency that had no significant equities in small business loan fraud or unemployment insurance fraud to assign an agent full-time to, in effect, work another office's investigations. That approach would divert investigative resources from their agency's mission.

Thinking through the task force gave me an opportunity to get to know more closely some of the finest investigative executives in the community of inspectors general. One of the things that stuck with me was something the head of investigations at Health and Human Services said to me early on.

"Bob," he said in an early planning meeting, "the IG community already works well together. The question is how can we work more closely together."

The solution we settled on was a virtual task force model. We would essentially deputize volunteers using the PRAC's umbrella pandemic fraud jurisdiction and staffing authorities. The premise of the PRAC fraud task force was this: If a special agent had bandwidth and the desire to join the fight against pandemic small business loan fraud, and if that agent's office could spare the resources, we would effectively deputize the agent with our jurisdiction, provide leads and cases, and support their efforts. Individual offices would remain responsible for conducting and supervising these investigations.

For task force agents, PRAC fraud task force cases would be what I called a side hustle. I was reminded of post 9/11 when many federal agents I knew wanted to contribute to the war on terror. I know I did. But that didn't necessarily mean I wanted to become a federal air marshal or work full-time on a joint terrorism task force. I just wanted to contribute in a meaningful way.

To garner support for a community-wide fraud task force, we reminded inspectors general that they were already sharing resources on a limited basis on law enforcement operations like search warrants. There was already a legal process by which, for example, an OIG investigator in Florida who was about to conduct a large search warrant and needed more bodies could get assistance from agents from other offices even though these assisting agents had no jurisdiction in the underlying case.

The PRAC fraud task force created an avenue for inspectors general to work more closely on pandemic fraud, and our collective efforts have resulted in arrests and the recovery of stolen funds.

We kicked off the PRAC fraud task force in February with a video meeting attended by around 100 federal investigators and Department of Justice attorneys. I did introductions and then explained how we envisioned working closely together. I told the attendees that we wouldn't be fighting the last war. This was not the Great Recession's Recovery Act, and we weren't the Recovery Board. Our problems were different from their problems and required a different approach. Agents alone wouldn't be able to address the problem.

For the task force to be successful, agents needed to be supported by analysts who could gather as much open-source and commercial-source intelligence as possible and by prosecutors who could streamline investigations and cut to the heart of the matter to avoid having agents go down rabbit holes.

One of the first task force cases was one we passed along to a Justice OIG special agent in New York. The investigation involved two career criminals in New York who used stolen identities to apply for fourteen Paycheck Protection Program and disaster loans seeking $10 million. One of the two was a French Canadian who was living large in Manhattan and Brooklyn, and aside from his distinct French accent and love of fine dining, investigators weren't initially sure of his actual identity. They had little to go on. The other was under indictment for separate fraud and identity theft charges during that time. The two converted much of the stolen funds into cryptocurrency, purchased stocks, and leased a luxury apartment and a Mercedes. The investigation was worked over the next months by the Department of Justice OIG task force agent who brought in other law enforcement partners.

In the end, one pled guilty and was sentenced to nine years in prison. The other was convicted by a jury (and was awaiting sentence as this book was being written).

$

The third COVID wave was receding by February 2021 but not before America crossed the awful marker of half a million deaths.

States rolled out vaccines in a variety of ways. In places like Arizona, parking lots were remade into mass vaccine centers with rows of portable drive-through car ports so drivers could pull right in.

In Maryland, Mom was able to sign up online and get a vaccine appointment for mid-February. On the appointed day, I wheeled her into a nearby high school gymnasium, which had been turned into a county Point of Distribution, or POD as they called it. The POD was well-organized, and the workers were solicitous as they cleared a path for the wheelchair and showed us where to go. This was a vivid example of good government at work delivering public services in an assembly-line manner in a time of need. There was a buoyant, carnival vibe.

Not everyone was equally civic-minded when it came to vaccine distribution. I would later learn about a Health and Human Services OIG investigation involving a West Palm Beach, Florida, nursing home. To prioritize vaccine distribution in nursing homes, the CDC allowed long-term care facilities to receive priority shipments of vaccines to distribute to residents and staff. This Florida nursing home's CEO decided to divert some of the vaccines instead to wealthy ineligible donors and potential donors to its foundation. To skirt the rules, these donors would be identified as "staff" or "volunteers."

In a text message to an employee and later uncovered by investigators, the CEO wrote, "Do not be weak be strong you have the opportunity to take advantage of everyone who needs the shot and figure out what they have and what we can go after and what their affinity [*sic*] as that's what I would do [*sic*] I was running the foundation."

I never found out how much they got in donations for selling vaccines, but I do know they paid a $1.75 million fine to settle the case.

11

A DOSE OF NORMALCY?
(SPRING 2021)

Another $2 trillion in relief to stimulate a stalled economy, and the White House tries a new approach to pandemic oversight. Finally, 100 million Americans receive their first dose of the COVID-19 vaccine.

In the spring of 2021, the third coronavirus wave was receding with declining trends in cases, hospitalizations, and deaths. Politicians and school officials around the country struggled with how to reopen schools safely and opinions varied widely.

California Governor Gavin Newsom was subject to a recall election in part over his handling of the pandemic and school shutdowns. Montgomery County, Maryland, public schools went back to limited in-person instruction in March, dividing grades into two groups, or A and B rotations. Students who chose to return to in-person instruction would attend classes four days a week, with Wednesdays off. Group A would attend in person one week and virtually the next, with Group B doing the opposite. Students could elect to remain virtual.

I was struck the first time I saw a school bus on the road outside my home office window for the first time in a year.

Our youngest decided to stay home during his senior year of high school and attend via Zoom, but otherwise things seemed to be largely getting back to normal. I felt like we turned the corner on the pandemic.

Apparently, nobody told that to the US economy. Our economic recovery stalled in the early spring. The 6 percent unemployment rate in March was less than half of the 14.7 percent at the height of the crisis but was higher than the prepandemic 3.5 percent. Too many Americans were out of work. When you adjust these figures, which do not count those not working and not actively seeking work, the adjusted number of unemployed was much higher. Research conducted by the Pew Research Center indicated that more women than men were out of the job market, and unemployment was disproportionately affecting Black and Hispanic women.

Our gross domestic product, or the value of all goods and services produced by the economy, was not growing as fast as we needed. In fact, it was lagging the G20 countries—not something you want to see in the world's largest economy. We were still reeling from the largest economic contraction in modern history during the period April to June 2020, when our gross domestic product decreased 32 percent.

Consumer sentiment, which is an index of how US consumers are feeling about their finances and state of the economy, had also dropped in February. In March, gasoline prices were up 9 percent from the previous month and up 22 percent from the previous year. You might have heard about this on social media.

To stimulate the economic recovery, the Biden administration decided to swing for the fences. In March Congress passed and President Biden signed into law the American Rescue Plan Act, which would—like all things Washington—be quickly reduced to an acronym and frequently referred to as ARP (A-R-P) or ARPA (Ar-pah) depending on your preference. The legislation passed along party lines in the Senate with Vice President Kamala Harris casting the tie-breaking vote and passed on almost party lines in the House of Representatives with one Democrat joining Republicans in voting against it.

The American Rescue Plan was a $1.9 trillion COVID stimulus package to speed up our recovery from the health and economic effects of the pandemic. The president signed the act into law on the anniversary of the day that the World Health Organization first declared COVID a pandemic. The White House also announced that Gene Sperling—who previously served in senior White House roles in the Clinton and Obama administrations—would oversee implementation of the act.

The intent and design of the American Rescue Plan was markedly different from the March 2020 CARES Act. In March 2020, the administration was facing dire death projections if immediate action was not taken and ominous economic data that suggested the US economy was in a free fall. The CARES Act was about coronavirus emergency response. The American Rescue Plan was about our nation's physical and economic well-being. The act would accelerate our recovery from the pandemic by funding over 400 federal programs.

To support state and local government, the act provided billions for schools to reopen safely within 100 days. The act provided transportation grants to Amtrak and the Federal Transit Administration for local subways that suffered significant reductions in ridership and revenue due to the pandemic. It provided billions to state, local, tribal, and territorial governments that could be used to support struggling families and businesses, to maintain public services in the face of declining tax revenues, and other purposes. This program was called the State and Local Fiscal Recovery Fund and carried my favorite Washington acronym, sometimes being referred to as the "slurf."

For individuals, the American Rescue Plan Act provided a $1,400 stimulus payment to individuals, including college students and those receiving social security benefits. It extended the 15 percent increased supplemental nutrition assistance, or SNAP, benefits through September. Millions of working families received their advance child tax credit as a monthly payment. Income-eligible seniors received reduced-fee internet access. The American Rescue Plan Act also targeted small business relief to sectors that were especially hit hard by the pandemic like restaurants and entertainment venues.

For the less fortunate and disadvantaged, the act extended the expanded $300 per week supplemental unemployment insurance benefits through Labor Day. It provided loan assistance to disadvantaged farmers, rural healthcare grants, block grants for substance abuse programs, emergency rental assistance, and homelessness assistance.

It's hard to get back to work without affordable child care, so the Department of Health and Human Services received billions for a child care stabilization grant program to help cover operating costs during and after the pandemic to stabilize that industry.

The act also provided the PRAC with $40 million in additional funding, bringing our total funding to $120 million to be spent over our five-year existence. This money was to be used to support oversight of all pandemic relief spending laws, now six in total, including the American Rescue Plan Act. This meant the PRAC was now responsible for overseeing $5 trillion in federal COVID-19 relief funding.

This also meant that the US would now be spending almost 25 percent of our 2019 GDP on pandemic response and recovery, more than any other country in the world.

The total tab was staggering. Between the now six pandemic relief bills, money was flowing to over 400 federal programs. I struggled to comprehend how some spending was related to pandemic relief. The American Rescue Plan Act, for example, provided over $70 billion to shore up one of the two pension programs run by the Pension Benefit Guaranty Corporation—the organization I had overseen before coming to PRAC. That pension program had been in the red for years and was facing insolvency.

We had our first video meeting with Gene Sperling and his small team on March 23, which included Deidre Harrison and attorney Jodie Morse. We started briefings and regular meetings the very next week. Sperling wanted to soak it all in, and he is one of those rare people who has the capacity to do just that. He's a lawyer and economist by training, having previously served as director of the White House National Economic Council for Presidents Clinton and Obama, and as a former consultant on the TV show, *The West Wing*. A native Michigander who now commutes to DC from Santa Monica, Sperling could be all over the place and then bring it all together. Within five minutes of first meeting him, in whatever setting, you'll likely learn that he's originally from Ann Arbor and that he loves Wolverines football.

Sperling wanted to better understand the watchdogs' concerns, so I arranged briefings from Mike Ware and Larry Turner at the Small Business Administration and Labor Department and their senior teams, along with others.

Turner was the deputy IG at the Labor Department when the pandemic hit and assumed the acting IG role when the prior IG retired in June 2020. Always impeccably dressed and unfailingly polite, Turner went on to lead a massive body of unemployment insurance oversight work and was rewarded by being nominated and confirmed to serve in the role permanently.

Sperling would open those first meetings repeating the story about his first cabinet meeting with the president. According to Sperling, President Biden opened that meeting retelling the story about how President Obama had tasked him with overseeing the Recovery Act, dubbing him Sheriff Joe.

Turning to Sperling, the president said, "I want you to work closely with the watchdogs." This direction would be for the benefit of the cabinet as much as it was for Sperling.

We had no word yet on when we would be eligible for vaccines, so in-person meetings between our two teams were out of the question. We met with the American Rescue Plan team over Zoom, which thankfully the White House got around to adopting.

We began meeting with Sperling and his team every Friday and regularly for what became known as the "gold standard" meetings. These open and consultative meetings became another defining success of the PRAC.

With these meetings, we figured out how to thread the needle of preserving our independence while maintaining a congenial and collaborative relationship with OMB and Sperling's ARP team. Government program officials and their watchdogs can both be committed to good government, even if we answered to two different bosses. This oversight philosophy was established through the tone at the top. Both Gene Sperling, as the senior administration official, and Michael Horowitz, the PRAC chair, modeled this philosophy in every interaction. We did not always agree on substantive issues, but we did always agree and acknowledge that we were all trying our best to ensure that emergency spending was well spent and not wasted.

With each gold standard meeting, the ARP team would prod agencies to share with us the key risks and actions they were taking to ensure program integrity and transparency of their spending. Respect breeds trust.

The gold standard meetings didn't just happen by accident. My recollection is that they were a direct result of an early fumble by the administration. SBA—repeating its earlier mistake of haste with the Paycheck Protection Program—raced to implement the $16 billion Shuttered Venues Program, a program created in December 2020 legislation and provided additional funding in the American Rescue Plan. The program was designed to help get relief to theaters, museums, music venues, and the like that had been shuttered due to social distancing. SBA launched the program on April 9, but the website portal crashed due to a technical glitch. Once again, there was a race with the first come, first served model.

The president of a large Los Angeles concert hall described the debacle to *Rolling Stone* magazine. "It just adds on to the fucked situation that we've been in this whole year. It's typical at this point. Every time you think there's a light at the end of the tunnel, something gets destroyed in the last minute."

Inspector general Mike Ware and his team had shared their concerns with the SBA administrator before the program launched. They were most especially concerned about whether SBA's controls were strong enough to prevent and detect fraud.

Sperling was none too pleased to hear about the website crash and to learn second-hand that the inspector general had serious concerns before the program launched. He personally intervened with the contractor running the website and helped ensure the portal was repaired quickly and operational. He then created the gold standard meetings to prevent this unpleasant surprise from happening again. He wanted to hear directly from inspectors general if there were any major concerns, and he didn't want it filtered through agency leadership.

Over the next year, I coordinated a couple of dozen meetings on behalf of the PRAC and the inspectors general. OMB would coordinate with senior agency leadership. We'd have everyone at the table to talk through antifraud and transparency concerns before major programs were implemented. These meetings were initially a culture shock to both sides, but I believe they played a key role in managing fraud risks.

It was in one of these gold standard meetings that the PRAC—along with the OIG—pushed SBA to tighten controls to block loan and grant applications coming from foreign internet protocol addresses. A foreign IP address doesn't mean an application is fraudulent, but it is an indicator to examine more closely. A subsequent audit by the inspector general found that SBA, in fact, was now blocking most applications from foreign IP addresses. Some still got through, but the situation was better than in the early days of the pandemic.

Our collaborative approach also resulted in an OMB-PRAC Joint Alert to federal agencies to raise awareness on key issues related to preventing waste, fraud, and abuse.

Michael Horowitz testified before the House Select Subcommittee on the Coronavirus Crisis on March 25. This was the first time the PRAC had been invited to testify before Congress. He spoke about our transparency efforts with the website and our coordination efforts across the IG community. He also called upon Congress to raise the jurisdictional amount for smaller civil fraud cases so we would have one more tool to combat pandemic fraud.

Congressional pandemic oversight was being conducted largely by that House subcommittee, and subcommittee staff did an exceptional job, in my opinion, in gathering facts. Their reports, unfortunately, had inflammatory titles that caused critics to question the objectivity of the report's important findings. In March 2021, the subcommittee issued "Lowering the Guardrails: How the Trump Administration Failed to Prevent Billions in Pandemic Small Business Fraud." They would later issue a report titled, "IDLE On EIDL Fraud: How the Trump Administration Wasted Taxpayer Dollars by Leaving the COVID-19 EIDL Program Vulnerable to Fraud."

In May, the Secret Service announced that they—in partnership with the OIGs and federal prosecutors and working closely with banks—had seized over $640 million in fraudulently obtained SBA funds and assisted in returning approximately $2 billion to state unemployment insurance programs. Secret Service special agent Roy Dotson and a federal prosecutor had come up with a creative workaround to seize funds efficiently.

Normally, to seize a bank account the government has to apply for an individual seizure warrant from a federal judge. Dotson and his team had discovered hundreds of bank accounts in the same banks belonging to various pandemic fraudsters but all fraudulent. It would take forever to do individual warrants and money may be lost by the time the paperwork was complete. The team submitted a bulk seizure warrant for multiple accounts at individual banks, and the federal judge reviewed the warrants for probable cause and signed off. I don't know if this was the first time this method was ever used, but nobody I knew ever heard of such a thing. Dotson and his team would later be awarded a prestigious Service to America award.

Another federal investigator who played a major role in the pandemic fraud crisis was SBA OIG desk officer Michelle Blank. In what may have been the worst timing ever, Blank transferred to SBA OIG from IRS Criminal Investigations a few weeks before the pandemic hit. Within months she was the center of the federal pandemic law enforcement universe as scores of agencies were asking her for assistance and data on small business loan fraud investigations.

$

The spring of 2021 was a time of personal and societal milestones. The CDC reported that over 100 million people had received their first dose of the COVID-19 vaccine. My wife and I got ours in the pharmacy department at the grocery store. We got the Johnson & Johnson single dose. I felt a little weird after the vaccine and my wife had chills and a fever.

The very next day, CDC placed a pause on the J&J vaccine due to some reported side effects with a small number of women who had received the vaccine. That development was a little unnerving, but the pause was lifted shortly thereafter and soon forgotten. When I told someone later which vaccine I got, they said, "Oh, the Walmart vaccine." Apparently, there was a half-in-jest social class distinction among the vaccines. Per CDC's latest guidance, though, being vaccinated now meant we could resume activities without wearing a mask if we wanted.

On a personal level, March was not a great month. We lost our beloved family dog Ginger in early March to old age and disease. We couldn't stand to see her suffer any longer. She had been our little chihuahua-terrier family pet for fourteen years. She was quirky and neurotic, but house trained and affectionate. I made an appointment with the veterinarian and took a midday break from pandemic oversight to say goodbye. Indoor COVID protocols were still in place at the vet's office, but I was allowed to sit masked and alone in a room while she passed. I got back to work but didn't feel much like turning my camera on during the afternoon of video calls.

Overall, I had not been taking care of myself and it was starting to show. I expended too much energy on work and not enough on maintaining my well-being. If I wasn't at my computer on a video call or doing work, I was thinking about work. By this point, I had reviewed countless résumés, conducted scores of interviews, and expended tremendous energy trying to acclimate new staff to this strange world and unifying the team. It was the background tape playing on a constant loop. I was no longer running at midday. I was eating garbage, and at my regular check-up my doctor politely but firmly told me to get it under control or else.

I had much on my mind on March 31, between the pandemic, work challenges, and all those zeros. I was receiving positive feedback on the progress we had made in pandemic oversight as we took stock in the PRAC's one-year anniversary, but there was still so much more to do. Some moments it felt like we were just getting started.

That night my wife and I were to celebrate our first-date anniversary, which we celebrate with as much pomp as our wedding day anniversary. After work I had planned to take her to a favorite restaurant up in Frederick County.

I had to first get through a busy day of meetings and an afternoon interview with two prominent podcasters who knew their stuff when it came to government oversight. They had been around during the Recovery Act days, and I could expect a thoughtful discussion. I had to be on my toes.

Shortly before the taping, I started getting weird power interruptions at the house. First one side of the house would lose power, then the other. The power blips caused the internet router to shut down, cutting off my connection without warning, and it would take a few moments to regain the internet connection. We later learned that the plumber's excavator who was doing work at our house nicked the underground power line into the house.

The podcasters made it clear that their style was to do a live recording. They would hit record and let it rip. No editing. No do-overs. I had warned them before we started that I was having some potential technical difficulties with the power at my house.

It happened about two minutes into the interview just as I had finished an answer with my tag line that policymakers need "insights now." The internet connection died. The hosts heard the click. When I later listened to the recorded podcast, I heard their reaction.

"Uh-oh."

"What should we do?" one asked.

"I don't know. We gotta do something and he's got no juice," said the other.

I got back on the call in less than one minute after sprinting downstairs with my iPhone and headphones. I jumped in the driver's seat of my car in the garage to block out construction noise at our house and dialed back in.

They heard me connect.

"We were just trying to decide whether you would try to call in," one said.

"Are you there?" said the other.

"I'm back on. Hey, my apologies."

"You're really a warrior," one replied.

"Flexibility and agility, man, that's what it's all about," I said, and we resumed the interview. I don't even remember what they asked. I was physically and mentally exhausted.

The podcast aired on April 12 with the title, "How much does $5 trillion weigh?"

Our power came back on, and after the podcast interview I went back to work for a few hours knocking out various tasks. I pushed myself away from the desk, though, to make sure we got out for our anniversary dinner. I bounded down to the kitchen where my wife was sitting and made a beeline to the garage without breaking stride.

"You ready?" I asked.

At that moment, I was hit with a bolt of pain in my right shoulder that shot up to the back of my skull. The pain was intense and felt like a bolt of lightning. I've pinched nerves and pulled muscles before but have never felt anything like this. I slowly lowered my body to the kitchen floor.

"What's wrong?" my wife asked.

"I don't know."

At that moment, the thought that came to mind was that I was stroking out, and any sudden movement would result in my immediate demise. I tried not to move. I told my wife I needed to go to the ER now. I'm not shy about going to the ER or my doctor when necessary, but I don't leap at the opportunity either. I needed to get to a doctor right away.

Instead of enjoying an anniversary dinner in a favorite restaurant, I spent the night alone in the emergency room, in a hospital gown, getting a CT scan and other tests. COVID visitor restrictions were still in place.

The pain had abated after a few hours, but I was shaken by the experience. While the doctor couldn't conclusively say what caused the pain, the CT scan showed an anomaly with an artery that pumps blood into the brain. I was discharged with instructions to see my primary physician and a vascular neurologist. When I showed the scan results to my doctor a few days later, he grimaced and said, "Yeah, you should get that looked at."

I didn't have time to celebrate my birthday in 2020 because of the pandemic. In 2021, I spent my birthday traveling to DC for the neurology consultation at GW University Hospital because of the pandemic. Thankfully, the neurologist found nothing significant. The episode was likely brought on by stress, he said. That was the best possible answer and didn't seem too implausible. Perhaps it was the combined effects of the power failure and the podcast and the daily tasks of building and running an organization. I heard the warning loud and clear.

12

MORE ZEROS THAN YOU CAN IMAGINE
(SUMMER 2021)

Delta comes to town and tempers once again boil over. America experiments with vaccine pleas, raffles, and mandates. The problem of identity fraud comes more sharply into focus.

I never got around to answering the podcast question: How much does $5 trillion weigh? I later tried to wrap my head around total federal pandemic relief spending with an alternative visual. If you take $100 bills and lay them end to end, in a mile you would have $1 million. If you stacked $100 bills end to end across America, you would have $3 billion. I have no idea if this is literally true, of course, but that's the answer I got from Google. I did know that a trillion is 1,000 billions and more zeros than I could imagine.

Our youngest son graduated from high school in June. He returned for in-person instruction for the last two weeks of his senior year, and his graduation ceremony was not any different from those of his older siblings. Our high school is one of the county schools that regularly holds its commencement in the school stadium, so few COVID adjustments were necessary. We prayed for good weather as we usually do, and when his name was finally announced toward the end of the alphabet and he walked across the stage, we cheered from the bleachers. It was almost normal, as I tried to forget that the pandemic had stolen his last two years of high school.

In June, we posted data on our website from the healthcare Provider Relief Fund, which was a $178 billion Department of Health and Human Services program created by the CARES Act to reimburse healthcare providers for lost revenue and other healthcare-related expenses resulting from the pandemic. This program was unusual from our perspective in at least two ways. First was the way that HHS distributed the funds.

To ensure money got out quickly, the program didn't require healthcare providers to do anything. HHS would automatically send federal money to providers who billed for Medicare automatically based on a formula of the provider's annual patient revenue. Second, the money was sent from HHS to healthcare providers across the country through a single service provider in Utah. This means that for all those federal funds, when you searched on the USASpending.gov federal spending public website, you would only find a single federal award to that Utah firm.

In other words, some doctors got pandemic money whether or not they wanted or needed it, and until we grabbed data directly from Health and Human Services, taxpayers couldn't even see who got what.

A new COVID-19 variant, Delta, came to town in the summer of 2021. This variant contained 1,000 times more virus than the previous variants and was as contagious as the chicken pox. It spread quickly. Delta started the fourth wave, which soon rolled over the US. Predictably, unvaccinated adults were hit the hardest, with one study indicating that they were twelve times more likely to be hospitalized. One Jacksonville, Florida, family lost four family members to COVID in a single week. The youngest was only thirty-five years old.

Montgomery County, Maryland, reinstated the mask mandates. This really didn't affect us as we were still wearing masks to the grocery store and the like.

Meanwhile, unlikely partners combined to encourage more Americans to get vaccinated. *Fox News* cable news host Sean Hannity urged his viewers to take the pandemic seriously and get vaccinated. In Michigan, Governor Whitmer held a month-long vaccination raffle where residents could win a total of $5 million (with one grand prize of $2 million and three prizes of $1 million) and $500,000 in college scholarships. West Virginia Governor Jim Justice spent $23 million on a state incentive program that gave away pickup trucks, rifles, and lawn mowers. The program was named after his dog and called the "Do It For Babydog" sweepstakes. Even with the incentives, West Virginia state auditors later reported that the sweepstakes didn't cause a noticeable bump in vaccine rates, and West Virginia vaccine rates were in the bottom 20 percent of states.

When public appeals and raffles didn't work, governments began vaccine mandates. In August, New York City became the first US city to mandate vaccines for indoor dining, gyms, and performances. Mandates and public health measures continued to divide the country and rage boiled over that summer.

In July 2021, a fifty-six-year-old West Virginia man pled guilty to making threats against physicians Anthony Fauci (chief medical adviser to the president at that time), Francis Collins (the former director of the National Institutes of Health), and others. The man used an anonymous email account from an encrypted email service company based in Switzerland to send a series of emails threatening harm to Dr. Fauci and his family. In one of his emails, the man threatened that Dr. Fauci and his family would be "dragged into the street, beaten to death, and set on fire."

In a separate case, a thirty-nine-year-old Mississippi man was so upset about vaccines that he called CDC Director Rochelle Walensky and left voicemails threatening to kill her. He later pled guilty and was sentenced to two years in prison.

In August 2021, in Williamson County, Tennessee, protesters heckled and harassed masked attendees at a school board meeting to discuss school mask mandates. Video of the parking lot mob scene went viral with over 3 million views on Twitter. With uniformed police protecting the attendees, the mob chanting "Will not comply!" and "There's a bad place in hell!" and "We will find you! We know who you are! We know who you are!"

A few days later President Biden publicly commented on the school board meeting.

"This isn't about politics; it's about keeping our children safe," Biden said in televised remarks. "I saw a video and reports from Tennessee of protesters threatening doctors and nurses who were before a school board making the case that, to keep kids safe, there should be mandatory masks. As they walked out, these doctors were threatened, those nurses were threatened. Our healthcare workers are heroes. They were the heroes when there was no vaccine. Many of them gave their lives trying to save others, and they're heroes again with the vaccine. They're doing their best to care for the people refusing to get vaccinated."

One of the aggressors was identified as a guy who didn't even have children.

I am not suggesting that all who opposed mandates condoned these extreme acts. Unquestionably in my view, these acts made civil discourse regarding the pandemic more difficult. Fellow citizens were unable to engage in a productive dialogue, respect differences, and reach a mutual understanding.

$

At the PRAC, a lot of our focus and energy during this season was on building out the Pandemic Analytics Center of Excellence now that the vision had been set. We needed the right data, the right tools, and the right people to help find fraud and support the OIGs in their pandemic oversight work.

We hosted a virtual OIG-wide data analytics expo in June. Spread out over two days, we had data experts share the details of their office's technology stack, what applications and software they used, and how they worked with their investigators and auditors. Over 300 oversight professionals attended the two expo sessions.

We awarded and kicked off the PACE contract in August, after reviewing the detailed bid packages from dozens of firms who wanted a piece of this high-profile and potentially lucrative federal contract. We initially needed a contractor to build a secure cloud-based data warehouse, with a scalable architecture, where we could load, transform, and extract federal spending data. We needed the software tools to do data mining and text scraping using natural language processing. We needed to be able to connect these data with third-party, commercial, and open-source data for investigative intelligence purposes—data such as credit information, phone records, and social media postings.

We also needed to make sure the system could talk to other systems, both within OIG offices and the larger federal law enforcement community.

One of the key data analytics players in the larger federal law enforcement community operates out of a six-story office building off Interstate 66 in DC's Virginia suburbs. The generic building looks like any one of a thousand similar office buildings in the area, although the dark black glass wrapping around the building like a cop's sunglasses does give off a hint of mystery and intrigue.

Inside the building sit 200+ data analysts along with the largest repository of criminal intelligence in the nation. Due to security protocols, personnel at the Justice Department's Fusion Center were not permitted to interact with the outside world through Zoom or Microsoft Teams, so we arranged for a masked meeting with Fusion Center leadership. Five members of my team joined me on this first in-person field trip.

After going through security and placing our iPhones in security lockers, we were escorted to the secure conference room. Our hosts arrived shortly thereafter, and we exchanged greetings and traded the obligatory law enforcement challenge coins, before taking our seats at the massive conference table, spread safely apart. We took turns briefing through masks on our respective activities and pledged to identify ways to work more closely.

The Fusion Center is part of the Organized Crime Drug Enforcement Task Force, and given their expertise in transnational financial crime and access to bank and other data, Fusion Center leadership redirected some of their efforts to providing pandemic fraud tips and leads to federal law enforcement agencies. They would later provide us with a massive report summarizing over 150,000 transactions that banks had flagged as being suspicious and possible pandemic fraud.

After the meeting wrapped up, I gathered with my team in the parking lot where we took a group picture in our masks. We had worked so closely together for almost a year, but this was the first time meeting in person. To celebrate the occasion, we found a restaurant a couple of blocks away with sidewalk seating and we sat for drinks and forgot about the pandemic for a little while, and just got to know each other as human beings.

One of the other major PRAC accomplishments from this season was posting pandemic oversight reports from state and local auditors on our public website. Federal spending data and federal inspector general audits only tell part of the story. We knew our state and local oversight partners were also identifying significant issues. Being on the ground closer to where the federal funds were being used gave them a different point of view.

Not all state and local auditors have an easily accessible website where the public and policymakers can find their reports. We brought it all together in one place. We started out manually crawling the internet and finding interesting state and local pandemic oversight reports to post. We then created a way for state and local auditors to submit newly issued reports to us. Over time our state and local oversight report library grew to over 200 audit reports.

In addition to combating historic levels of public fraud, federal law enforcement agents were also investigating pandemic-related fraud schemes that put people's lives at risk. In July, the Justice Department brought the first criminal charges in the nation against a Napa, California, woman for selling fake immunizations and counterfeit vaccine cards. A concerned family member had contacted the Health and Human Services OIG after their family members had purchased immunization "pellets" and a vaccine card that was marked with the Moderna vaccine. I never learned exactly what the pellets were, but just assumed that for proponents of holistic medicine, "pellets" were preferred to pharmaceuticals.

We continued to see high levels of identity fraud being reported particularly in the unemployment insurance program, including cases of insiders and prison-based groups.

In August, a thirty-five-year-old woman from New Bedford, Massachusetts, pled guilty in federal court to fraud and identity theft charges. The woman was what we call an insider threat; she was a contractor with the Massachusetts Department of Unemployment Assistance. If you can believe it, she applied for that position in April shortly after her release from federal prison following her conviction *for aggravated identity theft*.

While working for the department, she filed unemployment claims in her name and her husband's name, who—again if you can believe it—was at the time incarcerated in Texas. She submitted claims for herself and her husband claiming zero income and zero dependents. She then used her access to the state databases to increase their income to $240,000 and their dependents to seven, to maximize the benefits. She then improperly verified this income without supporting documentation.

When police later searched their apartment, they found the tools of the identity fraud trade: an ID laminator, blank ID cards, hologram overlays, sheets of blank checks, cash, and a notebook of personal information of other people. The couple were not amateurs.

Meanwhile in Virginia, five individuals pled guilty to filing fraudulent unemployment insurance claims on behalf of numerous inmates in southwest Virginia regional jails. The scheme involved a total of nineteen individuals.

A Patterson, New Jersey, man was arrested for submitting more than 100 fraudulent claims to the Massachusetts Department of Unemployment Assistance and obtaining over $1 million.

In August, a claims specialist with the Social Security Administration was arrested for unlawfully accessing agency databases, obtaining personal information from unsuspecting victims, and filing fraudulent unemployment insurance claims in their names.

Billions in federal tax dollars were being plundered from state unemployment insurance programs by professional criminals, experienced opportunists, and impulse novices.

We concluded we needed to be doing more on the issue of identity fraud in government benefit programs. We established a dedicated Identity Fraud Reduction and Redress working group.

A couple of federal agencies play a major role in addressing identity fraud. The US Secret Service and the US Postal Inspection Service, for example, provide significant investigative resources to detecting identity fraud and bringing those responsible to justice. The Federal Trade Commission is an independent federal commission responsible for protecting consumers. FTC's website, IdentityTheft.gov, is the place to go to file a complaint and report that your identity has been stolen. Unfortunately, there is no lead federal agency to prevent fraud across government benefit programs, and no office responsible for helping victims receive support like getting their government benefits quickly reinstated.

The new PRAC working group would focus on tackling identity fraud in pandemic response programs and more importantly strive to improve victim redress across government.

There are significant, long-standing structural challenges to addressing the identity fraud problem in the unemployment insurance program. It's a hard problem to solve.

Unemployment insurance is a program delivered through a federal-state partnership created in the Social Security Act of 1935. The Social Security Act is so seminal and comprehensive that it's a third rail in Washington. Few people are interested in opening it up and making legislative tweaks. The unemployment insurance program is funded through both the states and the federal government.

In normal times, employers contribute most of the funding through payroll taxes. States manage their own programs under broad federal mandates, and the federal government provides additional funding, if necessary, to stabilize local economies. As a former National Governors Association official once told us, "It doesn't matter whether the governor is an R or D, nobody likes the federal government telling them what to do."

While that sentiment is understandable, the federal government needed to find a way to better share information across states and between the federal and state governments.

The state unemployment insurance agencies are supported by an independent, nonprofit organization called the National Association of State Workforce Agencies. NASWA was originally born in 1937 as part of the Labor Department, but politics and lawsuits resulted in NASWA separating from the department in 1973.

This complicated history partly explains the inability or hesitancy of the US Department of Labor to fully engage with the state workforce agencies or NASWA on issues like fraud prevention and detection. The Labor Department, for example, funds an Unemployment Insurance Integrity Center that is operated in partnership with NASWA. This center can be used by states to determine whether a social security number is being used for a claim filed in another state. The Labor OIG found that one social security number was used to obtain benefits from twenty-nine states. If Congress mandated that all states use the Integrity Center, this would be much less likely to occur. The Labor Department would say under the current law they can only lead the states to the Integrity Center; they can't make the states drink its tools and services or mandate its use.

It was during this season I witnessed one of the most creative and significant antifraud contributions from Gene

Sperling and the American Rescue Plan team. Through the hard work of senior counsel Jodie Morse, the ARP team was able to work with the Labor Department and the inspector general on a way forward to both help the states fight fraud and help the OIG fight fraud and provide better oversight. It was in the form of grants.

In August 2021, to address the historic unemployment insurance fraud crisis and combat identity fraud, the administration awarded American Rescue Plan Act grants of up to $140 million to states to support fraud detection and prevention, including identity proofing and verification services. Some states that may have wanted to use the Integrity Center to conduct data matches to identity fraud were unable to do so because of their antiquated IT systems. States could use this grant money to modernize their IT systems. But to get the grant money, states had to agree to provide their unemployment insurance data to the OIG.

The ARP team also helped shepherd significant new guidance from the Labor Department to the states to require that they report suspected fraud to the OIG. Labor Department guidance is issued to the states in the form of an Unemployment Insurance Program Letter, or UIPL (pronounced *U-pull* and incidentally another one of my favorite Washington acronyms).

I worked as an intermediary between the ARP team and the Labor OIG as multiple drafts of the guidance went back and forth. The Labor Department OIG had been challenged before the pandemic to obtain unemployment data from the states. Many states flat out refused. At one point during the pandemic, the OIG was forced to issue fifty-four separate subpoenas to all the state workforce agencies to get these data and hope the states complied in a timely manner.

The ARP team expressly conditioned the new American Rescue Plan grants on the states agreeing to refer suspected fraud to the OIG and to provide unemployment insurance claim data to the OIG without need for a subpoena. This had been something the OIG had requested of Congress for many years. It was now a condition of receiving federal grant money. It was a win-win.

13

WHO'S BRANDON?
(FALL 2021)

Americans express wildly different views on returning to normal. Nursing home visitor restrictions are lifted; anti-mask protests disrupt school board meetings. "Let's Go, Brandon" is born, as social issues are combined into a hodgepodge of hate.

D elta, the fourth wave, peaked in September 2021. By that time, COVID had claimed 675,000 US lives, as many as we lost during the 1918 influenza pandemic.

In November, the federal government finally lifted restrictions on visitors and group activities in nursing facilities. Domino's Pizza may have been able to figure out contactless delivery in a matter of days, but our loved ones in nursing facilities were forced to live in relative isolation for twenty months.

Also in November, Big Bird from *Sesame Street*—the eight-foot two-inch six-year-old talking yellow bird—became eligible for the Pfizer vaccine. He tweeted, "My wing is feeling a little sore, but it'll give my body an extra protective boost that keeps me and others healthy."

President Biden replied, "Good on ya, @BigBird. Getting vaccinated is the best way to keep your whole neighborhood safe."

Some critics cried "fowl," objecting to messaging directed at minors.

"Government propaganda . . . for your 5-year-old!" Senator Ted Cruz tweeted.

The episode reminded me of the famous black-and-white picture of a smiling Elvis Presley with his sleeve rolled up as he got his polio shot on the *Ed Sullivan Show.*

In 2022, the senator would get mixed up with Mr. T after the actor tweeted about his personal choice of face masks.

"I just received my 2nd Moderna booster vaccine, and I feel good!" the actor tweeted. "I am still going to wear my mask and keep my distance because the virus ain't over, Fool! Grrr."

Cruz responded by tweet, "Bizarre. 535 Members of Congress can attend the State of the Union without wearing masks, but it's still not good enough for Hollywood."

"Mask mandates were brazenly wrong three years ago and they're wrong today," Cruz would later say in a January 2023 tweet.

From my perspective, this was another example of gratuitous, clumsy, and uncoordinated messaging from Washington that did little to unite the nation during the pandemic and make us safer. Words and tweets have consequences. This wasn't 1956 and Big Bird and Mr. T weren't Elvis. With the immediacy of Twitter, the concept of "choose your words carefully" had been all but lost along with the virtue of discretion.

With the widespread roll out of vaccines, though, life was starting to return to something resembling normal.

There was also a push to return to normal at work. For some, that meant returning to the office. I had no strong desire and had adjusted to working from home, but others thought it was time for the PRAC staff to meet in person.

In the early PRAC days, we signed a lease for a small office within the headquarters of the Government Accountability Office for when the stay-at-home order was lifted. This office had been unoccupied for the past year, but now some federal agencies were beginning to allow staff to return to the office with social distancing and mask restrictions. Horowitz, Martin, and I decided to go into town in September to visit the office space and meet in person.

At the time, GAO was requiring all employees and tenants to wear masks in common areas. I knew the two men for many years, but that first in-person meeting was awkward trying to figure out whether to shake hands, knuckle bump, or knock elbows and whether to keep the mask on inside the office, pull it down, or remove it completely. But I'll admit it felt great to be in the physical presence of coworkers again and to be able to communicate with my whole self and not just as a square on a screen.

Michael Horowitz and Paul Martin were fully engaged in PRAC business, and you would never know at that same moment Horowitz's day job had him preparing his testimony for a Senate hearing the next week that would be the lead story on most national news outlets. The Senate hearing was on the OIG's 119-page report on the FBI's handling of the Larry Nassar investigation, the longtime USA Gymnastics team doctor.

Over an eighteen-year period, Nassar sexually abused at least 265 USA gymnasts. One of our nation's elite gymnasts reported the abuse to the FBI, but worse than doing nothing, the FBI agent falsified the report. According to the OIG report, Nassar went on to abuse at least seventy more victims before his arrest.

As despicable as the subject matter of the investigation was, it made us all proud as oversight professionals that we worked in a system with independent watchdogs ready, willing, and able to take on powerful institutions.

$

COVID contradictions played out across the country and with various levels of intensity.

In Poway, in Southern California, the school board was forced to end a fall meeting early after a group of mask-protesters disrupted the proceedings. The board was planning to discuss updated mask guidance for students and staff. They abandoned this plan after protesters forced their way into the meeting room and refused to leave. The protesters were carrying signs that read, "Let Them Breathe!" and "Unmask our kids!" and "Recall Gavin Newsom" and "Critical Race Theory teaches hate, racism, division."

It was during this season that the nation was introduced to the phrase, "Let's Go, Brandon."

It was on October 2, during an NBC broadcast of a NASCAR race at the Talladega Superspeedway. Driver Brandon Brown had just won his first Xfinity series race and was being interviewed. The crowd behind him was chanting something loudly that was difficult to make out. The reporter suggested they were chanting "Let's go, Brandon," but they were really chanting "Fuck Joe Biden."

By the end of the month, the phrase went viral. Senator Ted Cruz posed with an LGB sign at the World Series, which he posted on Twitter. Representative Bill Posey ended a floor speech with the LGB phrase and a fist pump.

On the same day that the LGB slur was born, *Saturday Night Live* did a skit set at the fictitious Lucerne County's District 7 school board meeting.

"I am concerned and I am also crazy, let's begin," said one actor to open to skit.

"I don't have a child and I don't live in this town," said one parent.

"My son can't play football because they say the vaccine he got was not valid," said another.

"Which one did he get?" his straight man answered.

"Mike's Hard vaccine." Ba-dum-bump.

Another actor playing an outraged parent took to the podium. "I'm so mad I'm literally shaking right now. Forget COVID, the real threat is critical race theory being taught in schools. My question is, what is it and why am I so mad about it!"

School board protests in real life prompted Attorney General Merrick Garland to order the FBI to monitor the situation.

In a memo announced the next Monday, October 4, the attorney general cited increases in harassment, intimidation, and threats of violence against school board members, teachers, and workers in our nation's public schools. He ordered the FBI to provide training on how to understand the behavior that constitutes a threat, how to preserve evidence, and how federal tools can be used to prosecute cases.

Reporters were writing of compassion fatigue and burnout by medical professionals. One story from the *Washington Post* in September 2021 was about a pulmonologist in Michigan who had lost over 100 patients to COVID. The doctor posted on Facebook the comments he had received from patients over a two-day span at work. He had one critically ill patient who denied his COVID diagnosis.

"You're wrong doctor. I'm too healthy. I don't have COVID. I'm fine."

Another told him, "I'd rather die than take the vaccine."

From a woman whose husband died of COVID: "I would never feel comfortable recommending the vaccine for family or friends."

Another threatened to call his lawyer if he wasn't given ivermectin, the anti-parasite drug for scabies and roundworm that is more commonly prescribed for horses and which comes in apple flavor and was touted incorrectly as a treatment or preventive for COVID.

$

In November, the Small Business Administration OIG reported that the SBA did not take advantage of the Treasury Department's Do Not Pay service in the disaster loan program until April 2021, resulting in billions in payments to potentially ineligible recipients, and even still was not using all of Do Not Pay's capabilities to prevent fraud. This report followed the SBA OIG's January 2021 report regarding usage of Do Not Pay in the PPP program to prevent fraud, and the OIG's briefing in August 2020.

In other words, eight months and billions of dollars had been lost.

We issued a new kind of agile oversight report to identify and assess fraud risks, in partnership with one of our IG members. I don't recall any inspector general ever issuing a report quite like it.

The US Department of Housing and Urban Development (HUD) received billions in pandemic relief funds for grants for local communities and public and Indian housing. Historically, the agency does not have a strong track record of managing its fraud risks. It does not have a strong track record of welcoming independent oversight either, with former HUD secretary Andrew Cuomo once saying in congressional testimony that the HUD IG was viewed as "the embodiment of evil."

HUD inspector general Rae Oliver Davis had been quietly hard at work since her 2019 appointment to fundamentally change the risk culture at HUD. The engaging former federal prosecutor and oversight veteran was open to new thinking.

We proposed lending a member of our team to work with her office. This team member just happened to have spent years as a consultant to government agencies developing fraud risk management programs.

Fraud risk management is a responsibility of agency management, and inspectors general are required to maintain their independence so they can objectively conduct audits of programs when necessary. If you helped build it, you can't objectively audit it. The work we proposed to Davis's office was as close to the independence line as you can get. There is nothing wrong with that. In fact, it can be the sweet spot.

In my experience, I've found that a watchdog can be so distant from agency management, in the name of independence, that they become irrelevant. I've seen this at some agencies. One "tell" is if the agency has a large backlog of open audit recommendations from their watchdog. While that's not always the case, the more agency management trusts and values the professional opinions of their inspector general, the more likely they take their watchdog's advice and implement their audit recommendations—particularly the noncontroversial, low-cost, and easily implementable ones.

An inspector general who is closer to the action, so to speak, is in a better position to bark at the first sign of danger. So long as the inspector general knows where the independence line is, they can provide technical assistance to the agency and greatly enhance the agency's understanding of fraud risk, for example, with the inspector general's unique point of view.

Our PRAC in-house fraud consultant helped Davis's auditors and the HUD management team develop an inventory of housing program fraud risks. Our hope was that this kind of joint effort would inspire more work like this across government. Rather than just criticizing agency management teams for not doing enough to prevent and detect fraud, inspectors general could accelerate antifraud programs.

We also issued another major report during this season. This report identified the major gaps in public reporting of federal pandemic spending data that we were still observing.

Making accurate and complete federal pandemic spending data available to the public was still top of mind, as it had been since the very beginning. For this report we did a detailed analysis of the available pandemic spending data. We looked at over 50,000 federal awards worth nearly $350 billion. We found dead end after dead end. We found more than 15,000 awards worth over $30 billion with meaningless award descriptions that made it difficult to know how the money was used.

Most simply repeated the name of the federal program (for example, entitlement grant). Some used only technical jargon that the public wouldn't be able to understand (such as CCC5-2021), and some were just variations of the COVID-19 relief spending bills (such as the CARES Act).

We made some recommendations to OMB on ways to make incremental improvements in this area. It's a complicated problem with no easy solution. We recognized that. Our role is to draw attention to problems and suggest solutions. Clobbering OMB on an issue they alone couldn't fix wasn't constructive.

In addition to issuing reports, we were starting to get traction and see results with the Pandemic Analytics Center of Excellence (PACE). We were contacted by the director of public housing in a populous county in the Midwest. His office had received complaints that federal public housing participants had fraudulently obtained SBA Paycheck Protection Program loans. His staff could look up individual borrowers on our website, but individual searches were time consuming. He wasn't having it with participants in his program defrauding HUD or SBA. He had many needy and honest people on the public housing waiting list, he told us, and he wondered if there was a way to do a bulk data match.

Our data scientists obtained and cleaned his housing assistance participant data and matched it against the small business loan data. We identified a high percentage of individuals who appeared to have committed fraud. We found loans associated with the names and social security numbers of minors. We provided the results to the director for his office to conduct further inquiry, and we sent the results to the SBA and HUD.

We were careful to point out that a data match doesn't prove fraud. It's just an indicator of potential fraud. At the very least, we suggested these individuals should be flagged with a hold code in SBA's loan application system requiring additional steps to verify identity and eligibility before they are approved for any future SBA loans. This was a big early win for the PRAC and PACE.

To its credit, SBA management took immediate action in response to our findings. It took weeks for HUD management to even acknowledge receipt of my email. I had to shake the tree through multiple channels to get a simple acknowledgment.

We started making plans to hold our first all-hands, in-person staff meeting in DC in November. As the date drew closer, though, more and more staff were privately expressing concerns about the Delta variant. We had told staff that attendance in person was a personal choice. Given the choice, some told us they would not attend due to health concerns. Some staff were disappointed when we ultimately decided to postpone the gathering until the spring of 2022. We would often repeat that employee safety and well-being was our first concern, and I think most staff greatly appreciated that our actions matched our words.

In the meantime, our six PRAC senior leaders and I came together in DC for a leadership retreat. We asked them first if they felt comfortable doing so. All did, so we went forward.

With the smaller group, we had the physical space to maintain social distancing. We all agreed that if any one of us chose to wear a mask, then we would all abide by that person's personal decision and wear one also.

The seven of us got together for the first time in person and it was wonderful. We were able to see glimpses of each other's personalities after the exhaustion of being together for months of hours-long video meetings. Nobody is what you imagine on video calls when your brain fills in the missing pieces from the two-dimensional head and shoulder view.

Walking back from a group lunch, I was chatting with one of our managers on the sidewalk waiting for the crossing signal to change. As we started to cross, I caught a flash out of the corner of my eye. It was a twenty-something woman flying down Seventh Street on a motorized scooter and heading straight at us. I wish I could tell you I intentionally took swift and brave action to save the life of another, but I just reacted. I instantly froze with my arms out effectively holding back my colleague and successfully averting a high-speed collision, which would have been painful for all of us. The scooterist nodded sheepishly before adjusting her earbuds and accelerating on her journey.

Washington was getting back to normal, but social manners had apparently rusted a bit during the shutdown. On the positive side, it couldn't have been a better trust-building experience if it had been staged.

14

A GREEK ALPHABET OF WOE
(WINTER 2021–2022)

Omicron, the fifth wave, knocks America on its back. The Postal Service delivers millions of home COVID test kits.

I t's unlike anything we've seen, even at the peak of the prior surges of COVID," said James Phillips, MD, the chief of disaster medicine at George Washington University, in a media interview in December 2021, when the nation hit a new pandemic record high of over 300,000 average daily new cases. "What we're experiencing right now is an absolute overwhelming of the emergency departments in Washington."

"It feels like 2020 all over again," read one December 2021 headline from the *Washington Post*.

Maryland reported the highest number of new COVID cases recorded in a twenty-four-hour period: 6,218. We were experiencing the fifth wave: Omicron. More than 2,600 Americans a day were dying, and it was the elderly and unvaccinated who were most severely impacted.

Montgomery County government announced that because of the large number of firefighters and EMTs who were unable to work due to Omicron, it needed to make service adjustments. It asked for the public's patience and understanding.

I live on a main road, about a two-mile straight shot from the volunteer fire department, about thirty-two miles as the crow flies from the nation's capital. One winter afternoon, I heard a car crash outside my window, and I raced outside to assist. The woman passenger in one car was injured and wailing from the shock. Thankfully, she did not appear to be seriously injured.

It was then, as I waited outside for what seemed like an eternity for an ambulance to arrive, that I realized what "Omicron-related service adjustments" really meant. By this time other neighbors and travelers had stopped. We all felt helpless as did many Americans in similar situations.

Omicron and social disruption dampened the Christmas spirit. In a televised call on Christmas Eve with the president and first lady, an American dad used the opportunity to wish the president of the United States a Merry Christmas and a "Let's go, Brandon."

A few weeks prior, the president gave the inspectors general a welcomed present. The Office of Management and Budget issued new guidance titled, "Promoting Accountability through Cooperation among Agencies and Inspectors General." OMB had solicited the views of the community of inspectors general before issuing the guidance. It laid out the president's view on how independent oversight should be conducted and cited the experience of the PRAC and the ARP team as a best practice.

It was during this season that the federal government began deploying a new measure to address the pandemic: home COVID test kits. Americans could go to CovidTests.gov, a website managed by the Postal Service in partnership with the United States Digital Service, and order tests to be shipped to their home. The Postal Service would deliver hundreds of millions of tests to American households across the country.

$

My wife was feeling run down over the holidays and used one of the over-the-counter test kits. Her white plastic test strip came back with two lines. She was positive. She lost her sense of smell and taste for a while, but overall had a mild case. We were thankful for both vaccines and test kits, and she rested through it and quickly recovered.

Just as I was getting into my New Year's routine, I started to feel run down. I ended the week having to use one of those COVID tests from the Postal Service. After twenty months, I had finally caught the virus.

Thankfully, I was vaccinated and also had a relatively mild case that came and went in a few days. More than anything, once I tested negative, I felt a great unburdening. I was relieved. The waiting was over. The fear and uncertainty of how my body would respond was over.

For the past several years, I battled seasonal asthma that would linger and develop into serious coughing and shortness of breath. This would usually require a trip to the doctor and an inhaler and medicine. Many people have it far worse, but my fear had been that COVID would trigger one of these episodes. The image of being intubated and alone in an ICU was in the back of my mind. Thankfully that didn't come to pass, and within a few days I was back to normal. I knew people who were less fortunate and experienced longer-term symptoms.

For me, there was a pronounced sense of just being done with, and just so over, the pandemic. I wasn't over it in the sense that I no longer thought it was a physical threat. I did. I just meant over in the sense that it was no longer some mysterious threat stalking me. I was ready to move on with life . . . so I bought a new car.

The transmission on my 2002 truck was slipping badly and needed to be replaced. It was a costly repair in normal times, and the few shops I called mentioned car part shortages due to the pandemic. The pandemic significantly disrupted global shipping. At one point in January 2022, there were over 100 container ships stuck off the ports of Los Angeles and Long Beach, waiting to be unloaded, and there were 150 ships stuck outside other US ports.

In fact, supply chain shortages were so bad that the used car market was through the roof. A coworker mentioned that a neighbor bought a new car a few months ago, and the dealership was calling him offering to buy it back.

With the pandemic, my new car purchase was a completely online, socially distant business transaction. The salesperson drove the car to our home and handed me the keys in the driveway—both of us wearing face masks. I paid a fair price, and the dealership got the sale. The pandemic had changed how closely we interacted, but it didn't interfere with the flow of commerce.

The COVID-19 pandemic had rippled throughout the US economy, upending and transforming restaurants, movie theaters, home grocery delivery services, automobile sales, and so many other industries.

Sadly, for us, the Omicron surge meant there would be no first birthday party for our newest grandson.

$

At the PRAC, we put out two innovative oversight reports during this season.

Normally, senior staff would pitch me an idea for a project *before* they started work. One day, a few months prior, our staff brought me an idea that came from one of our junior staffers. At that time, he was an intern still finishing his graduate degree. He thought it would make an informative read if we summarized all the audit findings from state and local auditors on unemployment insurance programs. We had the reports on our website. This derivative product would require someone with the smarts to identify and summarize major themes across reports and across offices. While we had issued reports summarizing the work of federal inspectors general, nobody had thought that we could or should summarize the work of state and local auditors. It wasn't, after all, our work.

But this whole-of-government view made perfect sense in the context of pandemic oversight, and by the time they pitched me the idea, the report was nearly complete. They were getting my "approval" after the fact. How could I say no? How could I not relish that we had built a work culture where anyone at any level could surface a great idea and run with it?

The other innovative oversight report we issued was on the SBA's new $28 billion restaurant revitalization fund.

The restaurant fund was created in the American Rescue Plan Act. By this point, the SBA's shortcomings to prevent and detect fraud in the Paycheck Protection Program and the disaster loan program had been widely reported by independent auditors and the media. Gene Sperling and the ARP team needed some level of assurance with the restaurant program before they authorized release of the funds that the SBA had made significant improvements since the early months of the pandemic to stop fraud.

We tackled this project from an unconventional angle. Our auditors had no way to monitor the restaurant grant requests and approvals in real time, so all we had to go on was what SBA was telling us. We kicked the tires, knowing that the SBA inspector general and Government Accountability Office would also be looking at this program eventually. We had numerous meetings with SBA managers and the OIG and obtained documented proof of how SBA tightened some fraud controls since the early days of the pandemic. We ultimately found that while SBA's ability to stop fraud had improved, they still needed to do more to protect federal tax dollars.

Our findings were partially validated when the Justice Department announced the arrest of a former Oregon dentist who was charged with fraudulently obtaining $8 million from the restaurant program. He had previously filed dozens of disaster loan applications, using his personal residence as the business addresses. But he was lazy or sloppy and submitted all the applications from the same internet protocol number associated with his dental office. Most of these applications were denied. He then tried the restaurant program after it launched, filing three applications for fraudulent restaurants in Florida, but using his Oregon residence as the business address. He got $8 million before his fraud was discovered. He was prosecuted and forced to surrender the Maserati he bought with the proceeds. He was convicted of attempting to steal more than $170 million in pandemic relief and illegally distributing prescription drugs.

The Health and Human Services OIG was able to report a bit of good news. They audited the nearly $2 billion sole source contracts that the government awarded to national pharmacy and grocery stores for COVID testing. The auditors examined the sole source justification records and sample invoices and found the contracts were being appropriately managed in terms of performance and cost.

$

On February 1, the chief of the World Health Organization reported that there had been 90 million cases of coronavirus since Omicron was first identified ten weeks ago. More than all the number of cases in 2020. Thankfully, Omicron was trending down, and as the winter of 2022 came to a close, Montgomery County lifted its indoor mask mandate in late February. We were no longer in a high community level of transmission.

15

A GOOD NIGHT FOR GOOD GOVERNMENT
(SPRING 2022)

America passes 1 million COVID deaths. Airline mask mandates are lifted. The president acknowledges our work and pledges to do more to support the watchdogs.

P resident Biden addressed the nation in his State of the Union address on March 1.

To our surprise, about halfway through his one hour and one minute address, the president alluded to our work on pandemic oversight.

> The previous administration not only ballooned the deficit with those tax cuts for the very wealthy and corporations, it undermined the watchdogs—the job of those to keep pandemic relief funds from being wasted. Remember we had those debates about whether or not those watchdogs should be able to see, every day, how much money was being spent, where it—was it going to the right place?
>
> In my administration, the watchdogs are back. And we're going after the criminals who stole billions of relief money meant for small business and millions of Americans.
>
> And tonight, I'm announcing that the Justice Department will soon name a chief prosecutor for pandemic fraud.

That night, the White House issued a fact sheet with some additional details, including some important new anti-fraud initiatives including efforts to address identity fraud involving government benefits. The fact sheet also explicitly recognized how the PRAC, together with the inspectors general and the American Rescue Plan team, have helped fundamentally change the nature of federal disaster oversight. Specifically, the White House commended our gold standard meetings, which along with our antifraud technical assistance, were paying dividends, and now seen as the model moving forward.

The next morning, I sent an email to all staff sharing with them the comments from the White House. I've been with the federal government for twenty-eight years. It's not every day that your work draws the attention of the president.

"All in all," I told staff, "I'd say it was a good night for Good Government."

$

I noticed few people wearing masks in the grocery stores since Montgomery County had lifted its indoor mask mandate in late February, following the drop in cases after the Omicron wave. The county was no longer in the high community level zone. Masks were a personal choice, and I still couldn't understand the mental state of someone who would get openly frustrated, angry, or furious at others for exercising this personal choice.

In March 2022, Florida Governor Ron DeSantis was filmed at a press event chiding a group of high schoolers in his staged background for wearing face masks. Even though CDC was still recommending indoor masking, the governor told the students, "You do not have to wear those masks. I mean, please take them off. Honestly, it's not doing anything. We've got to stop with this COVID theater. So if you wanna wear it, fine, but this is ridiculous."

In April, a federal judge in Florida ruled that the mask mandate for airlines exceeded the authority of CDC. The judge ruled in favor of two women who claimed that wearing masks gave them anxiety. The thirty-three-year-old federal judge, who was rated as "Not Qualified" by the American Bar Association during her confirmation hearing in the Senate, was the youngest person President Trump appointed to a lifetime judicial appointment. Airlines responded immediately.

An Air Alaska pilot couldn't contain himself. In a viral tweet, the pilot is heard in a video gleefully making his announcement midflight: "Ladies and gentlemen, this is your pilot speaking. This is the most important announcement I've ever made," the pilot said. "The federal mask mandate is over. Take off your mask if you choose!"

In May, the Department of Homeland Security OIG released an audit report on what's called Enforcement and Removal Operations. This is the program responsible for housing and transporting migrants to Immigration and Customs Enforcement detention facilities. IG auditors found numerous instances where migrant adults, families, and unaccompanied minors were not tested for COVID before being put on domestic commercial flights.

It was not only traveling American citizens who were put at increased risk. An unrelated audit from the Health and Human Services OIG from this time found that most of the intake facilities for these migrants lacked procedures for COVID-19 testing of children, employees, and volunteers and lacked measures to protect against the spread of the coronavirus.

Our county school board dropped the mask mandate for schools. We are Maryland's largest school district and were one of the last in the state to still require masks.

As a nation, we passed 1 million deaths around May 9, 2022, but that grim milestone barely registered with people. For most, all that mattered was that the pandemic was winding down.

One of the data projects our PACE data scientists worked on was now ready for prime time. The Treasury OIG had oversight responsibility for the $150 billion Coronavirus Relief Fund that was paid out to over 960 state, local, and tribal governments. These prime recipients then paid some of the money to subrecipients. All told there were 79,000 entities receiving federal funds under this program. Too many to audit. Our data scientists developed a risk scoring model for Treasury OIG auditors to plan their work.

In the spring, Treasury OIG launched a series of desk reviews of recipients, large and small, all around the country. Announcements of these desk audits were posted on our website and showed we were providing oversight coverage in places like Ohio, Dallas, Beaver Village, Cherokee Nation, and the US Commonwealth of Northern Mariana Islands.

After postponing our first office in-person meeting due to Omicron, we decided to hold it in April—two years to the day after I started at the PRAC.

To be frugal, we used conference space at the Government Accountability Office headquarters. The historic GAO building was built in 1951, and its claim to fame is that it was at one time the largest air-conditioned building in Washington. The home of the congressional watchdog who sets the professional standards on government auditing was a fitting location to gather our nascent crew.

We ended the retreat on a high note. We arranged a field trip to the White House complex and met with Gene Sperling and his team right across from the West Wing in the Eisenhower Executive Office Building. Michael Horowitz, Gene Sperling, Deidre Harrison, Jodie Morse, and I sat at the front table in the storied, marble-paneled Indian Treaty Room. The ARP team arranged for everyone to get a small box of White House M&Ms as a memento of our visit, and on our way out, we took group pictures on the steps of the Eisenhower building. Our work felt historic.

I had missed my 2020 birthday because of the demands of the job. I spent my 2021 birthday at the neurologist's office because of the toll of the job. In 2022, I was at the White House enjoying some of the candied fruits of our labor.

There was one more surprise.

During our visit to the White House complex, Deidre Harrison quietly pulled me aside right before our group event.

"Keep this close hold," she said, "the president is having an event tomorrow on ARP and the infrastructure bill and is meeting with the IGs. We got you on the invite list." She forwarded me the email link to the Secret Service reservation clearance system.

The next day I met a handful of colleagues outside of the White House visitor's entrance. Before we were allowed to be in a room with the president, we had to be COVID tested by the White House medical unit. With our in-person conference that week, I had been around so many staff who traveled through airports around the country to attend our event. I was worried that I would test positive and be turned away at the door.

We were shepherded as a group to the medical unit in the Eisenhower building, and one after another were taken back to an exam room and swabbed by medical staff. It was so efficient and quick, and we were then taken up to a waiting area while we awaited the results. I privately shared with Deidre Harrison that I was worried about popping positive.

"Relax. You'll be fine," she assured me.

We were eventually given the all clear and then escorted through the West Wing, through the White House, to the State Dining Room for the meeting with President Biden.

The room can seat over 140 and is used for official dinners and receptions. Our small gathering was being held here to provide plenty of open space for social distancing. A large table with upholstered chairs sat in the middle of the room. Oak-leaf accents on the carpet matched the walls, and a portrait of a seated Lincoln stared down from above the fireplace. Gold candelabra decorated the fireplace and massive drapes lined the windows. I was seated closest to the door. Next to my chair was a rope barrier. The White House staffer warned me that this was the press corral and to "be ready."

President Biden entered the room a little after 3:30 p.m. through the door on the far end of the room from me, and we leaped to our feet as he walked around the table to his chair in the center. He sat down and removed his mask, and we followed suit and sat in our chairs.

I had seen Biden in person regularly when he was a senator and I was working on the Hill. I had never been in the same room with a president before, though, and was watching his every move. He paused and then gave an aide a slight, almost imperceptible nod.

A mob of reporters exploded into the empty space. Too many to count. The corral could not have been more than 10 feet deep by 20 feet around, and within a few seconds it was jammed with arms and lanyard passes and cameras and notebooks and shouting heads. I was startled and jerked back, then naturally scanned the faces of anyone I recognized from TV. As my brain was processing faces, the mob ebbed and flowed and jostled for positions. Faces were familiar, but I just couldn't place any names. The mob quickly settled down.

The president spoke slowly and softly, thanking us for joining him and he said a few words about the importance of the work of the watchdogs. He talked about his experience with the Recovery Act, and how closely he worked with former inspector general Earl Devaney. Devaney had passed away the week before at his home in Florida, and the president acknowledged his contributions to oversight.

"Earl was a stand-up guy," the president said. "And I would meet with Earl once a week. I didn't—I did not tell Earl what to do. But I found out from Earl what was happening, because he had carte blanche to know how every penny was being spent." Directing his comments to the reporters in the press corral, the president said, "And, you know, in my administration, the watchdogs are back. You're looking at them all here. All of you. And I really mean it. Look."

The president talked about pandemic oversight and the independent oversight that would be needed for the recently passed $1.2 trillion Bipartisan Infrastructure law to rebuild our nation's roads, bridges, rail, and access to clean water.

"And I want to make it clear to the press that's here: Nobody in my administration is telling the inspector generals what they have to do. They're totally independent. They make a judgment. If they want to investigate something, do it. If we—period. So, let's find out what's going wrong and what's going right and what help you need in order to determine if you're not getting the information you need."

As soon as the president ended his remarks, the reporters were given a sign and suddenly there erupted a babel of voices, reporters shouting over the top of each other in the hopes of getting the president's attention. In official transcripts this is called "cross-talk" and that term just doesn't do justice to the cacophony.

"Mister President, what about—?" I heard "president of Mexico" and "Ukraine," and it wasn't until I got home and searched the internet that I learned that the president had a call with the president of Mexico earlier in the day, and the media were separately reporting on the first US citizen killed in the fighting in Ukraine.

"Okay, that's enough," the White House aide said softly as he calmly shooed the reporters back out the door from which they entered. President Biden wasn't going to answer their questions.

The president's remarks in front of reporters lasted about ten minutes. The mob scene with the reporters probably a minute or two. It was just long enough for some reporters to get photographs of the meeting. MSNBC's Kristen Welker was one face I recognized. She lingered a bit longer than the rest of the mob making one last attempt to get the president to answer her question about the American who died in Ukraine.

"Your reaction to the American killed in Ukraine, sir?" Welker called out to the president as her peers were leaving the room.

"It's very sad. He left a little infant baby behind," the president said softly looking down at the table.

Once the door was closed and order restored, the president paused, looked up with a rueful smile and said, "I just wish they'd ask questions about why we're here today."

The president then heard from Gene Sperling and Michael Horowitz who talked about our pandemic oversight work and from former New Orleans mayor Mitch Landrieu who serves as senior adviser to the president and infrastructure coordinator.

The Office of Management and Budget released that day new federal guidance on management and oversight of the

Bipartisan Infrastructure law. The new guidance required agencies to proactively engage with their watchdogs before implementing new and changed programs to ensure risks were identified. The administration was using the gold standard meetings from our pandemic oversight as the gold standard for infrastructure spending.

The president asked questions and stayed for longer than I would have thought. When he left and we concluded the meeting, Gene Sperling and Mitch Landrieu took a small group of us on a private tour of the White House—the People's House. It was like two kids sneaking around the place. They were equal parts reverent and mischievous, and always under the watchful eye of the patient Secret Service.

16

PANDEMIC EMERGENCY WINDS DOWN
(JUNE 2022 TO APRIL 2023)

More about vaccine hesitancy, mandates, and conspiracy theories. The president gets COVID—twice. Inflation hits Americans in the gas tank. Promising technology is underutilized as the availability of home tests results in poorer public health surveillance data. Another apparent uptick in cases in July, but you wouldn't know it. Congress extends the statute of limitations for pandemic fraud prosecutions. The pandemic emergency winds down, and the president declares it over.

It should have been an easy lay-up for the former president. The Trump administration was largely responsible for Operation Warp Speed, which was an overall success for his administration in the sense that as of August 2022, 67 percent of our population was fully vaccinated. This public-private partnership was announced by his administration in May 2020 to accelerate the manufacture and distribution of vaccines.

The federal government provided funding for six promising options and shortened the FDA approval process from the typical seventy-three months to fourteen months using large-scale clinical trials to analyze the safety and efficacy of the vaccine. Its mission was to deliver 300 million doses by January 1, 2021. By December 2020, the FDA had issued emergency use authorizations to Moderna and Pfizer.

But former president Trump just couldn't go there with vaccines. In a July 2022 rally in Alaska, the former president wouldn't even mention the word.

"We did so much in terms of therapeutics and a word that I'm not allowed to mention . . . but I'm still proud of that word," the former president told the crowd. "We did in nine months and it was supposed to take five years to twelve years, nobody else could have done it but I'm not mentioning it in front of my people. But someday we're gonna have to all sit down and have a little talk but you know what, we did a hell of a job."

Truer words may have never been spoken: *someday we're gonna have to all sit down and have a little talk.* Speaking before that crowd, the former president had to thread the needle between rightfully taking credit and distancing himself from COVID-19 vaccines.

I knew a few people who had concerns about all types of vaccines due to personal reasons and experiences. I respect that. COVID vaccine hesitancy seemed to come from a different place.

COVID vaccine hesitancy was a slow burn. A Wisconsin pharmacist had been arrested in December 2020 for intentionally spoiling trays of 500 Moderna vaccines by removing them from refrigeration. He was later sentenced to three years in prison. Other medical providers were arrested for selling fake vaccine cards.

Claims that the vaccine caused AIDS, infertility, and contained microchips so the Bill & Melinda Gates Foundation could track your movements were amplified by social media. Tucker Carlson told viewers that the vaccine mandate in the military was designed to identify the sincere Christians, free thinkers, and men with high testosterone.

"It's a takeover of the US military," Carlson explained to his audience.

Twenty-six Navy SEALs took the Secretary of Defense to court over the vaccines. The case went to the US Supreme Court who ruled that the SEALs could be reassigned if they refused the COVID vaccine. New recruits to the Armed Services are required to take seventeen vaccinations against diseases before initial entry or basic training, but for some reason, these SEALS took exception to this particular one.

To some, the religious objection of the SEALs and others to the vaccine was dubious. Pope Francis publicly said that the COVID vaccine was a "moral obligation" and "an act of love."

First Baptist Dallas pastor Robert Jeffress told reporters, "Since there is no credible biblical argument against vaccines, we have refused to offer exemptions to the handful of people who have requested them. People may have strong medical or political objections to government-mandated vaccines, but just because those objections are strongly felt does not elevate them to a religious belief that should be accommodated."

Those twenty-six SEALs weren't the only prominent anti-vaxxers.

An anti-vaccine group led by Robert F. Kennedy Jr., the son of the late RFK, was kicked off Instagram in August. Kennedy himself had been banned from Instagram and Facebook in February 2021. He resurrected himself through the Child Health Defense and continued spreading misinformation. Kennedy believes Dr. Fauci was "orchestrating fascism" and "personally profiting" from the pandemic. Kennedy shared other misinformation like a video that falsely attributed the death of baseball great Hank Aaron to the vaccine.

These weren't just occasional comments. Kennedy had published a book in November 2021 called *The Real Anthony Fauci: Bill Gates, Big Pharma, and the Global War on Democracy and Public Health*. The book alleges Dr. Fauci sabotaged treatments for AIDS and conspired with Bill Gates and Facebook to suppress information about COVID-19 cures. Kennedy wrote about an alleged "powerful vaccination cartel" and called Dr. Fauci "a powerful technocrat who orchestrated and executed the historic 2020 coup against Western democracy."

At an anti-vaccine event in DC in January 2022, Kennedy told the crowd that they can't even "hide in an attic like Anne Frank did." This comment forced Kennedy's wife, Cheryl Hines, the actress from HBO's *Curb Your Enthusiasm*, to issue a public statement on Twitter distancing herself from her husband's political views.

"My husband's reference to Anne Frank at a mandate rally in D.C. was reprehensible and insensitive," Hines wrote in a post. "The atrocities that millions endured during the Holocaust should never be compared to anyone or anything. His opinions are not a reflection of my own."

$

Despite the health precautions I witnessed at the White House in late April, President Biden tested positive for COVID-19 in July 2022.

Some of his critics were delighted by the news. Despite being vaccinated and having access to the best possible medical care, President Biden had a breakthrough case that for anti-vaxxers proved the point that vaccines didn't prevent infection. Vaccine proponents were left shaking their heads in dismay, as nobody claimed vaccines would categorically prevent infection. When caught in a rainstorm, umbrellas may keep you mostly dry, but you're still bound to get a little wet. Some conservatives were doubly delighted when President Biden tested positive shortly after testing negative. He had a so-called rebound case.

Trump took to Truth Social, the Twitter alternative platform he launched after getting kicked off Twitter.

"Joe Biden's second bout of Covid, sometimes referred to as the China Virus, was sadly misdiagnosed by his doctors," Trump said.

"He instead has Dementia, but is happily recovering well. Joe is thinking of moving, part time, to one of those beautiful Wisconsin Nursing Homes, where almost 100% of the residents miraculously, and for the first time in history, had the strength and energy to vote—even if those votes were cast illegally. Get well soon, Joe!" Trump wrote.

President Biden responded in kind.

"When my predecessor got COVID he was taken to the hospital by helicopter. When I got it, I worked for five days."

Americans deserve better than this.

$

In July 2022 I took my first business trip in over two years since the pandemic hit. I went to Anaheim, California, for a conference of government accountants and financial managers. My traveling skills were rusty.

I took an Uber to the airport, wearing a mask in a stranger's car. While Uber stopped requiring masks in April, the CDC recommended masking in high transmission communities. Both Montgomery County and my destination in Anaheim were back to high levels of transmission, so I wore a mask.

When my driver picked me up in my driveway and saw my mask, he seemed slightly annoyed as he fished through his center console for his mask. A small price to pay for a large fare, which included a sizable fuel surcharge to reflect the high price of gasoline. Average gas prices across the nation went from under $3.50 a gallon in January 2022 to over $5 per gallon by June.

My flight had too many connections and got me to my destination late Saturday night. My Uber driver drove past the Disneyland gate on the way to the hotel. You wouldn't know there was a recession or any worries about inflation. Hordes of tourists were leaving the park at dark, arms stuffed with overpriced concessions. You also wouldn't know that Anaheim was a high transmission community by the crowds. Not a mask in sight.

Several hundred people attended the conference. When I checked in, I could pick up a green, yellow, or red lanyard to signal to other attendees my comfort level on social distancing. Green, for example, meant I was comfortable with handshakes and hugs, while red meant to keep your distance. I took the middle option and spent the week in various states of masked and unmasked. In one-on-one conversations where I could keep my distance, I'd pull down my mask. Whenever the crowd emerged after session breaks when there were people shoulder to shoulder, I'd pull it up.

I mostly wore my mask on the airplane and in the airports. I noticed distinct regional differences. I saw few masks at the Dallas–Ft. Worth airport but saw plenty in DC.

Three days after I returned, I received an alert on my iPhone. I must have set up a feature in settings and forgotten about it. It was an exposure notification saying that the DC Health Department believes it is likely I was exposed to someone with COVID-19 with a "15–59-minute exposure." DC Health, along with other local health departments, was using Bluetooth to communicate with other phones near you that had also been enabled for this feature. My iPhone was exchanging random IDs with other devices in an exposure log for fourteen days.

This technology was co-created by Apple and Google in 2020 to automate contact tracing. This phone notification app has great potential, but unfortunately few people I knew reported their home test results to public health officials. Unless and until large segments of a population enabled the COVID exposure alert system on their phone and publicly reported their results, the impact of these apps would be limited. Like the more low-tech measure of masking, exposure notification apps will only work in the next pandemic if people care enough about their neighbors, or the common good, to put it on.

As I had been throughout the pandemic, I continued to follow the Johns Hopkins University COVID-19 tracker to look for trends. I didn't notice anything noteworthy on the tracker in July, but more and more of our staff were testing positive. And even with up-to-date vaccines, they were getting sick. Nobody was hospitalized, but a few were sick enough to warrant a trip to urgent care and a prescription for Paxlovid, the antiviral medicine recommended by the CDC for early treatment.

Home test kits were a major step in getting the pandemic under control, but one downside was that the public reporting of infection rates was becoming less reliable.

$

In late July, Congress passed a bipartisan bill and the president signed into law a measure to extend the statute of limitations for Paycheck Protection Program and disaster loan fraud from five to ten years. SBA inspector general Mike Ware told the media that his office had enough cases for "100 years."

On Thursday, August 4, my work cell phone buzzed after hours. It was Michael Horowitz calling from vacation. I knew it must have been something important.

He had received a call from Gene Sperling. The White House was putting together the bill signing ceremony for the new law on Friday at 1:00 p.m. There was one snag. President Biden was still testing positive for COVID-19, so this would be a hybrid signing ceremony, unlike the traditional ones where people stand hovering around the president signing the bill into law on the portable signing desk. It seemed fitting for the Pandemic Response Accountability Committee that this bill would be signed into law by the president in a virtual ceremony.

On Friday, I drove into DC. The weather was an oppressive 90 degrees and humid with no wind. The night before, a freak thunderstorm hit the White House area killing two tourists who were taking cover across the street in historic Lafayette Square. That was the somber small talk of the day.

Our group met up with Ware and his team. We gathered outside the White House visitors' entrance, cleared security at the Secret Service security booth, then made our way up West Executive Way.

With the West Wing on the right, we entered through the ground-floor entrance of the Eisenhower Executive Office Building and made our way to the South Court Auditorium. We were joined by a couple of Justice Department officials including the lead prosecutor for the DOJ's COVID-19 fraud task force.

The auditorium was set up like a TV sound stage with arena seating. While we waited for the event to start, we made subdued small talk and took selfies with the White House backgrounds.

When it came time, Gene Sperling walked in wearing a mask around his neck, accompanied by the SBA administrator. Sperling told us there had been a last-minute change in plans due to the president's health condition. We would watch the president on the video monitors while he commented on some major economic news of the day. The latest job numbers had been released, and they were better than expected: 528,000 jobs were added in July. For a White House that was faced with bad break after bad break, they were going to savor this good news. Speaking from the Blue Room Balcony, the president then took his seat at the portable signing desk.

"The American people deserve to know that their tax dollars are being spent as intended," Biden said via teleconference. "My message to those cheats out there is this: You can't hide. We're going to find you. We're going to make you pay back what you stole and hold you accountable under the law."

Later in August, the Secret Service, working with the SBA OIG, recovered $286 million in fraudulent SBA disaster loans. This money was from loans that used stolen or fake identities. Thankfully the money was still sitting in 15,000 accounts at an online bank where a customer can establish his identity and open an account entirely online. Secret Service agent

Roy Dotson and his boss printed a giant Publishers Clear-inghouse–size check and posed for pictures with Mike Ware presenting the check to an SBA official.

$

I enjoyed a personal milestone in August. Our son—the ER nurse who started his career the very week in March 2020 that COVID-19 shut down the US—got married. After two and a half years, the pandemic crisis was in the rear view but not forgotten. I was especially careful in the two weeks leading up to the wedding, avoiding unnecessary contact. I postponed one work lunch until after the special day. My wife would murder me, I admitted to a colleague, if I tested positive right before the special day. The wedding went off without a hitch. We had an outdoor ceremony with an indoor reception with family and friends and not a mask in sight.

The week after, my wife and I went to an outdoor Rod Stewart and Cheap Trick concert, our first public social event since COVID. Full disclosure: we're not super fans or any-thing. It just sounded like a fun night of familiar hits in a post-pandemic world. We were surrounded by 18,000 or so fans at Merriweather Post Pavilion in Columbia, Maryland, and I saw only a handful of people with masks.

Merriweather and I go back forty years to my teens. I've spent many a summer evening in the covered pavilion or sitting on the lawn listening to favorite, familiar, and new bands. Like many concert venues, Merriweather had to shut-ter its doors during the pandemic. In between sets, I couldn't resist looking up on our website how much pandemic relief Merriweather received. It got $10 million in federal pandemic aid as part of the federal shuttered venues grant program, and that may be the only reason it's still in operation and was able to host me and Rod Stewart in late August 2022.

$

I later joined one of our audit teams on a field visit to White Earth Nation reservation in White Earth, Minnesota, before the cold fall weather hit the Midwest. This tribal government was selected as one of our case studies to examine and compare how federal pandemic funding streams affected local communities. We selected two small-medium cities, two rural counties, and two tribal governments.

On this trip we learned firsthand how this or that billion--dollar federal program paid for medical supplies and internet access for home schooling at the community level. I was struck when tribal leaders explained how they grappled with vaccine hesitancy among their elders. For them, stories of smallpox blankets were not learned from history books but were part of their family's history. The tribal government successfully combined traditional medicine with vaccines and vaccine rates increased accordingly.

$

In August, the CDC modified its COVID-19 guidance, no longer recommending that people self-quarantine for five days after exposure. The new guidance recommended that after exposure you just wear a mask and test after five days.

In a major sign that the pandemic was winding down, the head of the CDC, Rochelle Walensky, MD, MPH, announced that the time was now right for the CDC to examine how it could improve its public health response for the next pandemic.

"For 75 years, CDC and public health have been preparing for COVID-19, and in our big moment, our performance did not reliably meet expectations," Dr. Walensky said in a statement. "As a longtime admirer of this agency and a champion for public health, I want us all to do better."

The Department of Justice announced the establishment of three new COVID fraud strike force teams: one in Baltimore, one in Miami, and one in California. These interagency teams would work the more complex fraud cases.

By September, it was clear that the US pandemic crisis was ending. As if any more signs were needed, a couple of prominent contemporaneous public announcements made the point. New York announced that masks would no longer be required on its subways, and the Pentagon told its workers they could all come back to work in person. The risk of COVID-19 infection was at its lowest since the beginning of the pandemic.

President Biden declared it over in a taped interview broadcast on *60 Minutes* on September 18.

"The pandemic is over," the president said as he walked the floor of the first Detroit Auto Show in three years. "We still have a problem with COVID. We're still doing a lot of work on it. But the pandemic is over."

Twelve days earlier, his White House Coronavirus Response Coordinator, Ashish Jha had told reporters, "The pandemic isn't over. And we will remain vigilant, and of course, we continue to look for and prepare for unforeseen twists and turns."

The COVID-19 pandemic of 2020–2023 was winding down just as it began: with clumsy and uncoordinated public messaging from our nation's leaders. Dr. Jha's science-based view was as well-grounded as President Biden's common-sense-based view. They were both partly right, but an unforgiving public often won't look at intentions.

In March 2023, the Department of Justice OIG issued a capstone review on the Federal Bureau of Prisons' response to the pandemic. Over the past three years, this office conducted sixteen remote inspections of federal corrections facilities. The capstone summarized their findings and included recommendations to help the bureau prepare for any future public health emergencies.

The GOP-controlled House of Representatives announced their intentions to increase pandemic oversight in 2023 and symbolically chose the issue as the topic for the first hearing of the new House Oversight and Accountability Committee. The committee invited PRAC chair Michael Horowitz, Comptroller General Gene Dodaro, Labor inspector general Larry Turner, and Secret Service assistant director David Smith to testify.

On the eve of the hearing, the PRAC's Pandemic Analytics Center of Excellence released a fraud alert identifying $5 billion in SBA small business loans that were associated with over 69,000 questionable social security numbers. These were numbers that were either not issued by the Social Security Administration, issued by SSA under a different name, associated with a different date of birth, or otherwise not verified by the SSA. We had to haggle with SSA lawyers for months to get them to verify these SSNs used in a government benefit program. They first refused and then came back and said they would have to charge us a fee for this service.

The hearing was somewhat overshadowed when Rep. Marjorie Taylor Greene used her allotted time to ask Dodaro, the head of the US Government Accountability Office, "How much money went to CRT." Dodaro, who's testified countless times in his forty-nine years at GAO, was taken by surprise and asked, "CRT?" Greene explained the term stood for critical race theory in education.

Dodaro politely explained that he did know that there was a provision generally that federal funds are not to be used for curriculum. Representative Taylor Greene interrupted his answer stating in Illinois an elementary school received "$5.1 billion" for these things. Her communications director later told reporters that she misspoke, and the congresswoman was referring to the entire state school system. A YouTube video of the exchange has been viewed by millions.

The Health and Human Services OIG issued its report on the gaps in our national approach to COVID-19 vaccines. State and local immunization programs were challenged getting vaccination data from retail pharmacies and federal agencies that administered vaccines. Without complete individual-level data, you can't accurately measure vaccine coverage or target outreach to unvaccinated and vulnerable populations. If left unresolved, the IG report concluded, "These challenges will likely hinder the ongoing COVID-19 vaccination campaign, *responses to future public health emergencies*, and routine vaccination campaigns (e.g., flu shots)." (emphasis added)

The Centers for Disease Control and Prevention did not agree—what we call in the business "nonconcurred"—with the OIG's recommendations. In my mind, it was a sad, but fitting, bookend to the HHS OIG's pulse survey report in April 2020 that had been criticized and had received a "nonconcur" from the prior president.

In April 2023 President Biden signed legislation officially declaring an end to the COVID-19 national emergency.

$

As the pandemic emergency was winding down, I realized it was time to say goodbye. The Pandemic Response

Accountability Committee—which will be around until September 30, 2025, unless Congress grants it an extension—needed someone with fresh eyes and fresh legs as pandemic oversight enters a new stage.

I had spent day after day on endless Zoom meetings, switching from one big topic to the next, constantly thinking about how to find win-wins with various partners who often had competing interests. Quite simply, the pandemic emergency was mentally, physically, and emotionally exhausting; and you can only set yourself on fire so many times before there's nothing left to burn.

I helped build a fifty-plus-person, $30 million/year oversight organization from scratch under incredibly challenging conditions like stay-at-home orders and global supply chain shortages. We were, in my view, the exemplar of both "coordinated, comprehensive oversight" and the next generation federal workforce. We were a distributed team in a virtual workspace.

Whether we would be a paragraph or a footnote in a future public administration textbook about the pandemic, we had met the moment. I witnessed the work of the oversight community being cited by the White House and members of Congress and being referenced on the national TV news. I enjoyed the many one-on-one talks with OIG colleagues and staff during my virtual office hours. All the pieces were in place, and I knew we had knocked it out of the park.

And yet there is still so much work to be done with $1 trillion in unspent pandemic relief funds still on the table. Oversight of the federal pandemic response and relief spending will continue for years, and I look forward to learning more from the future work of the PRAC, the inspectors general, the Government Accountability Office, public interest groups, the media, and congressional oversight committees.

PART III

17

THE FINANCIAL AND OTHER COSTS OF THE PANDEMIC

The pandemic crisis exacted a heavy toll on our nation, some of which we can see now but some costs may not be revealed for years to come.

For those of you who skipped ahead to Part III, this is the heart of my soapbox speech. For those of you who have read everything up until this point, thank you for going on that journey back in time as we all weathered shortages of toilet paper, wiped off groceries, bought things small and large (such as new cars) online, ordered masks on Amazon, considered vaccines, figured out how to work from home if we could, stopped traveling and seeing friends and family, and grieved those we lost.

I have a few observations I'd like to share from my unique point of view.

The three-year pandemic emergency exacted a heavy toll on our nation, some of which we can see now and some costs may not be revealed for years to come. There are enough data points available now, though, and we should be asking ourselves whether the federal pandemic response was successful or not.

Let me give you the good, the ugly, and the bad from my perspective.

Did shutting down schools save lives or set back children's learning? Probably both.

Did handing out $900 billion in forgivable Paycheck Protection Program loans save jobs or would those jobs have been saved or lost regardless? Probably both.

Did the expanded unemployment insurance benefits keep food on the table or keep workers from getting back to work? Probably both.

One of the most challenging problems for politicians, policymakers, and government auditors to solve is proving causation. It's rarely direct. How do you prove that a certain federal program is achieving its intended result? Answer: reliable and publicly available performance information.

Unfortunately, the federal government is challenged in reporting its spending data accurately and completely. Performance data are, in some respects, an even harder nut to crack. You can easily enough report *outputs*, but it's often hard to measure actual *outcomes*. This is a complex science with interdependent elements.

About a year before the pandemic hit, President Trump signed into law the Foundations for Evidence-Based Policymaking Act, which is a good start. This act aims to strengthen policymaking by tying policies to data and evidence of effectiveness. But until we get to a point where we have accurate and complete spending and performance data publicly available, people will look at various limited data points with their conscious and hidden biases and see what they want to see.

The Good

First the good news. If you're reading this, you survived the pandemic crisis. I survived the pandemic crisis. The US economy didn't crater. The national unemployment rate in March 2023 was back down to 3.6 percent—about where it was before the pandemic hit.

Our nation proved that it's able to accelerate and scale on many fronts. We fast-tracked the vaccine approval and production process and made vaccines available many months before the World Health Organization or other experts believed possible. You were able to get vaccinated at your local retail pharmacy. We successfully mobilized various instruments of government in a time of crisis. Military health professionals were sent to staff hospitals when surges hit. The Postal Service delivered millions of masks and home testing kits.

The pandemic forced government to be flexible and businesses to adapt. These innovations are likely here to stay. In the early days of the pandemic, for example, the Montgomery County Board of License Commissioners approved a change allowing restaurants to sell beer and wine for off-premise consumption. Our favorite place in town began selling a 32-ounce craft beer Growler To-Go to enjoy with your take-out. The restaurant is thriving, post pandemic, having weathered the long storm with curbside delivery and beer to go.

Contactless delivery of food and groceries is here to stay.

Telehealth, online education, and voting by mail are among the many activities that were fundamentally altered by the pandemic.

One of the most profound impacts was felt in the workplace. Remote work for knowledge workers soared. Work is no longer a physical place you arrive at after battling rush hour traffic. It's an activity that can be done from any place. Your zip code is no longer a legitimate job qualification. In many organizations, conference room meetings have been replaced by video calls.

Before the pandemic, some federal managers would hold their noses and allow someone to remote work full-time from their basement only in extreme cases. That attitude has changed. Even the Internal Revenue Service is considering allowing more remote work. The IRS, like other government agencies and private-sector employers, is facing a changing workforce who have tasted a better work-home life. If the workforce has anything to say about it, they are not going back to the old way. Progress does not move in a straight line, though, and time will tell how much remote or hybrid work is here to stay.

Finally, Washington got a little smarter over time and took a more surgical approach with subsequent pandemic relief legislation. In March 2021 the American Rescue Plan Act focused on hard-hit industries, like concert venues and restaurants. It provided significant funding to get kids safely back in schools. It expanded broadband to the poor for work, school, telehealth, and more. It funded programs to get nutritious food on the table for children and low-income Americans.

The American Rescue Plan Act provided direct payments to Americans. There are data to support that these payments had the desired impact, at least in the short term. The Census Bureau collects data through various surveys, and beginning in April 2020 it conducted the Household Pulse Survey to collect data in near real time on how families were faring. The survey measures hardship rates, which include whether the household has enough to eat, whether they are caught up on rent, and whether they have money left over to pay other bills. The survey showed that hardship rates declined following the direct payments in the American Rescue Plan, even if some problems still persist.

The Ugly

At the same time, the American Rescue Plan Act (like the CARES Act) was a massive amount of money—not all of which was strictly related to the pandemic—and components of the act like the stimulus checks likely had little effect on the economy, according to some researchers. Questions remain over whether such massive federal spending was necessary.

The New Jersey state auditor found, for example, that as of March 2023, the state had only spent $1 billion of the $6 billion provided to the state under the American Rescue Plan's state fiscal recovery fund program. In April 2023, House Republicans floated a proposal to claw back the billions of pandemic relief dollars that Congress approved but had not been spent.

At the PRAC, we previously reported on the rental assistance program, which distributed about $46 billion to pay for rent and utilities. The federal government initially allocated these funds to the states based on population instead of need, with a minimum allocation of $200 million per state. This resulted, for example, in Rhode Island state officials reporting that they should have received less than half of the $200 million they were allocated. Wyoming state officials returned 97 percent of their allocation.

I personally experienced the government's largesse when my local county recreation department, suddenly flush with cash, was now paying county gym fees (or rather waiving the fees thereby making gym use free) for residents. It was only a modest fee to begin with, but still. Gym fees didn't strike me as needed or necessary for national pandemic relief.

Regarding the Paycheck Protection Program, a 2022 report by a team of economists reported on the cost to the taxpayer for each job saved. The researchers found that the cost per job saved for one year was $169,000 to $258,000, significantly higher than the average amount—$58,200—paid in wages and benefits to small business employees in 2020.

The researchers also concluded that the Paycheck Protection Program "cost taxpayers roughly $4 for every $1 of wages and benefits received by workers in 'saved' jobs. The 'leakage'—$3 out of every $4 distributed through the program—went to small-business owners."

That was what I heard in my social circle: so-and-so small business owner was able to buy a new boat. Money's fungible. Some small business owners didn't need PPP relief but took the government money because it was available and they saw everyone else taking it. It was a boon that became a boat. When I write of waste (as in fraud and waste), this is what I'm referring to.

The Bad

The most important measurement, of course, is the loss of life. Over one million American souls lost their lives to the pandemic. According to the Kaiser Family Foundation, more than 230,000 deaths could have been avoided if individuals had gotten vaccinated. Over 200,000 American children lost one or both parents to COVID-19.

The World Health Organization, the CDC, and others are still studying and gathering data on the long-term effects for those who recovered. It goes by different names—long COVID or long-haul COVID—its physical and mental effects can be felt for weeks, months, or longer.

In September 2022, researchers at Washington University School of Medicine published the results of their study on the long-term neurological effects of COVID-19. They found that COVID-19 infection increases the risk of brain problems including stroke, seizures, depression, anxiety, and movement problems.

"We're seeing brain problems in previously healthy individuals and those who have had mild infections," the report's senior author said. "It doesn't matter if you are young or old, female or male, or what your race is. It doesn't matter if you smoked or not, or if you had other unhealthy habits or conditions."

Mayo Clinic, among other medical centers of excellence, has established a twelve-week program to treat post-COVID symptoms in patients who continue to experience health issues after COVID infection.

According to a WHO study, the pandemic triggered a 25 percent increase worldwide in prevalence of anxiety and depression. According to numerous studies, the mental health implications from the pandemic will be with us for many years.

The pandemic shutdowns rippled through our communities in countless ways. Some of our seniors lost over a year in isolation when no visitors were permitted in nursing homes from March 2020 until the federal restrictions were lifted in November 2021. For the estimated 1.3 million Americans in recovery programs like Alcoholics Anonymous or Narcotics Anonymous, it meant the suspension of meetings in church basements across the country, where so many gather over coffee and cigarettes and work on their sobriety one day at a time. Healing and recovery was put on pause for those in residential addiction treatment programs across America.

Despite the best efforts with remote learning, the pandemic set our nation's children back in both book learning and socialization. In September 2022, the National Center for Education Statistics issued its 2022 report card. The organization has been conducting national assessments since 1969 to track learning progress and trends of school-age students' progress. In 2022, it conducted a special assessment of nine-year-olds' progress in reading and math during the 2020–2021 school year. Student scores dropped 5 points in reading, the largest drop since 1990. Math scores dropped 7 points, the first ever drop.

The study found that higher performing students had access to a computer or tablet all the time, had a quiet place to learn some of the time, and had a teacher available every day. Most concerning was that the declines were much greater for lower performing students. Millions of children were being left behind.

It wasn't just book learning that was affected by the pandemic. According to another National Center for Education Statistics study, more than 80 percent of US public schools reported that the pandemic has negatively affected student socioemotional development. In other words, schools were seeing higher rates of classroom disruptiveness, acts of disrespect toward teachers and staff, and rowdiness outside the classroom.

Numerous studies pointed to profound mental health effects of the pandemic on school-age children, with increased rates of stress, anxiety, and depression. "School connectedness"—a student's sense of being cared for, supported, and belonging in school—was an important factor for learning and socialization. Remote learning reduced the risk of physical illness while the isolation increased the risk to mental health. As Education Secretary Miguel Cardona said, kids need to not only catch up academically but catch up with their friends.

The pandemic also took a heavy toll on our nation's educators. Teachers retired in massive numbers, and local school systems around the country are experiencing serious shortages. According to the Bureau of Labor Statistics, the pandemic precipitated the largest drop ever in the number of teachers, and there are about 300,000 fewer teachers now than in February 2020. Some states were required to lower the educational requirements to attract more teachers.

It wasn't just teachers. Stress, compassion fatigue, and burnout caused nurses and other healthcare professionals to exit the profession in droves leaving significant shortages. I knew from the nurses in my family that hospitals were forced to pay large shift bonuses to keep units sufficiently staffed.

The rise of remote work was a boon for many workers but a bust for others. One of my colleagues told me about how the pandemic shutdown and remote work affected her mother. My colleague is from South America, and her mother, who lived with her, had worked full-time as an office building custodian before the pandemic. It was physically hard and thankless work, but her mother was proud to work every day.

For many, work provides meaning and offers the dignity of self-sufficiency. With the pandemic shutdown, this building custodian was out of work and suddenly unable to fend for herself. Now she was dependent on others. Remote work may have ultimately been a boon for knowledge workers, but many others would lose their livelihood as our offices and cities emptied.

The December 2022 omnibus federal spending bill that Congress passed and the president signed into law ended the additional SNAP benefits for thirty-two states that were still using them. In a state like Michigan, over one million citizens or 13 percent of the state's population depend on this food program. The vast majority are working families, people with disabilities, and the elderly. Their monthly food benefits were cut $95 effective March 1, 2023.

"We are in the midst of heading into a very dark time with families struggling," one Michigan anti-poverty advocate said in a press interview referring to the SNAP cuts.

Our society is experiencing its own long-haul COVID effects.

And then there was the fraud problem—which warrants its own separate chapter.

18

AN INCONCEIVABLE AMOUNT OF FRAUD

In response to the COVID-19 pandemic, the federal government distributed an unfathomable amount of money in the trillions, through a jumble of federal programs in the hundreds, to a menagerie of recipients in the millions. The internet reduced barriers to fraud and made it harder and sometimes nearly impossible to follow the trail.

W hen I started my federal law enforcement career as a postal inspector, we were trained how to conduct a proper loss ascertainment, or "count" as it was called. Suppose a local post office was burglarized overnight. Soon after securing the crime scene and preserving the tool-mark evidence of the forced break-in, postal inspectors would then start counting.

You count the money. You count the stamps. You compare your counts to what is supposed to be on hand according to the last reconciliation forms. The task was so tedious that after all these years I still remember the Postal Service form number for the reconciliation forms: 1412. Any postal inspector worth his or her salt knew how to do a proper loss ascertainment.

This technique is not the most adrenaline-pumping law enforcement work, but it is necessary to prove how much money was stolen in a burglary. I'd like to say we usually got the count down to the penny, down to the stamp, but the truth is that, even with this tedious exercise, even in the best of times, all you can give is an informed guess on the loss. You can never get it down to the penny. This is true with many financial crimes.

As I was closing out my twenty-eight-year federal law enforcement career leading pandemic oversight, the most common question I was asked was this one: How much of the $5 trillion in COVID-19 relief spending was lost to fraud? It's the loss ascertainment exercise on a cosmic scale.

The honest answer to the pandemic fraud question is this: I don't know for sure. Nobody does and nobody will ever be able to say with any degree of precision. My best guess is that when it's all tallied up, we will have lost around $500 billion or more taxpayer dollars to fraud and waste (based on the

10 percent rule of thumb, which is supported by anecdotal yet ample evidence).

Determining the amount is way more complicated than filling out form 1412 and counting stamps. It's a complex question with a complex answer. Here's what I can tell you.

Transparency and Accountability Go Hand-in-Hand

Making government spending and other data publicly available is a sign of a healthy democratic republic. I believe there are six "c" north star design principles with government data. It should be **comprehensible**, or easy to understand. It should be **citizen-focused** and concentrated on their interests. It should be **comprehensive**, or as complete as practicable. It should be **connected**, with contextual links to other government data. It should be **contemporaneous**, or as timely as possible. Finally, government data need to be **correct** and accurate.

The federal government is too big and has too many working parts for any one watchdog. Oversight is a team sport, and publicly available government data are needed to engage the public, public interest groups, the media, government auditors, inspectors general, and the Congress. We all have a right to know whether the government's business is being carried out in the public's interest. Congressional staff, the media, and groups like the Project on Government Oversight, ProPublica, and USAFacts are key players and need transparent data to fulfill their important mission.

Before the pandemic, I used to think of transparency for members of the general public as a noble aspiration but largely hypothetical pursuit. That was before I met Jim Richards. Richards happens to be a former prosecutor and the former global head of financial crimes risk management at a large bank. He now runs a small consultancy and knows more about PPP and disaster loan fraud than just about anyone I know outside of government.

I connected with Richards on LinkedIn, and over the years I've raptly read post after post. I think he's posted over 185 "episodes" now. In each one, he expertly dissects the individual fraud case, identifying where the bank and SBA went wrong and providing commentary that only he can. This is the power of transparency, and I'm grateful that we live in a country where members of the public like Richards have access to government data.

Fraud Happens Even in the Best of Times

In normal times, the federal government estimates an overpayment rate of around 5 percent across all federal programs, a portion of which may be fraud. For another 2 percent of payments, agencies can't tell if they overpaid or not because of a lack of documentation, a portion of which, again, may be fraud. That is, if you believe these estimates.

The US Government Accountability Office does not have confidence in the accuracy of these estimates and is concerned these estimates are understated. That is in normal times.

But COVID was the worst of times.

There is a long-standing rule of thumb regarding rough estimates of fraud and error in high-risk government benefit programs. It's the rule of 10 percent. It goes back years. A 1979 Department of Justice report titled "Fraud and Abuse in Government Programs" put it this way: "Fraud and abuse in government programs is widespread but there is no certain tally of the enormity of the losses," but the rate is assumed to be up to "10 percent" for high-risk programs.

The 10 percent rule of thumb is also baked into the federal payment integrity law, which flags agencies that report an improper payment rate greater than 10 percent.

These Were Not the Best of Times

The CARES Act was introduced, debated, and signed into law in a matter of days, and in some instances implemented in a matter of weeks. This happened while large sections of our country were under stay-at-home orders, and we were facing the specter of the collapse of our economy and very way of life. The six COVID-19 relief laws are the largest infusion of emergency relief spending in US history, involving more than $5 trillion in federal spending through 426 programs run by forty agencies.

Massive new programs like the Paycheck Protection Program were created overnight. Other programs like the SBA's disaster loan program or the Labor Department's unemployment insurance program received massive infusions of federal funds that they were not able to effectively handle and made the programs almost unrecognizable.

New programs and a massive influx of funding in existing programs increases agency fraud risks by expanding the attack surface. Agencies were under pressure to get money out quickly to parties with whom they never before had any dealings.

Congress wanted the money to go out quickly to avert a public health and economic catastrophe, so some programs were designed for expediency at the expense of payment integrity.

Congress chose speed over scrutiny. Congress directed the small business loan programs and unemployment insurance programs to accept the honor system, or self-certification. The oversight community knew self-certification was not an effective fraud control. We knew this before the pandemic. It was not a secret.

Congress was aware of the inadequacy of self-certification in federal contracting and women-owned small business certifications. Outside of the pandemic, helping small businesses, including women-owned small businesses, compete for federal contracts is one of the other responsibilities of the Small Business Administration. Qualifying businesses are eligible for preferential, sole source, noncompetitive federal contracts.

For many years prior to the pandemic, the SBA OIG reported on the problems with the way businesses were able to establish that a woman, in fact, controlled the day-to-day operations of the business. One could go to a website, self-certify they were a woman-owned small business, and voilà you were certified and eligible to receive noncompetitive federal contracts.

Recognizing the ineffectiveness of self-certification, Congress changed the law in 2015 to require these businesses to be certified by a third party. It took SBA five years to implement this change.

With the Paycheck Protection Program, the quickest way for SBA to disburse funds was by using their existing network of approved third-party small business loan lenders who would process the loans for a fee. Unfortunately, SBA did not effectively manage their third-party risk. Loan approvals were too often being rubber-stamped with little regard for fraud. The algorithms used by some FinTech lenders for quickly approving PPP loans are still under review. Lenders did not even have to put any of their own capital at risk for these government loans. Lenders could rely on the borrower's self-certification and were held-harmless for any underwriting deficiencies.

SBA's disaster loan program is technically run by the agency and not by approved third-party lenders. I say technically because SBA's IT system couldn't handle the disaster loan application volume brought on by the pandemic, so they turned to a contractor to create a new system for loan processing.

According to the SBA OIG and a report from the House Select Subcommittee on the Coronavirus Crisis, SBA failed to implement basic fraud controls with this new disaster loan system. SBA initially directed the contractor to employ a "batch" approval process where they would send up to fifty applications at a time for approval by an SBA loan officer. Loan officers could not even open the individual applications in the batch. SBA's guidelines for loan officers directed them to approve applications even if the application "failed online identity verification" without taking action to address the fraud flag.

This procedure was eventually changed to require government identification to prove identity. In addition, the CARES Act prohibited SBA from using tax return transcripts to verify income even if they wanted to.

Fraud vulnerabilities were sometimes a bug and sometimes a feature of these programs.

Inspectors General Warned Early and Often about the Increased Fraud Vulnerabilities

Within a week after the CARES Act was passed, the SBA inspector general issued its first warning. SBA leadership failed to heed this warning, and over the next year the OIG issued a series of reports pointing out gaps in fraud controls. One of the basic and available fraud controls is the Treasury Department's Do Not Pay program. A prepandemic statute passed by Congress ordered agencies to use Do Not Pay, but the SBA OIG found that the agency was not using the system, until the OIG pointed it out.

Through its audit work, SBA OIG identified that SBA paid duplicate PPP loans, approved loans to businesses possibly created after the February 15, 2020, requirement, and approved loans to large businesses that exceeded employee size limits.

Through its audit work of pandemic-related disaster loans, the SBA OIG identified billions in potentially fraudulent loans, including loans to potentially ineligible borrowers who were flagged in Treasury's Do Not Pay system, loans where the applicant changed bank accounts between application and approval, and loans that involved duplicate names, addresses, emails, internet protocol numbers, and vague borrower names like "N/A," "None," or "Uber."

Through its audit work, the SBA OIG identified hundreds of millions in emergency disaster grants (about 2 percent of the total) that were provided to applicants who were found in the Do Not Pay system, and billions in potential overpayments to independent contractors and sole proprietors. This included fifteen sole proprietors who received grants claiming to have one million employees.

Within a month after the CARES Act was passed, the Labor Department OIG issued a report identifying several concerns with the unemployment insurance program questioning the ability of the states to process the expected large number of claims, the states' ability to prevent and detect fraud, and the inherent challenges of relying on self-certification of income from the self-employed and gig workers.

Through its audit work of the $800 billion in pandemic unemployment insurance benefits, the Labor OIG identified more than $45 billion of potentially fraudulent benefits paid to individuals with social security numbers filed in multiple states, to individuals with social security numbers of deceased persons and federal inmates, and to individuals with social security numbers used to file for unemployment insurance claims with suspicious email accounts.

Fraud Happened Across
COVID-19 Relief Programs

Criminal prosecutions do not tell the whole story. They are not a complete representation of all the fraud that occurred, but rather represent those instances where someone has been caught and where a prosecutor has decided to prosecute. They are just the tip of the iceberg. Even with that limitation, prosecutions are publicly reported and can provide valuable insights.

Landlords have been prosecuted for defrauding the Treasury's emergency rental assistance program, like the Dayton, Ohio, man who submitted false claims for rental reimbursement for abandoned homes and properties receiving HUD Section 8 rental benefits.

Corrupt local public officials have been prosecuted for defrauding the Treasury's Coronavirus Relief Fund, like the former mayor of Stonecrest, Georgia, who set up a company behind the scenes and used this company to funnel funds to himself and associates to pay for personal expenses.

Healthcare providers have been charged with fraudulently billing Medicare for moderately complex office visits for COVID-19 testing that took five minutes or less, and for keeping pandemic healthcare provider funds for medical practices no longer in operation. There was a prosecution of a convicted healthcare fraudster who had been excluded from participating in Medicare due to prior healthcare fraud convictions. He controlled a lab testing company and submitted millions in fraudulent Medicare claims for COVID-19 and respiratory tests without regard to medical necessity and paying kickbacks to marketers.

In a separate case, a Florida advanced nurse practitioner was prosecuted for submitting millions in fraudulent claims by taking advantage of relaxed telemedicine rules and ordering medically unnecessary tests and durable equipment.

With the IRS stimulus checks, members of a Myrtle Beach family were convicted of fraud by holding themselves out as tax preparers and targeting foreign individuals, usually Bulgarian immigrants, to file false returns.

Cross-program fraud is also common, where someone steals from more than one program in more than one agency. Fraud prosecutions involving the trifecta of PPP, disaster loans, and unemployment insurance are not uncommon.

For example, a prison inmate was charged with submitting more than 240 fraudulent unemployment insurance claims to twenty states and obtaining a PPP loan, all while he was within the confines of the Allenwood Federal Correctional Complex. A US Army warrant officer stationed at Fort Stewart was convicted of submitting 150 fraudulent PPP loan applications, while defrauding the Department of Veterans Affairs through false disability claims and the Education Department through obtaining fraudulent discharge of student loans.

Three COVID-19 Relief Programs Were Especially Attractive and Vulnerable Targets for Criminals

The unemployment insurance program, the SBA disaster loan program, and Paycheck Protection Program account for about half of the $4 trillion in pandemic relief that has been disbursed to date. These programs also had some of the weakest fraud controls.

For years, unemployment insurance has been highly susceptible to fraud. Prior to the pandemic, the reported improper payment estimate for the regular unemployment insurance program has been above 10 percent for fourteen of the last seventeen years. The massive infusion of funding coupled with the self-certification requirement made it an irresistible target.

A California rapper and his co-conspirators—who obtained over $1 million in fraudulent unemployment insurance benefits from California—summed it up in a music video he posted on YouTube and Instagram, titled EDD. "You gotta sell cocaine. I just file a claim—"

California estimates it lost at least $20 billion to unemployment insurance fraud. Texas officials reported a fraud and error rate of 15 percent and losses of over $2.5 billion. Pennsylvania reported over $4 billion in losses. An audit by the Illinois state auditor general found that $1.9 billion out of $3.6 billion paid out during the period July 2020 to June 2021 was fraudulent. Arizona paid over $4 billion in fraud—30 percent of payments, but were fortunate to recover more than $1.4 billion it had paid out.

A couple of billion here and a couple of billion there, and it starts to add up.

There are no definite and comprehensive loss figures yet on the Paycheck Protection Program, but losses are likely well in excess of $100 billion or more. PPP lenders took on minimal risk on these 100 percent government-guaranteed loans and received fees for their efforts.

The Internet Reduced Barriers to Fraud

The government made it too easy to commit fraud and the internet was the great facilitator. As the old saying goes, "On the internet nobody knows you're a dog." The availability and relative or perceived anonymity of the internet reduced geographic, criminal competency, and rational choice barriers that would otherwise limit fraud.

Criminals could file COVID-19 relief claims from literally anywhere in the world. In the early months, for example, SBA did not flag or block foreign internet protocol addresses. Only an amateur criminal would use their own IP address, of course. Competent criminals would have enough sense to use a virtual private network or proxy to conceal their true location and spoof a domestic location. Unemployment insurance claims were filed online from out of state with minimal verification. Criminals could file unemployment insurance claims in multiple states.

A novice fraudster with an internet connection and a curiosity could easily find step-by-step instructions (or "sauce") on how to commit fraud. Stolen personal information from prior data breaches (or "fullz") is readily available for sale for cheap on the dark web. Criminals regularly posted information on efforts by federal and state agencies to tighten fraud controls and instructions on how to defeat or avoid these attempts. The information was so commonplace that it wasn't even kept hidden. In addition to the YouTube video from the California rapper, a Korean couple in Atlanta who were charged with disaster loan fraud had posted instruction videos in Korean on YouTube.

Experienced and professional criminals could commit fraud at scale. A Maryland fraud ring was responsible for 600 unemployment insurance fraud claims in nineteen states. A Nigerian national fraud recidivist was sent back to prison after hacking into tax preparation firms and using stolen personal information to file SBA disaster loans and unemployment insurance claims. Another Nigerian national was arrested after using the stolen identities of over 100 Washington residents and filing fraudulent unemployment insurance claims. A Fort Lauderdale man pled guilty to stealing $24 million in PPP funds, using complex computer storage and virtualization machines to manufacture synthetic IDs, automatically open bank accounts and shell companies, and monitor bank activity.

The internet also unfortunately reduced the rational choice barrier. Under this theory, people choose to commit crime or not based on their perceptions of reward and risk. The fear of getting caught and punished deters criminal acts. The visibility and minimalization of fraud on social media, in my opinion, desensitized too many individuals who may not have otherwise committed fraud.

We saw impulsive novices committing fraud. In unrelated cases we saw the Los Angeles college football player who committed unemployment insurance fraud and then convinced some of his teammates to do the same; the Coral Springs, Florida, police officer who submitted a fraudulent SBA disaster loan and used the proceeds for his vintage car; and the former president of the Anaheim Chamber of Commerce who submitted a fraudulent disaster loan application and used the proceeds for clothes and back taxes.

The Total Fraud Losses Are Difficult to Measure and Hard to Exaggerate

In 2021, federal agencies estimated they paid $281 billion in improper payments. That's a 7 percent overall error rate not counting SBA's Paycheck Protection Program or DOL's pandemic unemployment insurance programs (which were not included in the estimations). In 2022, federal agencies estimated they paid $247 billion in improper payments across all government programs, or 5.1 percent. The rates are significantly higher in certain programs, and it is important to note that not all improper payments are fraud, but—.

In 2021, the Department of Labor reported an improper payment rate for the overall unemployment insurance program of 18.71 percent, but that didn't include the pandemic program most susceptible to fraud due to the self-certification feature. Moreover, the 18.71 percent figure didn't include any improper payment testing from the months of March to June 2020, when we know that state workforce agencies were getting bombarded with fraudulent claims. In 2022, the Department of Labor reported an improper payment rate for all unemployment insurance programs of 21.52 percent.

Labor Department inspector general Larry Turner uses a phrase that I like. The phrase is "a significant portion attributable to fraud." Regarding the pandemic unemployment insurance programs, Turner testified before a March 2022 House hearing that his office believes, based on the administration's own 2021 estimates, that the low-range estimate of COVID-19 unemployment insurance fraud and error is $163 billion, with "a significant portion attributable to fraud."

In his February 2023 testimony at a House hearing titled "The greatest theft of American tax dollars: Unchecked unemployment fraud," Turner provided an updated estimate. Based on the administration's own 2022 estimate, Turner said his office believes "at least $191 billion in pandemic UI payments could have been improper payments, with a significant portion attributable to fraud."

The SBA reported a 13 percent improper payment rate in 2021 for the disaster loan programs generally, or about $49 billion. In 2022 it reported an implausible improper payment rate for COVID-19 disaster loans of 4.5 percent, and 4.24 percent for the PPP.

On the other hand, some COVID-19 relief programs have been audited and found to have experienced generally lower rates of fraud. The IRS made around $800 billion in stimulus payments to individuals. These were not without fraud and error. The IRS's inspector general identified payments to prisoners, dead people, and nonresidents and found that in some instances IRS made some duplicate payments.

But we know from one audit by the IRS's inspector general that for $800 billion—around 16 percent of total COVID-19 relief spending—the payment accuracy rate was around 98 to 99 percent. Why? Because the individual payment amounts were calculated by IRS. Moreover, IRS coordinated with other agencies like the Social Security Administration and Veterans Affairs to associate verified bank accounts for direct deposits, limiting the number of paper checks.

$

If it brings any consolation, you should know we weren't the only nation targeted by domestic and international fraudsters. In April 2022, the UK House of Commons Committee of Public Accounts sharply criticized the UK government for its complacency in preventing what it described as "eye-watering" levels of fraud. In March 2023, the watchdog for the European Union warned member countries that they too were at risk and were not doing enough to prevent and detect fraud with their pandemic-related stimulus funding.

The cold hard truth is I'm not confident we will ever have a complete and accurate accounting of how much pandemic relief spending was lost to fraud and waste. This doesn't mean that we, as taxpayers and oversight professionals, should not ask the question or seek the answer. It's just that the answer is unknowable with any degree of precision.

It would be comforting to throw out a number, and, of course, an odd number would be more believable, would seem more authentic, and would bring comfort to Americans who want the answer. But the truth is: we just don't know. When it's all tallied up, we will have likely lost roughly $500 billion or more taxpayer dollars to fraud and waste. And we, the taxpayers, are left shouldering that debt and holding that bag.

19

BEFORE THE NEXT
NATIONAL CRISIS

Memo to Congress and the President (and the people who elected them):

As a former inspector general with twenty-eight years of public service and as an American who cares deeply about the future of our great nation, here are my recommendations on what we need to do before the next national crisis:

- Do more, now, to combat disinformation on social media.
- Overhaul the federal government's approach to improper payments.
- Make antifraud activities a national priority, ensure fraud risks are considered and basic controls put in place, even in emergency situations, and require that agencies improve their understanding of fraud and control effectiveness over time.
- Embed in legislation the pandemic oversight lessons learned so we're prepared to face the next crisis.

If Washington doesn't act, memories will fade and our pandemic experience will likely be repeated when the next crisis hits. If Washington doesn't act, the American people will once again be left holding the bag and shouldering the consequences to our fiscal and physical well-being.

Here's what Congress and the president should do.

Combat Public Health Misinformation and Disinformation on Social Media

Although fraud turned out to be a major part of our national pandemic story and the predominant theme of this book, there were other critically important themes. Transparency of federal pandemic spending and the public health aspect of the federal pandemic response, for example, were other major themes examined by the oversight community and detailed in the earlier chapters. The constant undercurrent throughout the pandemic years, though, was the deepening divisions within our country and misinformation. To quote a phrase: we're gonna have to all sit down and have a little talk.

In a public health crisis, Washington needs to speak with one voice, effectively communicating public health information to the American people in a clear, trusted, and unifying voice. The after-action review of CDC's role that Dr. Walensky ordered in September 2022 will hopefully go deep enough to identify actionable steps for federal public health officials before the next crisis.

At the same time, we have to recognize that Russia, China, and other foreign adversaries have and are expending considerable resources to distract and destabilize our nation and its political leaders.

On March 19, 2020, eight senators led by Senator Richard Durbin sent a letter to Secretary Pompeo urging the State Department to take the Russian COVID disinformation campaign more seriously and to refrain from using derogatory terminology as it plays into their hands. In April 2020, Pentagon officials warned us that under the rubric of "not wasting a good crisis," Russia, China, and others were using the coronavirus pandemic to spread disinformation to further their goals. Their efforts have led to what the nonpartisan think-tank RAND Corporation calls Truth Decay.

Our enemies attack us with troll farms and automated bots. A technological whack-a-mole approach to block disinformation alone will not solve the problem. Like something out of the Book of Genesis and the Garden of Eden, long-standing enemies have tricked some Americans into believing they are not an adversary but a true ally.

Distrust runs deeper than issues of public health. Too many Americans ignore warnings like the September 2020 public service announcement from the FBI and the Cybersecurity & Infrastructure Security Agency, "Foreign Actors and Cybercriminals Likely to Spread Disinformation Regarding 2020 Election Results", or their October 2022 announcement, "Foreign Actors Likely to Use Information Manipulation Tactics for 2022 Midterm Elections."

Russian President Putin is enjoying his return on investment, as some popular cable television hosts and podcasts don't just ignore his malign intentions; they parrot his talking points.

In April 2023, an Air National Guard technician was arrested for leaking top-secret material in an internet chat room. Among the top-secret documents: statements from Russian operators of thousands of social media accounts—the ones used to spread misinformation about vaccine safety— bragging that they are detected only about 1 percent of the time. While this is likely an exaggeration, we apparently are currently not very good at stopping Russian misinformation.

The pandemic hit at a time when trust in government was already low. At times it seemed like America lost its common sense, as well as its sense of the common good. COVID-19 disinformation propagated or amplified by our adversaries has targeted and sometimes been welcomed by the right. Like cigarette smoking, disinformation is hazardous to your health.

A November 2022 study by the Harvard T. H. Chan School of Public Health was the first to study the relationship between political ideology and COVID-19 impacts. The researchers specifically focused on the political ideology of elected members of Congress, those members' voting records on the pandemic response laws, and the concentration of political power in one party.

The researchers found that the higher the exposure to conservatism, the higher one's chances of dying from COVID-19 and the greater the use of one's community hospital's intensive care unit facilities. As the author of the study, a professor of social epidemiology, noted, this data point is not about pointing fingers, but rather "to understand how politics, and political polarization, are affecting population health."

In January 2023, Oklahoma Senator James Inhofe retired from the US Senate after serving twenty-eight years. He told reporters that the effects of long COVID were the reason for his retirement. He had originally tested positive a year earlier after being fully vaccinated and boosted. "Five or six others [senators] have [long COVID], but I'm the only one who admits it."

Following 9/11 there was a period, however too brief, when the "us vs. them" mentality in our political system became "US vs. them," and Americans largely united as one against an enemy who attacked us and wished to do us more harm. Even now over twenty years later, I choke up—not as an independent or member of this or that party but as an American—when I see the clip of President Bush atop the rubble at Ground Zero surrounded by first responders and rescuers, raising the bullhorn: "I can hear you. The rest of the world hears you!"

Some politicians and public officials will have to explain why they literally demonized public health officials, which caused extremist followers to act on their impulses and threaten to kill these officials and their families.

Poor Emma Lazarus, the nineteenth-century American poet whose sonnet is engraved on the pedestal of the Statue of Liberty. I picture her shaking her head, AYFKM-style, upon learning that her line about the "huddled masses yearning to breathe free" had been co-opted to defend a Florida man who got kicked off a flight for protesting the airline mask mandate by wearing a woman's thong on his face. Political speech and protests are as American as apple pie; I'm just suggesting this cultural appropriation may be a bit over the top.

Responding to misinformation is not my area of expertise, so I defer to experts. Here's what they recommend.

The bipartisan US Advisory Commission on Public Diplomacy issued a report in September 2020 titled, "Public Diplomacy and the New 'Old' War: Countering State-Sponsored Disinformation." The commission report quotes Facebook CEO Mark Zuckerberg who described efforts to combat disinformation on his platform as an "arms race." Social media are global, but the federal government is restricted by law on the communication activities it can take in the US. The report recommends Washington do more now to define the challenge, invest in digital capabilities, and compete in the information space.

A senior scholar with the Johns Hopkins Center for Health Security—who has worked for over a decade on pandemic preparedness and health misinformation—has called for national strategy to combat health-related misinformation and disinformation. She recommends that such a strategy be the responsibility of the National Security Council and contain four pillars. As a nation, we need to: intervene against false content on social media, promote factual information, increase the public's resilience to misinformation, and coordinate the national strategy with input with a variety of groups.

For what it's worth, our European allies have experienced the exact same problem, prompting the European Commission to issue a report in 2023 from its Joint Research Centre. This paper called on EU members to take similar actions to fight this "infodemic."

Fix the Federal Improper Payment Law

The federal law designed to ensure the government is paying the right payees in the right amount is, shall we say, complicated. The inspectors general and the Government Accountability Office have been suggesting improvements for years.

Under the Payment Integrity Information Act and OMB guidance, agencies are required to estimate the rate of improper payments in individual programs and have corrective action plans if the rate is above the prescribed threshold (10%). In general, though, agencies are not required to estimate improper payments in the initial year of the program. OMB says this is to give the agency sufficient time to hire a statistician and develop an estimation and testing methodology and to review a year's worth of data.

If the agency determines that the program is susceptible to improper payments, then the agency must do public reporting on their actions to reduce improper payments the following year. That means, in effect, neither the public nor Congress may know how the agency is managing its improper payment and program fraud risk for two to three years after the next emergency spending bill.

None of this works too well with emergency spending. I think we can safely assume emergency spending is at a higher risk for fraud.

But it's not just the timing gap that is the problem. In 2020, the Department of Labor initially took the position that the temporary emergency nature of the pandemic unemployment insurance programs, regardless of the considerable amount of federal dollars, made it impracticable and unnecessary to estimate improper payments.

Congress should designate all emergency federal spending programs over a certain amount (GAO recommends $100 million) as susceptible to significant improper payments in their first year of operation. This would require agencies to cut to the chase.

Agencies would be required—beginning the year emergency money is spent—to report to the Office of Management and Budget the specific actions they are taking to address fraud and their progress on estimating the levels of improper payments. These reports should be made available to the OIGs and Government Accountability Office.

Make Antifraud Activities a National Priority

Before federal money goes out the door, fraud risks must be considered and basic controls put in place, even in emergency situations, and agencies must improve their understanding of fraud and control effectiveness over time.

I wrote about public trust in earlier chapters. Public trust is more than just expecting that public servants don't lie, cheat, or steal. Public trust is also having faith in government and confidence that officials are competent, good stewards, and give their best efforts to keep criminals from picking our pockets.

The federal government needs to make antifraud activities an enduring national priority. Getting relief aid out quickly in an emergency and stopping preventable fraud is not an either/or proposition. Program delivery and program integrity are not mutually exclusive. It's critical that Washington balances the need to quickly distribute targeted emergency aid with ensuring the money gets into the right hands. We can walk and chew gum.

As a nation, we can learn a lot from the UK and Australian governments. The UK boasts of having formed the world's first government profession specializing in public-sector anti-fraud activities (they call it counter fraud) in 2018. In March 2022, the UK took their antifraud game up a notch. After considering their experiences with pandemic-related fraud, the UK government created what they call the Public Sector Fraud Authority to coordinate antifraud activities across government agencies. The Authority is staffed with experts who help agencies apply the latest practices and technology to reduce "fraud and error."

In 2019, the Australians established the Commonwealth Fraud Prevention Centre within its attorney general's department. The center similarly helps agencies improve their antifraud activities.

The US federal government is too vast and varied, in my view, for a centralized antifraud office. The American taxpayer and federal agencies, though, would benefit greatly from a national antifraud strategy, and we should be looking to our allies in the west and the east to copy what's working well for them and may work for us.

Unless there is a life-threatening emergency, and by that I mean a "throwing bread off the back of a truck" type of emergency, OMB should not allow federal agencies to release any funds unless and until there is an associated funding code to track the spending. While OMB assigned codes to programs under the six pandemic relief laws, we found some programs that fell through the cracks.

Agencies should ensure basic fraud controls are in place, even in emergency situations, prior to disbursing funds. This is a recommendation from the UK National Audit Office from their COVID lessons learned and is just as appropriate in the US. Self-certification should be stricken from our lexicon. Appealing to the better angels of humankind to not commit fraud is not a fraud control strategy, and relying solely on self-certification for program eligibility is not an effective fraud control.

I learned from a Canadian counterpart that they also relied on what they call "attestation." But the Canadian authorities combined that with what they described as light-checks (verifications) up front and after-care. What a great term: after-care. In an emergency situation, performing light-checks up front, verifying after payment, and providing after-care (including clawing back improper payments when necessary) strikes me as the right approach.

During the pandemic years, I found little appetite among federal agencies to claw back money that had been improperly paid. In his March 2023 testimony before the House government operations subcommittee, SBA deputy inspector general Sheldon Shoemaker reiterated his office's concerns with SBA's plan to discontinue or defer collecting on delinquent disaster loans under $100,000. Senator Joni Ernst wrote to the SBA administrator demanding that the SBA continue collections. This is after-care.

While there is no one-size-fits-all solution, agencies should be required to prepare a fraud control plan up front identifying the specific actions they are taking to ensure accountability. Fraud control plans don't have to be complicated and should evolve over time. At a minimum, the plans document how the agency is (1) verifying that an identity used is valid (and not fake or stolen), (2) determining whether a claimant is eligible for the program, and (3) calculating the correct benefit amount. Fraud control plans should be designed to deter and deny fraud attempts from being successful (blocking) and to detect and disrupt as early as possible those fraud schemes that get through to minimize losses (tackling).

These plans should be shared with OMB, the inspector general, and the Government Accountability Office. This is the general approach, by the way, used in Australia and the UK and is similar to what we later accomplished with gold standard meetings that we used prior to implementation of American Rescue Plan programs. We didn't require this information in written plan form, but it was the same thought process.

The fraud control plan should document what fraud risks are being accepted by management in the early stages and include a phased control approach to add antifraud controls in as exigencies wane. Any existing controls that management is overriding for an emergency should be identified.

One key component of a fraud control plan is monitoring and feedback. Agencies should be continuously scanning the environment, evaluating the effectiveness of their fraud controls, and hardening their defenses. GAO recommends monitoring in its fraud risk management guidance to US federal agencies. The UK calls this "intelligence and analysis," and the Australians call it "strategic fraud intelligence."

Whatever we call it, I can tell you federal agencies typically do a poor job in this area. Like the old Ronco rotisserie commercials, federal agencies during the pandemic emergency tended to adopt a "set it and forget it" approach. Once a program was implemented and funding went out the door, some agencies didn't want to hear about fraud and were slow to make changes.

Monitoring without closing the feedback loop is meaningless. A good fraud control plan spells out roles and reporting routes so agencies can adapt to prevent, detect, and disrupt fraud.

Where appropriate, the fraud control plan may include staffing for an antifraud purple team of attackers and defenders to conduct live testing and provide real-time intelligence to agency management on the effectiveness of their fraud controls. For agencies committed to reducing fraud in government benefit programs, such an approach would greatly enhance their ability to adjust on the fly. This would only require a few people. It would be an infinitesimal investment that could pay potentially huge dividends—or rather prevent massive financial losses and damage to agency reputation. The UK calls this proactive detection activities.

Embed in Legislation the Lessons Learned During the Pandemic So We'll Be Ready When the Next Crisis Hits

As of April 2023, the federal inspector general community had issued over 550 pandemic oversight reports and the Government Accountability Office had issued over 200. In addition, the PRAC has accumulated over 280 pandemic oversight reports from state and local auditors. That's a lot—an overwhelming amount—of findings and recommendations. Where to start?

Healthcare policy experts, I hope, have been carefully considering the reports from the OIGs at Health and Human Services, Veterans Affairs, Justice Department, GAO, and others to identify actionable, incremental steps that can be taken to better prepare the nation for a public health emergency.

In terms of my primary area of focus, emergency spending oversight and accountability, I recommend Congress pass legislation to do the following.

- Make permanent the data analytics function created in the PRAC's Pandemic Analytics Center of Excellence now.

The Pandemic Response Accountability Committee is set to expire on September 30, 2025. Unless Congress takes action, this means that its data analytics function, the Pandemic Analytics Center of Excellence (PACE), will cease to exist. The PACE, which took months to construct, will disappear just like its predecessor, the ROC, that was built following the financial crisis of 2009.

When the pandemic hit, we had to rebuild the data analytics function from scratch. Setting up a data analytics function can't be done overnight. Even if you know exactly what you want built, federal contracting takes time. Hooking up the data "plumbing and wiring" takes time. Ensuring that sensitive data are gathered and secured in compliance with federal privacy laws takes time. There's no switch to flip. The wrong time to start this process is during a crisis.

Congress needs to make this data analytics function permanent and provide it with legal authorities to ensure access to agency data and authority to share data with OIGs and its law enforcement partners. We lost too much time during the early days of the pandemic acquiring data. I don't want the next person (who is tasked with my role) to be spending time during a national emergency hammering out data use agreements.

A whole-of-government data analytics function will unquestionably enhance law enforcement's capabilities to prevent and detect fraud.

- Include in future emergency spending legislation increased penalties and alternative remedies for accountability to deter fraud.

One of the thorniest problems springing from the pandemic fraud crisis in my view is the issue of low-grade fraud. By that I mean cases involving relatively small-dollar losses with the absence of aggravating factors (like someone using the money to buy a Lamborghini). Not all of these cases will end up getting prosecuted, but there are remedies short of criminal charges that should be authorized by statute and encouraged.

Congress can, for example, increase the dollar ceiling for administrative cases handled by agencies outside of the courtroom and provide funding for more attorneys to handle these cases (under the Program Fraud Civil Remedies Act).

Congress can make it easier for agencies to ban someone found to have committed fraud from obtaining additional federal funds. This is called suspension and debarment. We tried desperately to pursue this as an option but discovered the system is just not set up to handle large numbers of S&D referrals. To send a strong deterrence message up front, Congress can increase the penalties for fraud related to a specific emergency spending bill and extend the statute of limitations on prosecutions. There is already a federal law with increased penalties for false statements in connection with benefits offered during a presidentially declared national emergency. It was rarely charged by federal prosecutors.

Congress can also require or encourage agencies to set up voluntary self-disclosure programs. These programs mitigate fraud risk by providing a pathway for impulsive novices to repay ill-gotten funds. Such programs are hugely successful at the IRS and the Department of Health and Human Services.

Let's face it, people sometimes panic in a crisis and sometimes do stupid things. Once the smoke clears and they come to their senses, the government should have a way for them to resolve their noncompliance and limit their criminal exposure—in other words, put the cookies back in the cookie jar. In addition, their punishment might include going without government cookies for a while, along with an affordable monetary fine that stings just enough to hurt.

- Include in future emergency spending legislation additional agency transparency requirements so the public can see who is getting taxpayer dollars and how it's being used.

During the pandemic, we learned that current federal spending processes have too many holes and gaps. The Treasury Department's USASpending website is an important tool for standardized government spending data but may not be suitable for the reporting of nuanced emergency program data.

To their credit, during the COVID crisis some agencies gathered and posted supplemental data on their agency website. Enhanced data transparency must be baked into all emergency spending programs from the very beginning. Congress should specifically identify what supplemental data are expected to be collected and publicly reported, along with accountability mechanisms if these requirements are ignored, like the SBA did with demographic data on small business loan borrowers. The American people deserve better than a mixed bag of voluntary reporting.

$

Quite simply, before the next national public health crisis, Washington needs to figure out how to speak with one voice, effectively communicating public health information to the American people in a clear, trusted, and unifying voice. Washington also needs to figure out how to make it easier for the American people to see who is getting federal tax dollars and how tax dollars are being used. We need to narrow the opportunity for fraud and make it harder to steal. As tempting as it may be for us to view this pandemic as a one-off experience and move on with our lives, we do so at our peril.

Otherwise, what happens? Once again, whether it's another pandemic or a hurricane that wipes out the west coast of Florida or an earthquake that takes a chunk off the coast of California or [a disaster, you fill in the blank], when the federal government comes in to make things better for us, the American people, we want the funding to go where it's needed—not to criminals and fraudsters and people gaming the system. Because, after all, this is *your* money, this is *our* money, and we American taxpayers don't want to be left holding the bag.

EPILOGUE

While the Pandemic of 2020–2023 is officially over, the threat of another public health emergency will cast a shadow for some time to come. Serving as executive director of the Pandemic Response Accountability Committee during that moment in American history was the privilege of a lifetime.

I took a hiatus for a few months after retiring before getting back to the business of accountability, assisting government organizations here and abroad. It's wonky work, I know, but it's what I was made for.

While I haven't been successful in persuading any of my kids to join me in the "family business," we now have three kids who are hospital nurses serving the public in their own way.

NOTES

U nless otherwise indicated in the text, statistics regarding COVID-19 cases, deaths, and vaccinations were obtained from the Johns Hopkins Coronavirus Resource Center.

The following notes are provided for information that does not have individual attribution in the text.

Indictments or criminal charges are merely an allegation. All defendants are presumed innocent until proven guilty beyond a reasonable doubt in a court of law.

Former President Trump's tweets from 2020 are no longer accessible on Twitter. They can be found online at any number of unofficial archive websites including TheTrumpArchive.com.

CHAPTER 1

First pandemic fraud prosecution: United States Attorney's Office, District of Rhode Island Press Release, "Two charged with stimulus fraud: First in the nation to be charged with fraudulently seeking CARES Act Paycheck Protection loans." Criminal Complaint Affidavit (May 5, 2020).

Forgetting our pandemic stories: Mary Kekatos, "Why people may be forgetting their COVID pandemic memories: Experts say it's not just the passage of time that makes us forget." ABC News Health (April 8, 2023).

Nation awash in grief: Lena H. Sun, "My mom died while I was covering COVID. It changed my views on grief." *Washington Post* (March 9, 2023).

Total pandemic relief spending: Available at https://www.pandemicoversight.gov/.

Percentage of GDP: Presentation by Dan White, Moody Analytics, AGA Professional Development Training Conference (July 2022).

National public debt: Available at https://www.fiscaldata.treasury.gov/.

Social security number used to file for unemployment insurance benefits in forty states (and was successful in getting benefits from twenty-nine states): US Department of Labor, Office of Inspector General, "Alert Memorandum: The Employment and Training

Administration (ETA) needs to ensure State Workforce Agencies (SWA) implement effective unemployment insurance program fraud controls for high risk areas." (Report # 19-21-002-03-315) (February 22, 2021).

Fraudster blocked from obtaining benefits in one agency program turned to another program in the same agency: United States Attorney's Office, District of Oregon Press Release, "Oregon dentist faces federal charges for stealing nearly $8 million in COVID-relief program funds." (December 15, 2021).

Former NFL player: US Department of Justice, Office of Public Affairs Press Release, "NFL player fraudulently obtained $1.2 million in Small Business Administration Paycheck Protection Program loans." (September 10, 2020).

Former U.S. Olympic figure skater: United States Attorney's Office, Southern District of New York Press Release, "Former Olympic figure skater arrested for role in defrauding US Small Business Administration of over $1.5 million." (June 8, 2021).

Rapper: United States Attorney's Office, Central District of California Press Release, "Rapper who bragged about unemployment benefits scam in music video arrested for allegedly bilking COVID-19 Jobless Relief Program." (October 16, 2020).

Reality TV star: United States Attorney's Office, Northern District of Georgia Press Release, "Reality TV personality charged with bank fraud." (May 13, 2020).

Pastors: United States Attorney's Office, Southern District of Georgia Press Release, "South Georgia pastor, tax preparer admits CARES Act fraud." (March 25, 2022).

Prisoners: United States Attorney's Office, Western District of Pennsylvania Press Release, "33 inmates and accomplices charged with illegally obtaining Coronavirus unemployment benefits." (August 25, 2020).

Police officers: United States Attorney's Office, Southern District of Florida Press Release, "Coral Springs police officer charged with COVID relief fraud, using loan money to service and repair his vintage car." (June 16, 2022).

Politicians: United States Attorney's Office, Northern District of Georgia Press Release, "Former mayor of Stonecrest sentenced to prison for stealing COVID-19 relief funds." (July 13, 2022).

College students: United States Attorney's Office, Central District of California Press Release, "College football player arrested on federal charges of orchestrating fraudulent scheme to obtain COVID-related jobless benefits." (December 20, 2021).

International fraudsters: United States Attorney's Office, Western District of Washington Press Release, "Nigerian citizen pleads guilty to COVID-19 unemployment fraud on Washington and seventeen other states." (May 3, 2022).

Red Power Ranger: United States Attorney's Office, Eastern District of Texas Press Release, "18 arrested, charged in east Texas Paycheck Protection Program-related fraud." (May 18, 2022).

Largest pandemic fraud prosecution: US Department of Justice, Office of Public Affairs Press Release, "US Attorney announces federal charges against 47 defendants in $250 million Feeding Our Future fraud scheme; nonprofit Feeding Our Future and 200+ meal sites in Minnesota perpetrated the largest COVID-19 fraud scheme in the nation." (September 20, 2022).

US Secret Service confirmed the investigation of members of a hacker group associated with the Chinese military who were linked to the loss of millions of dollars: Timothy Nerozzi, "Chinese hackers exploited US COVID relief funds for millions, Secret Service claims; The Secret Service confirmed the involvement of Chinese hacking group APT41 but did not disclose details." Fox News.com (December 6, 2022).

CHAPTER 2

The December–January timeline was constructed from the following sources:
US Department of Defense timeline, available at https://www.defense.gov/Spotlights/Coronavirus-DOD-Response/Timeline/
Centers for Disease Control and Prevention, available at https://www.cdc.gov/museum/timeline/covid19.html.
Mark Zanin, et al., "The public health response to the COVID-19 outbreak in mainland China: A narrative review." *Journal of Thoracic Disease* (August 2020),

available at https://www.ncbi.nlm.nih.gov/pmc/arti
cles/PMC7475588/.
Joint Testimony of Anthony S. Fauci, MD, Robert R.
Redfield, MD, and Admiral Brett P. Giroir, MD, House
Select Subcommittee on Coronavirus Crisis (July 31,
2020), available at https://www.cdc.gov/washington/
testimony/2020/t20200731.htm.
Congressional Research Service, "COVID-19 and China:
A chronology of events (December 2019-January 2020)."
Updated May 13, 2020, available at https://crsreports
.congress.gov/product/pdf/r/r46354.

Raccoon dogs: Katherine Wu, "The strongest evidence yet
that an animal started the pandemic: A new analysis
of genetic samples from China appears to link the pandemic's origin to raccoon dogs." Atlantic (March 16,
2023).

Michael Atkinson: "Statement of Michael K. Atkinson,
Inspector General of the Intelligence Community, on
his removal from office." (April 5, 2020).

Atkinson's removal: Kyle Cheney, "Atkinson: Trump fired me
because I handled whistleblower complaint properly."
Politico.com (April 5, 2020).

Postal Service delivering COVID tests: Courtney Rozen,
"Biden mailed 737 million COVID tests but mum on
who got them." Bloomberglaw.com (February 2, 2023).
US Postal Service, Office of Inspector General, "Audit
Report: COVID-19 test kit distribution." (Report #22-
076-R22) (September 28, 2022).

Obama's Removal of Inspector General: Project on Government Oversight, "Lessons learned from Obama's removal of CNCS inspector general." (June 15, 2009). The Associated Press, "Obama fires AmeriCorps' inspector general." NBCNews.com (June 12, 2009).

Pandemic Playbook: Executive Office of the President of the United States, "Playbook or early response to high-consequence emerging infectious disease threats and biological incidents." Available at: https://s3.document cloud.org/documents/6819268/Pandemic-Playbook.pdf.

Event 201: "Event 201, A Global Pandemic Exercise." *Event 201.* Available at: https://www.centerforhealthsecurity.org/ our-work/exercises/event201/.

CHAPTER 3

2019 government improper payment: Government Accountability Office, "Payment integrity: Federal agencies' estimates of FY 2019 improper payments." (GAO-20-344) (March 2, 2020).

PBGC Procurement Fraud case: US Attorney's Office, Eastern District of Virginia Press Release, "Government official and contracting executive plead guilty to bribery conspiracy." (May 4, 2020).

PBGC-related Paycheck Protection Program fraud case: United States of America v. James Nicholas Girardi, No. 1:22-CR-39 (AJT), United States District Court, Eastern District of Virginia. Statement of Facts. (March 17, 2022).

Bureau of Prison survey: Department of Justice, Office of Inspector General, "Staff perceptions of the Federal Bureau of Prisons' management of the coronavirus disease 2019 pandemic: A follow-up survey of BOP staff." Available at: https://experience.arcgis.com/experience /582f32f0127c4c86870b2e129c05b9bc.

Coronavirus Supplemental Request: Russell T. Vought, acting director, Office of Management and Budget, letter dated February 24, 2020, available at https://www. whitehouse.gov/wp-content/uploads/2020/02/Corona virus-Supplemental-Request-Letter-Final.pdf.

Messonnier CDC briefing: Transcript for the CDC telebriefing update on COVID-19 (February 26, 2020). Available at https://www.cdc.gov/media/releases/2020/t0225 -cdc-telebriefing-covid-19.html.

CHAPTER 4

Congress authorizes $8 billion: Emily Cochrane, "House passes $8.3 billion Emergency Coronavirus Response Bill: The spending package dwarfs what the Trump administration requested to confront the outbreak." *New York Times* (March 4, 2020).

COVID case at CPAC: Michael Leveson, "CPAC attendee has the coronavirus, officials say the Conservative Political Action Conference was attended last week by President Trump, Vice President Mike Pence and other administration officials." *New York Times* (March 9, 2020).

Christ Church Georgetown: Michelle Boorstein, "The Georgetown church quarantined by D.C.'s coronavirus outbreak." *Washington Post* (March 9, 2020).

Midland Texas hate crime: United States Attorney's Office, Western District of Texas Press Release, "Texas man sentenced on hate crime charges for attacking Asian family." (August 4, 2022).

Trump declares national emergency: White House, "Proclamation on Declaring a National Emergency Concerning the Novel Coronavirus Disease (COVID-19) Outbreak." (March 13, 2020). Available at https://trump whitehouse.archives.gov/presidential-actions/procla mation-declaring-national-emergency-concerning-no vel-coronavirus-disease-covid-19-outbreak/.

15 days to slow the spread: White House, *1600 Daily News-letter,* archived at https://trumpwhitehouse.archives. gov/articles/15-days-slow-spread/.

Largest Dow drop in history: Jonathan Garber, et al., "Dow drops 2,997 points on word coronavirus crisis could extend until August." FoxBusiness.com (March 16, 2020).

White House proposes $1 trillion: Jennifer Shutt, et al., "Mnuchin: White House plan will inject $1 trillion into economy: The Treasury secretary discussed the proposal at Senate Republicans' weekly policy lunch." Rollcall.com (March 17, 2020).

Trump orders hospital ships: "Navy hospital ship could take weeks getting to New York as coronavirus cases soar." Military.com (March 18, 2020).

Domino's Pizza: Joanna Fantozzi, "Domino's launches custom contactless delivery during coronavirus crisis." *National Restaurant News* (March 16, 2020).

Vanity Fair article: Katherine Eban, "'That's their problem': How Jared Kushner let the markets decide America's COVID-19 fate." *Vanity Fair* (September 17, 2020).

Nursing home deaths: US Department of Health and Human Services, Office of Inspector General, "Certain life care nursing homes may not have complied with federal requirements for infection prevention and control and emergency preparedness." (Report No. A-01-20-00004) (September 2022).

CARES Act: The Coronavirus Aid, Relief, and Economic Security Act (the CARES Act), enacted on March 27, 2020, as Public Law 116-136.

San Quentin death row case: Treasury Inspector General for Tax Administration Press Release, "California woman pleads guilty to the fraudulent use of inmates' personally identifiable information to obtain stimulus checks." (April 27, 2022).

Remarks by President Trump in a meeting with supply chain distributors: (March 29, 2020). Available at: https://trumpwhitehouse.archives.gov/briefings-state ments/remarks-president-trump-meeting-supply-cha in-distributors-covid-19/.

Project Airbridge: Benjamin Swasey, "'Project Airbridge' to expedite arrival of needed supplies, White House says." *NPR News* (March 29, 2020).

USS Roosevelt: US Department of the Navy, "Command Investigation concerning chain of command actions with regard to COVID-19 onboard USS Theodore Roosevelt (CVN 71)." (June 19, 2020).

CHAPTER 5

New York salutes: Gary Harcastle, "Every night, New York City salutes its health care workers." *NPR News* (April 10, 2020).

Hell of a bad two weeks: Andrew O'Reilly, "White House projects 100K to 240K coronavirus deaths as Trump tells US to prepare for 'very painful two weeks.'" FoxNews.com (March 31, 2020).

New York funeral homes: Chris Irvine, "Dozens of bodies found in unrefrigerated U-Haul trucks outside NYC funeral home." Foxnews.com (April 30, 2020).
Dana Kennedy, "Dead bodies pile up outside NYC funeral home: 'We've got no more room inside.'" NYPost.com (April 18, 2020).

New York nursing home deaths scandal: New York State Office of the Attorney General, Letitia James (Revised January 30, 2021), "Nursing home response to COVID-19 pandemic report."

Bernadette Hogan, "Cuomo aide Melissa DeRosa admits they hid nursing home data so feds wouldn't find out." *New York Post* (February 11, 2021).

Office of the New York State Comptroller, Department of Health, "Use, collection and reporting of infection control data audit." (Report #2022-S-5) (March 2022).

Glenn Fine appointed PRAC Chair: Council of the Inspectors General on Integrity and Efficiency Press Release, "Glenn A. Fine appointed Chair of CIGIE's Pandemic Response Accountability Committee: Will lead CIGIE's efforts to oversee federal funds used for coronavirus response." (March 30, 2020).

John Kamensky, "Where's the money? Keep an eye on the CARES Act: With the passage of the $2.3 trillion economic relief bill, things are happening at break-neck speed." GovExec.com (April 2, 2020).

SBA OIG stimulus loan fraud report: US Small Business Administration, Office of Inspector General, "White Paper: Risk awareness and lessons learned from prior audits of economic stimulus loans." (Report No. 20-11) (April 3, 2020).

Unemployment and jobless claims in April: Department of Labor News Release, "Unemployment insurance weekly claims." (April 9, 2020), available at https://oui.doleta.gov/press/2020/040920.pdf.

US Bureau of Labor Statistics, TED: The Economics Daily, available at https://www.bls.gov/opub/ted/2020/ unemployment-rate-rises-to-record-high-14-point-7- percent-in-april-2020.htm.

Jeff Cox, "A record 20.5 million jobs were lost in April as unemployment rate jumps to 14.7%." CNBCNews. com (May 8, 2020).

David Gura, "US jobless claims reach 26 million since coronavirus hit, wiping out all gains since 2008 recession." NBCNews.com (April 23, 2020).

Niels Lesniewski, "Senate Democrats back oversight efforts after Trump removal of IG." RollCall.com (April 8, 2020).

Health and Human Services OIG Pulse Survey: US Department of Health and Human Services, Office of Inspector General, "Hospital experiences responding to the COVID-19 pandemic: Results of a National Pulse Survey March 23-27, 2020." (Report No. OEI-06-20-00300) (April 3, 2020). Note: This report was dated April 3 but publicly reported on April 6.

Individual PPP loan records: Available at https://www.pan demicoversight.gov/data-interactive-tools/interactive -dashboards/paycheck-protection-program.

SBA OIG flash report: US Small Business Administration, Office of the Inspector General, "Flash Report Small Business Administration's implementation of the Paycheck Protection Program requirements." (Report No. 20-14) (May 8, 2020).

Stimulus checks as of May 2020: US Department of Treasury Press Release, "Treasury, IRS announce delivery of 159 million Economic Impact Payments." (June 3, 2020).

IRS Income Verification Service and SBA loans: SBA Procedural Notice, "Changes to 4506-T Tax Transcript Verification Procedures during the COVID-19 emergency." (Control No. 5000-20016) (April 8, 2020).

Small Business Administration, "Interim Final Rule on business loan program temporary changes; Paycheck Protection Program." Federal Register, Vol. 85, No. 73, p. 20811 (April 15, 2020).

SBA blanket approval for members of Congress: Small Business Administration, "Paycheck Protection Program loans frequently asked questions (FAQs)" (as of July 8, 2022), p. 13.

Jonathan O'Connell, et al., "SBA exempted lawmakers, federal officials from ethics rules in $660 billion loan program." *Washington Post* (June 26, 2020).
Associated Press, "Congress created PPP loans—then at least twelve members reaped their benefits." (July 8, 2020).

Project Airbridge: US Department of Homeland Security, Office of Inspector General, "FEMA did not provide sufficient oversight of Project Airbridge." (Report # OIG-23-14) (June 7, 2023).

CHAPTER 6

Trump ousts Fine: Charlie Savage, et al., "Trump ousts pandemic spending watchdog known for independence: The official had been leading the office of the inspector general for the Pentagon: In removing him from that role, the president stripped him of his pandemic relief oversight duties as well." *New York Times* (April 7, 2020).

Recovery Act: American Recovery and Reinvestment Act of 2009 (ARRA or Recovery Act), enacted on February 17, 2009. Public Law 111-5.

Additional Paycheck Protection Program funding: Paycheck Protection Program and Health Care Enhancement Act, enacted April 24, 2020. Public Law 116–139.

Lessons learned from the Recovery Board: Government Accountability Office, "Recovery Act: Grant implementation experiences offer lessons for accountability and transparency." (GAO-14-219) (January 2104).

Encino businessman: US Department of Justice, Office of Public Affairs Press Release, "Man convicted for $27 million PPP fraud scheme." (March 29, 2022).

CHAPTER 7

South Brooklyn Marine Terminal: Dave Davies, "Reckoning with the dead: Journalist goes inside an NYC COVID-19 disaster morgue." *NPR News* (May 28, 2020).

Protest at Michigan State Capitol: Mallory McMorrow, "Protesters at the Michigan Capitol can't just play politics with a pandemic or we'll all lose; The cacophony this week was just the most public expression of a movement driven by well-organized right wing groups and egged on by the president." NBCNews.com (May 2, 2020).

Black Lives Matter protests: Gregory Neyman, et al., "Black Lives Matter protests and COVID-19 cases: Relationship in two databases." Journal of Public Health, Volume 43, Issue 2, June 2021, Pages 225–227 (originally published November 20, 2020).
Dhaval M. Dave, et al., "Black Lives Matter protests, social distancing, and COVID-19." Research Briefs in Economic Policy, CATO Institute. (October 14, 2020).

Maryland Governor gives authority to counties: Order of the Governor of the State of Maryland (May 5, 2020), amending and restating the Order of March 30, 2020, "Prohibiting large gatherings and events and closing senior centers, and all non-essential businesses and other establishments, and additionally requiring all persons to stay at home." (No. 20-05-06-01).

Office of Management and Budget initial COVID spending guidance: Office of Management and Budget, "Implementation guidance for supplemental funding provided in response to the coronavirus disease 2019." (M-20-01) (April 10, 2020).

Department of Interior OIG flash report: US Department of Interior, Office of Inspector General, "Where's the money? DOI use of CARES Act funds as of April 28, 2020." (May 5, 2020).

OMB initial guidance under the Recovery Act: Office of Management and Budget, "Initial implementing guidance for the American Recovery and Reinvestment Act of 2009." (M-09-10) (February 18, 2009).

President's order invoking Defense Production Act: Executive Order 13917 of April 28, 2020 (published in the Federal Register, Vol. 85, No. 85, May 1, 2020), "Delegating authority under the Defense Production Act with respect to food supply chain resources during the national emergency caused by the outbreak of COVID–19."

Operation Warp Speed: US Government Accountability Office, "Operation Warp Speed: Accelerated COVID-19 vaccine development status and efforts to address manufacturing challenges." (GAO-21-319) (February 11, 2021).

Secret Service law enforcement bulletin: Mike Baker, "Feds suspect vast fraud network is targeting US unemployment systems; Investigators see evidence of a sophisticated international attack they said could siphon hundreds of millions of dollars that were intended for the unemployed." *New York Times* (May 16, 2020).

Department of Labor alert memo: US Department of Labor, Office of Inspector General, "Alert Memorandum: The Pandemic Unemployment Assistance Program needs proactive measures to detect and prevent improper payments and fraud." (Report No. 19-20-002-03-315) (May 26, 2020).

Veteran Affairs health care facilities: Tiffany Stanley, "Why was the COVID death toll so high at some veterans homes? How Charlotte Hall in Maryland, like other veterans facilities across the country, was devastated by the pandemic." *Washington Post Magazine* (November 3, 2021).

Trump fires State Department IG: Jennifer Hansler, et al., "Pompeo says he asked Trump to fire inspector general because he was 'undermining' the State Department." CNNNews.com (May 18, 2020).

Governor Hogan lifts stay-at-home order: Amending and restating the Order of March 30, 2020, "Prohibiting large gatherings and events and closing senior centers, and all non-essential businesses and other establishments, and additionally requiring all persons to stay at home." (Order No. 20-05-06-01).

George Floyd killing:
Evan Hill, et al., "How George Floyd was killed in police custody." *New York Times* (May 31, 2020).
Hollie McKay, "George Floyd case: Protests erupt across the country after Minnesota man's death." FoxNews.com (May 28, 2020).

Oakland courthouse federal guard murder: US Attorney's Office, Northern District of California Press Release, "Steven Carrillo sentenced to 41 years in prison for murder and attempted murder for role in drive-by shooting at federal courthouse in Oakland." (June 3, 2022). Associated Press, "Alleged 'boogaloo' member pleads guilty to killing federal guard during 2020 protests." *NPR News* (February 11, 2022).

CHAPTER 8

Economic impact payments: John B. Taylor, "The economic impact of the Economic Impact Payments." *Hoover Institute Economics Working Papers* (May 2021). Data story on the three rounds of stimulus checks available at https://www.pandemicoversight.gov/news/articles/update-three-rounds-stimulus-checks-see-how-many-went-out-and-how-much.

Miami father and sons: US Attorney's Office, Southern District of Florida Press Release, "Father and sons charged in Miami federal court with selling toxic bleach as fake 'miracle' cure for COVID-19 and violating court orders." (July 8, 2020).

Governor DeSantis rejects mask mandate: Zack Anderson, "Gov. DeSantis rejects statewide mandatory masking policy." *USA Today Network* (June 23, 2020).

Governor DeSantis press conference: Andrew Atterbury, "DeSantis called a 'bully' after he scolds students for wearing masks." Politico.com (March 3, 2022). Video

available on YouTube at https://www.youtube.com/
watch?v=N9syRGE51HE.

Trump Arizona youth rally: Colby Itkowitz, "Trump again
uses racially insensitive term to describe coronavirus."
Washington Post (June 23, 2020).

Asian hate crime statistic: Center for the Study of Hate
and Extremism, California State University, San
Bernardino.

Asian hate crime research: Sungil Han, et al., "Anti-Asian
American hate crimes spike during the early stages
of the COVID-19 pandemic." *Journal of Interpersonal
Violence*. 2023 Feb; 38(3-4): 3513–3533.

United States Commission on Civil Rights letter: May
8, 2020, available at https://www.usccr.gov/files/
press/2020/05-14-CLhamon-Letter-to-Senators-re-An-
ti-Asian-Discrimination.pdf.

FBI warning on Asian hate crime: Josh Margolin, "FBI
warns of potential surge in hate crimes against Asian
Americans amid coronavirus: Critics say rhetoric has
fueled ill will." ABCNews.com (March 27, 2020).

Project Airbridge audit: US Department of Homeland
Security, Office of Inspector General, "FEMA did not
provide sufficient oversight of Project Airbridge."
(Report # OIG-23-14) (June 7, 2023).

Black Lives Matter protests: Larry Buchanan, et al., "Black Lives Matter may be the largest movement in US history." *New York Times* (July 3, 2020).

Public health research on protests: Madeleine Schachter, et al., "Black Lives Matter and COVID-19: Lessons in coincidence, confluence, and compassion." The International Journal of Information, Diversity, & Inclusion 4(3/4) (2020).

Rittenhouse interview: Eric Litke, "Fact check: Rittenhouse appears to have bought gun with unemployment funds, not stimulus check." ["I got my $1,200 from the coronavirus Illinois unemployment because I was on furlough from YMCA," he said. "And I got my first unemployment check so I was like, 'Oh, I'll use this to buy it.'"] *USA Today* (November 25, 2020).

PRAC June 3, 2020 Virtual Listening Forum: Video available at: https://www.pandemicoversight.gov/news/events/virtual-listening-forum-stakeholder-perspectives-oversight.
Witness statements available at: https://www.pandemicoversight.gov/media/file/prac-virtual-listening-forum-witness-statements.

Government Accountability Office report: Government Accountability Office, "Report to Congress: COVID-19 opportunities to improve federal response and recovery efforts." (Report No. 20-625) (June 2020).

PRAC's June 11 letter to Congress: Tom Hamburger, et al., "Inspectors general warn that Trump administration is blocking scrutiny of coronavirus rescue programs; As uproar over small-business disclosures intensifies, watchdogs tell Congress the White House is trying to shield how money is being spent." *Washington Post* (June 15, 2020).

Treasury reverses course: Aaron Gregg, et al., "In big reversal, Treasury and SBA agree to disclose details about many small business loan recipients." *Washington Post* (June 19, 2020).

November release of PPP data: "Judge orders the release of data on emergency loans for small businesses." *ProPublica* (November 2020).

PRAC's top pandemic challenges report: Pandemic Response Accountability Committee, "Top challenges facing federal agencies: COVID-19 emergency relief and response efforts." (June 2020).

OMB controller alert: Award description data quality for financial assistance awards (August 2020).

Unemployment Insurance Program: Outlook President's Budget 2020, available at https://oui.doleta.gov/unemploy/pdf/prez_budget_20.pdf.

Maryland uncovers fraud: Governor's Office of Homeland Security, "Hogan administration uncovers massive criminal fraud scheme." (July 16, 2020).

Oklahoma case: US Attorney's Office, Northern District of Oklahoma Press Release, "Nearly 3,800 fraudulently filed Unemployment Insurance claims blocked by the US Department of Labor: US Attorney and Oklahoma Attorney General encourage Oklahomans to report false claims filed in their name." (June 29, 2020).

FBI bulletin: Federal Bureau of Investigation Press Release, "FBI sees spike in fraudulent unemployment insurance claims filed using stolen identities." (July 6, 2020).

Equifax case: US Department of Justice, Office of Public Affairs Press Release, "Chinese military personnel charged with computer fraud, economic espionage and wire fraud for hacking into credit reporting agency Equifax: Indictment alleges four members of China's People's Liberation Army engaged in a three-month long campaign to steal sensitive personal information of nearly 150 million Americans." (February 10, 2020).

US Secret Service confirms investigation: Timothy Nerozzi, "Chinese hackers exploited US COVID relief funds for millions, Secret Service claims; The Secret Service confirmed the involvement of Chinese hacking group APT41 but did not disclose details." FoxNews.com (December 6, 2022).

SBA disaster loans: US Small Business Administration, Office of Inspector General, "Serious concerns of potential fraud in economic injury disaster loan program pertaining to the response to COVID-19." (Report #20-16) (July 28, 2020).

CHAPTER 9

HHS OIG nursing home report: US Department of Health and Human Services, Office of Inspector General, "Onsite surveys of nursing homes during the COVID-19 pandemic: March 23–May 30, 2020." (Report No. OEI-01-20-00430) (December 2020).

According to reports, state unemployment insurance systems: Pandemic Response Accountability Committee, "Key insights: State Pandemic Unemployment Insurance Programs." (December 16, 2021).
Tony Romm, "A magnet for 'rip-off artists': Fraud siphoned billions from pandemic unemployment benefits." *Washington Post* (May 15, 2022).
AP News, "Colorado deals with widespread fraud in unemployment claims." (September 10, 2020).

SBA disaster loan report: US Small Business Administration, Office of Inspector General, "Inspection of Small Business Administration's initial disaster assistance response to the coronavirus pandemic." (Report No. 21-02) (October 28, 2020).

FinCEN SARS: Government Accountability Office, "COVID-19 critical vaccine distribution, supply chain, program integrity, and other challenges require focused federal attention." Page 215 (Report GAO-21-265) (January 2021).

Fake farm schemes: Celia Hack, "Nearly $1 million in fraudulent pandemic relief loans leave Johnson County victims searching for answers." *Shawnee Mission (KS) Post* (February 11, 2021).

Eli Sherman, et al., "'Take immediate action:' Reed calls on SBA's Carranza to investigate disaster loan fraud." WPRI.com (December 22, 2020).

SBA financial statement audit report: US Small Business Administration, "Independent auditors' report on SBA's FY 2020 financial statements." (December 18, 2020).

Lessons learned from the Recovery Board: Government Accountability Office, "Recovery Act: Grant implementation experiences offer lessons for accountability and transparency." (GAO-14-219) (January 2104).

PPP data: Lydia DePillis, "Judge orders the release of data on emergency loans for small businesses." (November 6, 2020).

MITRE study: MITRE Corp., "Transparency in pandemic-related federal spending: Report of alignment and gaps." (99-D-00005/PRAC-20-A-0002) (2020). Available at https://www.pandemicoversight.gov/media/file/transparency-pandemic-related-federal-spending-full-report.

Agile oversight toolkit: Pandemic Response Accountability Committee Agile Products Toolkit (2020). Available at https://www.pandemicoversight.gov/media/file/agile-products-toolkit2022pdf.

President and First Lady test positive: Christine Wang, "President Trump, First Lady Melania test positive for coronavirus." *CNBC News* (October 2, 2020).

Statement by First Lady Melania Trump, "My personal experience with COVID-19." (October 14, 2020), available at https://trumpwhitehouse.archives.gov/articles/first-lady-melania-trump-personal-experience-covid-19/.

White House video, "'Don't be afraid of coronavirus': Trump removes mask as he returns to White House." (October 5, 2020), available at https://www.youtube.com/watch?v=FBtP8yWd7Qg.

Rose garden event: DC Government, Department of Health, "DC Health and nine local jurisdictions ask individuals connected to recent White House events to contact their local health department." (October 8, 2020).

David Nakamura, et al., "Rose Garden event suspected of virus outbreak alarms DC officials." *Washington Post* (October 3, 2020).

Janie Haseman, et al., "Here's everyone at the White House Rose Garden SCOTUS event now called a likely 'super-spreader.' Help us ID them all." *USA Today* (October 7, 2020).

Wisconsin response: Adam Raymond, et al., "Teens, politics, and fatigue: Why Midwest COVID cases have surged." SpectrumNews1.com (October 30, 2020).

Michigan case: The Department of Justice, Office of Public Affairs Press Release, "Six arrested on federal charge of conspiracy to kidnap the Governor of Michigan; The Michigan Attorney General charged seven additional individuals following a coordinated disruption of the plan." (October 8, 2020).

State governor travel restrictions: Stephen Caruso, "Pa. lays out COVID travel restrictions ahead of holidays, without guarantee of enforcement." *Penn Capital Star News* (November 17, 2020). New York Department of Health, "Interim guidance for quarantine restrictions on travelers arriving in New York State following out of state travel." (November 3, 2020).

Ben Leonard, "Maryland reports 2,910 new coronavirus cases, by far the highest daily total during pandemic." *Baltimore Sun* (November 19, 2020).

Alabama, "Order of the state health officer suspending certain public gatherings due to risk of infection by COVID-19 (applicable statewide) (amended December 9, 2020)."

Melissa Brown, "Alabama mask mandate extended amid worsening COVID-19 spread." *Montgomery (AL) Advertiser* (December 9, 2020).

Mnuchin returns funds: Reuters staff, "Mnuchin will put clawed-back fed funds out of Yellen's reach -Bloomberg." (November 24, 2020).

CHAPTER 10

Oregon protests: Lauren Dake, et al., "Far-right protesters disrupt Oregon Legislature special session." *Oregon Public Broadcasting* (December 21, 2020).

Consolidated Appropriations Act: Consolidated Appropriations Act, 2021, enacted on December 27, 2020, as Public Law 116-260.

FDA approval: US Food & Drug Administration News Release, "FDA takes key action in fight against COVID-19 by issuing emergency use authorization for first COVID-19 vaccine; Action follows thorough evaluation of available safety, effectiveness, and manufacturing quality information by FDA career scientists, input from independent experts." (December 11, 2020).

New York, Times Square: Michael Gold, "No crowds, but Times Square ball drop is still happening. Here's how." *New York Times* (December 30, 2020).

Capitol riot: Select Committee to Investigate the January 6th Attack on the United States Capitol, "Final Report." (House Report 117-663) (December 22, 2022), available at https://www.govinfo.gov/content/pkg/GPO-J6-REPORT /pdf/GPO-J6-REPORT.pdf.

McConnell statements: "McConnell says Jan. 6 Capitol attack was 'provoked' by Trump and others in power," (with video link). *PBS NewsHour* (January 19, 2021).
Sahil Kapur, "McConnell calls Jan. 6 a 'violent insurrection,' breaking with RNC: The Republican National Committee recently referred to the events of Jan. 6 as 'legitimate political discourse.'" NBCNews.com (February 8, 2022).

Graham statement: Office of Senator Lindsey Graham Press Release, "Graham Statement on January 6." (January 6, 2022).

Trump impeachment: Todd Ruger, "Senate votes to acquit Trump for incitement of Jan. 6 insurrection; Seven Republicans voted with all Democrats, but fell ten short of the votes needed to convict." RollCall.com (February 13, 2021).

Horowitz testimony: Statement of Michael E. Horowitz, Chair, Pandemic Response Accountability Committee, Before the US House of Representatives Committee on Oversight and Government Reform, Select Subcommittee on the Coronavirus Crisis concerning "The Pandemic Response Accountability Committee's role in combating fraud in pandemic relief and small business programs." (March 25, 2021).

US rejoins WHO: White House Executive Order 13987, "Organizing and mobilizing the United States Government to provide a unified and effective response to combat COVID-19 and to provide United States leadership on global health and security." (January 20, 2021).

DOJ Opinion on Special IG for Pandemic Recovery: US Department of Justice, "Authority of the Special Inspector General for Pandemic Recovery to oversee programs established under the CARES Act, Memorandum Opinion for the Acting General Counsel, Department of the Treasury, and the Special Inspector General For Pandemic Recovery." (April 29, 2021).

SBA OIG report on SBA's use of Do Not Pay system: US Small Business Administration, Office of Inspector General, "Paycheck Protection Program loan recipients on the

Department of Treasury's Do Not Pay List." (Report No. 21-06) (January 11, 2021).

PRAC February Listening Forum: Pandemic Response Accountability Committee, "Pandemic response: Perspectives from small business borrowers." (February 17, 2021), available at https://www.pandemicoversight .gov/news/events/pandemic-response-perspectives -small-business-borrowers.

DOD OIG report on Navy response: US Department of Defense, Office of Inspector General, "Evaluation of the Navy's plans and response to the coronavirus disease-2019 onboard Navy warships and submarines." (Report No. DODIG-2021-049) (February 4, 2021).

New York task force case: United States Attorney's Office, Southern District of New York Press Release, "Recidivist fraudster convicted at trial of over $10 million COVID-19 loan fraud scheme." (November 1, 2022).

Palm Beach Florida nursing home case: United States Department of Justice, Office of Public Affairs Press Release, "MorseLife Nursing Home Health System agrees to Pay $1.75 million to settle false claims act allegations for facilitating COVID-19 vaccinations of ineligible donors and prospective donors." (June 30, 2022).

CHAPTER 11

Employment rate in March 2021: US Bureau of Labor Statistics, "TED: The Economic Daily." (May 4, 2021).

Contraction of GDP in 2020: Bureau of Economic Statistics, "Gross Domestic Product." Available at https://www.bea.gov/data/gdp/gross-domestic-product.
Jeff Cox, "Second-quarter GDP plunged by worst-ever 32.9% amid virus-induced shutdown." CNBCNews.com (July 30, 2020).

American Rescue Plan Act: The American Rescue Plan Act of 2021 (ARP), enacted on March 11, 2021, as Public Law 117–2.

PRAC/OMB Joint Alert: "Payment Integrity Alert: The use of automation and data analytics from the Office of Management and Budget (OMB) Office of Federal Financial Management and the Pandemic Response Accountability Committee (PRAC)." (July 21, 2021).

Horowitz testimony: Statement of Michael E. Horowitz, Chair, Pandemic Response Accountability Committee, Before the US House of Representatives Committee on Oversight and Government Reform, Select Subcommittee on the Coronavirus Crisis concerning "The Pandemic Response Accountability Committee's role in combating fraud in pandemic relief and small business programs" (March 25, 2021).

Secret Service May 2021 announcement: US Secret Service Press Release, "US Secret Service helps recover $2B through investigations into COVID-19-related financial fraud." (May 12, 2021).

Secret Service bulk forfeitures: Service to America Award, "Roy Dotson and the CARES Act Team: Conducted a nationwide criminal investigation that recovered $1.2 billion in stolen federal pandemic relief payments meant for small businesses and the unemployed, and halted the dispersal of $2.2 billion more in fraudulently requested funds." Available at https://servicetoamericamedals.org/honorees/roy-dotson-and-the-cares-act-team/.

CHAPTER 12

HHS Provider Relief Fund: Pandemic Response Accountability Committee Press Release, "Provider Relief Fund data now available on PandemicOversight.gov." (June 3, 2021).

Jacksonville family: Emily Bloch, "Their family was scared of the vaccine. They lost 4 members to COVID-19 within 1 week." *Florida Times-Union* (August 3, 2021).

Michigan sweepstakes: Michigan Governor Press Release, "Gov. Whitmer highlights 'Outstanding Success' of MI Shot to Win Sweepstakes, which increased vaccinations every week during July." (August 23, 2021).

West Virginia incentive program: Governor's website: https://doitforbabydog.wv.gov/
Amelia Ferrell Knisley, "Guns, trucks and more: Governor's 'Do It for Babydog' campaign spent $23M in federal COVID relief funds." *Bluefield (WV) Daily Telegraph* (February 14, 2023).

New York City mandate: Laurel Wamsley, "New vaccine mandates are coming for government employees and health care Workers." *NPR News* (July 26, 2021).

West Virginia man: United States Attorney's Office, District of Maryland Press Release, "Man who made threats against Dr. Anthony Fauci and other federal officials sentenced to over three years in federal prison." (August 4, 2022).

Mississippi man: United States Attorney's Office, Southern District of Mississippi Press Release, "Ridgeland man sentenced to two years in prison for making threats against CDC Director Rochelle Walensky." (March 8, 2023).

Williamson County School Board meeting: Caroline Sutton, "'We know who you are.' Group threatens doctors, others wearing masks outside Williamson Co. school board meeting." *NewsChannel5 Nashville* (August 21, 2021). Matt Masters, "No charges in 2021 viral school board meeting that saw anti-mask protests devolve into mob." *The News/Williamson (TN) Homepage* (August 4, 2022).

California woman: US Department of Justice, Office of Public Affairs Press Release, "Woman arrested for fake COVID-19 immunization and vaccination card scheme." (July 14, 2021).

Massachusetts couple: United States Attorney's Office, District of Massachusetts Press Release, "Former

Department of Unemployment Assistance employee pleads guilty to fraud and identity theft charges related to COVID-19 pandemic." (August 30, 2021).

Virginia individuals: United States Attorney's Office, Western District of Virginia Press Release, "Five plead guilty to pandemic unemployment fraud, mail fraud charges." (August 27, 2021).

New Jersey man: US Attorney's Office, District of Massachusetts Press Release, "New Jersey man pleads guilty to unemployment fraud relating to COVID-19 pandemic." (November 12, 2021).

Social Security Administration employee: US Attorney's Office, Middle District of Pennsylvania Press Release, "Social Security employee charged with pandemic fraud scheme." (August 13, 2021).

American Rescue Plan unemployment insurance counter-fraud grants: US Department of Labor, Employment and Training Administration, Unemployment Insurance Program Letter No. 22-21, "Advisory: Grant opportunity to support states with fraud detection and prevention, including Identity Verification and Overpayment Recovery Activities, in all Unemployment Compensation (UC) Programs." (August 11, 2021).

Labor employment insurance guidance: US Department of Labor, Employment and Training Administration, Unemployment Insurance Program Letter No. 04-17, Change 1, "Subject: Requirement for states to refer allegations of Unemployment Compensation (UC) fraud, waste, abuse, mismanagement, or misconduct to the Department of Labor's (Department) Office of Inspector General's (DOL-OIG) and to disclose information related to the Coronavirus Aid, Relief, and Economic Security (CARES) Act to DOL-OIG for purposes of UC fraud investigation and audits." (August 3, 2021).

CHAPTER 13

Lifting of nursing home restrictions: Centers for Medicare & Medicaid Services Nursing Home Visitation – COVID-19. (Ref: QSO-20-39-NH) (Revised Sept. 23, 2022). American Hospital Association CMS lifts restrictions on nursing home visitation. (Nov. 16, 2021).

Big Bird: Rachel Pannett, "Big Bird got his Pfizer shot, and conservatives are calling it vaccine 'propaganda.'" *Washington Post* (November 8, 2021).

Elvis Presley and polio vaccine: Hal Hershfield, et al., "How Elvis got Americans to accept the polio vaccine." *Scientific American* (January 18, 2021).

Senator Cruz and Mr. T: Bruce Lee, "Ted Cruz trolls Mr. T COVID-19 Face Mask Tweet; Here's the reaction." Forbes.com (April 7, 2022).

DOJ Report on Nassar investigation: US Department of Justice, Office of the Inspector General DOJ Press Release, "OIG releases report of investigation and review of the FBI's handling of allegations of sexual abuse by former USA Gymnastics physician Lawrence Gerard Nassar." (July 14, 2021).

Melissa Mahtani, "US gymnasts testify before Congress about FBI's Nassar investigation." *CNN News* (September 15, 2021).

Poway California School Board meeting: Elizabeth Himchak, "Protesters disrupt Poway Unified board meeting, cause its adjournment." *San Diego Union Tribune* (September 9, 2021).

Let's Go Brandon: Colleen Long, "How 'Let's Go Brandon' became code for insulting Joe Biden." AP News (October 30, 2021).

Saturday Night Live: Caroline Vakil, "'SNL' pokes fun at rowdy school board meetings." TheHill.com (October 3, 2021).

Attorney General Garland order to FBI: US Department of Justice, Office of Public Affairs Press Release, "Justice Department addresses violent threats against school officials and teachers." (October 4, 2021).

Michigan pulmonologist: Andrea Salcedo, "Doctor who has lost over 100 patients to COVID says some deny virus from their deathbeds: 'I don't believe you.'" *Washington Post* (September 24, 2021).

PRAC and HUD OIG report: US Housing and Urban Development, Office of Inspector General, "Fraud risk inventory for the CDBG and ESG CARES Act funds." (Report No. 2022-FO-0801) (October 12, 2021).

PRAC pandemic spending data report: Pandemic Response Accountability Committee, "Increasing transparency into COVID-19 spending." (October 19, 2021).

CHAPTER 14

Omicron surge: Aya Elamroussi, "Omicron surge is 'unlike anything we've ever seen,' expert says." CNNNews.com (December 31, 2021).

***Washington Post* headline:** Marissa Lang, "'It feels like 2020 all over again': As COVID cases climb, DC-area residents take extra precautions." *Washington Post* (December 18, 2021).

President's call: Rick Rouan, "Oregon man who told Biden 'Let's go, Brandon' on call says it was 'innocent jest.'" *USA Today* (December 27, 2021).

OMB IG cooperation guidance: Office of Management and Budget memo, "Promoting accountability through cooperation among agencies and Inspectors General." (M-22-04) (December 3, 2021).

Postal Service/US Digital Service home tests: Natalie Alms, "USPS, USDS collaborate on new COVID-19 test website." FCW.com (January 14, 2022).

PRAC unemployment insurance report: Pandemic Response Accountability Committee, "Key Insights: State Pandemic Unemployment Insurance Programs." (December 16, 2021).

PRAC restaurant program report: Pandemic Response Accountability Committee, "Small Business Administration Paycheck Protection Program Phase III fraud controls." (January 21, 2022).

Oregon dentist case: United States Attorney's Office, District of Oregon Press Release, "Former Oregon dentist sentenced to federal prison for stealing millions in COVID-relief funds and illegally distributing controlled substances." (February 16, 2023).

HHS OIG audit on COVID testing contract: US Department of Health and Human Services, Office of Inspector General, "The Assistant Secretary for Administration awarded and managed five sole source contracts for COVID-19 testing in accordance with federal and contract requirements." (Report No. A-05-21-00014) (January 2022).

WHO chief announcement: World Health Organization, COVID-19 Virtual Press conference transcript – 1 February 2022. Available at https://www.who.int/publications/m/item/covid-19-virtual-press-conference-transcript-1-february-2022.

CHAPTER 15

White House Fact Sheet: White House, "Fact Sheet: President Biden to announce new steps to combat criminal fraud and identity theft in pandemic relief programs." (March 1, 2022).

Florida press event: Zac Anderson, "'Stop bullying kids': Gov. Ron DeSantis widely criticized over mask confrontation with students." *Sarasota (FL) Herald-Tribune* (March 3, 2022).

Judge strikes mask mandate: Health Freedom Defense Fund, Inc., et al. v. Joseph R. Biden, Case No. 8:21-cv-1693-KKM-AEP, United States District Court, Middle District of Florida. Order. Kathryn Kimball Mizelle, US District Judge.
Jessica Wehrman, "Federal judge overturns travel mask mandate: Ruling comes just days after the CDC extended the requirement amid concern about latest virus variant." RollCall.com (April 18, 2022).

Air Alaska pilot: Yaron Steinbuch, "Judge's decision to void mask mandate prompts mid-flight cheers among fliers." NewYorkPost.com (April 19, 2022).

DHS OIG audit report on transporting migrants: US Department of Homeland Security, Office of Inspector General, "ICE did not follow policies, guidance, or recommendations to ensure migrants were tested for COVID-19 before transport on domestic commercial flights." (Report No. OIG-22-44) (May 18, 2022).

Health and Human Services OIG report: US Department of Health and Human Services, Office of Inspector General, "Office of Refugee Resettlement's influx care facility and emergency intake sites did not adequately safeguard unaccompanied children from COVID-19." (Report No. A-06-21-07002) (June 6, 2022).

White House meeting with IGs: White House "Remarks by President Biden with Inspectors General on commitment to oversight, accountability, and transparency." (April 29, 2022), available at https://www.whitehouse. gov/briefing-room/speeches-remarks/2022/04/29/re marks-by-president-biden-with-inspectors-general -on-commitment-to-oversight-accountability-and -transparency/.

OMB guidance on Bipartisan Infrastructure Law: Office of Management and Budget memo, "Advancing effective stewardship of taxpayer resources and outcomes in the implementation of the Infrastructure Investment and Jobs Act." (M-22-12) (April 29, 2022).

One million COVID deaths in the US: Maria Caspani, "COVID claims 1 million US lives." Reuters News (May 11, 2022).

CHAPTER 16

Percentage vaccinated as of August 2022: USAFacts. org, available at https://usafacts.org/visualizations/ covid-vaccine-tracker-states\.

Trump rally in Alaska: C-SPAN video at 00:10:47. Available at https://www.c-span.org/video/?521436-1/president -trump-rally-anchorage-alaska.

Wisconsin pharmacist case: United States Attorney's Office, District of Wisconsin Press Release, "Hospital pharmacist to plead guilty to attempting to spoil hundreds of COVID vaccine doses." (January 26, 2021).

Tucker Carlson statement: "Tucker Carlson says the military's vaccine requirements are a plot to purge 'sincere Christians' and 'men with high testosterone.'" *Media Matters for America* (September 20, 2021).

Navy SEALS case: Austin v. US Navy Seals, 1-26, 595 US ___ (2022).

Pope Francis statement on vaccines: Pope Francis urges people to get vaccinated against COVID-19, "Pope Francis launches a powerful appeal for people to get vaccinated with approved COVID-19 vaccines, calling it 'an act of love.'" *Vatican News* (August 2021).

Robert Jeffress statement on vaccines: Tom Steele, "First Baptist's Robert Jeffress: 'There is no credible religious argument against the vaccines': The downtown Dallas megachurch's senior pastor is among faith leaders across the country who aren't endorsing vaccine exemptions for their congregants." *Dallas Morning News* (September 17, 2021).

Robert F. Kennedy, Jr.: David Klepper, "RFK Jr.'s anti-vaccine group kicked off Instagram, Facebook." APNews.com (August 18, 2022).
Olga Robinson, "Instagram bans Robert F Kennedy Jr over COVID vaccine posts." *BBC News* (February 11, 2021).

Biden tests positive: "Biden again tests positive for COVID-19 in rare 'rebound' case." *PBS News* (July 30, 2022).

Trump and Biden statements: Emily Jacobs, "SEE IT: Trump mocks Biden, claims he has dementia in wild post." *Washington Examiner* (July 31, 2022).
Rob Crilly, et al., "'When my predecessor got COVID he was taken to the hospital by helicopter. When I got it, I worked for five days': Biden mocks Trump's COVID diagnosis as he tests negative and leaves WH isolation." Daily Mail.com (July 27, 2022).

COVID fraud statute of limitations: COVID-19 EIDL Fraud Statute of Limitations Act of 2022, enacted August 5, 2022, as Public Law No: 117-165. PPP and Bank Fraud Enforcement Harmonization Act of 2022, enacted August 5, 2022, as Public Law No: 117-166.

$286 million recovered: United States Attorney's Office, District of Colorado Press Release, "US Secret Service returns $286M in fraudulently obtained funds to the Small Business Administration." (August 26, 2022).

CDC guidance: Centers for Disease Control and Prevention Press Release, "CDC streamlines COVID-19 guidance to help the public better protect themselves and understand their risk." (August 11, 2022).

COVID-19 Strike Forces: US Department of Justice Press Release, "Justice Department announces COVID-19 Fraud Strike Force Teams." (September 14, 2022).

Dr. Jha statement: White House, "Press Briefing by White House COVID-19 Response Team and public health officials." (September 6, 2022).

DOJ OIG capstone report: US Department of Justice, Office of Inspector General, "Capstone Review of the Federal Bureau of Prisons' response to the coronavirus disease 2019 pandemic." (Report No. 23-054) (March 21, 2023).

PRAC Fraud Alert: Pandemic Response Accountability Committee, "FRAUD ALERT: PRAC identifies $5.4 billion in potentially fraudulent pandemic loans obtained using over 69,000 questionable Social Security numbers." (January 30, 2023).

House oversight hearing: US House of Representatives, Committee on Oversight and Accountability hearing, "Federal pandemic spending: A prescription for waste, fraud and abuse." (February 1, 2023). Video available at https://oversight.house.gov/hearing/federal-pandemic-spending-a-prescription-for-waste-fraud-and-abuse/.

Health and Human Services OIG report on vaccines: US Health and Human Services, Office of Inspector General, "Challenges with vaccination data hinder state and local immunization program efforts to combat COVID-19." (Report No. OEI-05-22-00010) (January 2023).

CHAPTER 17

Evidence-based policymaking: Foundations for Evidence-Based Policymaking Act of 2018, enacted January 14, 2019, as Public Law 115-435.

IRS remote work: Jory Heckman, "IRS considers pilot expanding remote work, amid hiring challenges." FederalNewsNetwork.com (September 7, 2022).

Census Household Pulse Survey: US Census, "Household Pulse Survey collected responses just before and just after the arrival of the first CTC checks." (August 11, 2021).

New Jersey audit report: New Jersey State Auditor, "American Rescue Plan state fiscal recovery fund Information Report." (March 31, 2023).

House GOP plans to claw back: Catie Edmondson, "House GOP eyes rescinding unspent COVID money as part of its fiscal plan: Estimates put the amount of leftover money between $50 billion and $70 billion. But even if Republicans could claw it back, it would not make much of a dent in the deficit." *New York Times* (April 20, 2023).

PRAC finding on rental assistance program: Pandemic Response Accountability Committee, "Lessons learned in oversight of pandemic relief funds." (June 8, 2022).

Paycheck Protection Program 2022 report: David Autor, et al., "The $800 billion Paycheck Protection Program: Where did the money go and why did it go there?" *Journal of Economic Perspectives*, Vol. 36, No. 2 (Spring 2022). William Emmons, et al., "Was the Paycheck Protection Program effective?" Federal Reserve Bank of St. Louis, available at https://www.stlouisfed.org/publications /regional-economist/2022/jul/was-paycheck-protection -program-effective.

Kaiser Family Foundation study: Krutika Amin, et al., "COVID-19 mortality preventable by vaccines." Peterson-KFF Health System Tracker (April 21, 2022).

Washington University study: Washington University, School of Medicine in St. Louis News Release, "COVID-19 infections increase risk of long-term brain problems: Strokes, seizures, memory and movement disorders among problems that develop in first year after infection." (September 22, 2022).

WHO study: World Health Organization, "COVID-19 pandemic triggers 25% increase in prevalence of anxiety and depression worldwide." (March 2, 2022).

National Center for Education report: Available at https://www.nationsreportcard.gov/highlights/ltt/2022/.

Miguel Cardona statement: Brad Dress, "Education secretary: Dramatic drops in reading, math scores should be call to action." TheHill.com (September 1, 2022).

Teacher shortages: "Facing shortages, US states lower teachers' requirements." *Voice of America News* (August 30, 2022).

Bureau of Labor statistics: Kathryn Dill, "Teachers are calling it quits: Educators say they are worn down by the COVID-19 pandemic, understaffed schools and political battles. Districts warn of a worsening shortage." *Wall Street Journal* (June 20, 2022).

Nursing shortages: National Council of State Boards of Nursing (NSCBN), "Examining the impact of the COVID-19 pandemic on burnout & stress among US nurses." (April 13, 2023).

December 2022 omnibus bill: Consolidated Appropriations Act, 2023, enacted on December 29, 2023, as Public Law 117-328.

Effect of SNAP cuts: Anna Gustafson, "'A very dark time': SNAP cuts leave Michigan families, food banks struggling." *Michigan Advance* (March 19, 2023).

CHAPTER 18

GAO's general views on payment integrity and accuracy of government estimates: Government Accountability Office, "Payment Integrity: Federal agencies' estimates of FY 2019 improper payments." (Report No. GAO-20-344) (March 2020).

Self-certification in women-owned business program: "Women-Owned Small Business and Economically Disadvantaged Women-Owned Small Business-Certification." Federal Register, Vol. 80, No. 243 (December 18, 2015).
US Small Business Administration, Office of Inspector General, "SBA'S implementation of the Women-Owned Small Business Certification Program." (Report No. 22-20) (September 29, 2022).

SBA OIG and House Select Subcommittee on the Coronavirus Crisis reports: US Small Business Administration, Office of Inspector General, "Inspection of Small Business Administration's initial disaster assistance response to the coronavirus pandemic." (Report No. 21-02) (October 28, 2020).
Select Committee on the Coronavirus Crisis, "Staff Report: IDLE on EIDL fraud: How the Trump administration wasted taxpayer dollars by leaving the COVID-19 EIDL Program vulnerable to fraud." (June 2022).

Do Not Pay requirement: Payment Integrity Information Act of 2019, enacted March 2, 2020, Public Law 116–117.

SBA OIG report on duplicate loans: US Small Business Administration, Office of Inspector General, "Duplicate loans made under the Paycheck Protection Program." (Report No. 21-09) (March 15, 2021).

SBA OIG report on Do Not Pay: US Small Business Administration, Office of Inspector General, "Paycheck Protection Program loan recipients on the Department of Treasury's Do Not Pay List." (Report No. 21-06) (January 11, 2021).
US Small Business Administration, Office of Inspector General, "COVID-19 EIDL Program recipients on the Department of Treasury's Do Not Pay List." (Report No. 22-06) (November 30, 2021).

Department of Labor report citing concerns with UI program: Department of Labor, Office of Inspector General Alert Memorandum, "The Employment and Training

Administration (ETA) needs to ensure State Workforce Agencies (SWA) implement effective unemployment insurance program fraud controls for high-risk areas." (Report No. 19-21-003-03-315) (February 22, 2021).

Department of Labor report reporting $45 billion in potential fraud: Department of Labor, Office of Inspector General Alert Memorandum, "Potentially fraudulent unemployment insurance payments in high-risk areas increased to $45.6 billion." (Report No. 19-22-005-03-31) (September 21, 2022).

Dayton landlord case: Josh Sweigart, "Local landlord pleads guilty in federal rental assistance fraud case." *Dayton (OH) Daily News* (March 21, 2023).

Stonecrest mayor case: United States Attorney's Office, Northern District of Georgia Press Release, "Former Mayor of Stonecrest sentenced to prison for stealing COVID-19 relief funds." (July 13, 2022).

Medicare false billing cases: United States Department of Justice Press Release, "Justice Department announces nationwide coordinated law enforcement action to combat COVID-19 health care fraud." (April 19, 2022). United States Attorney's Office District of Maryland Press Release, "Maryland doctor facing federal indictment for COVID-19 healthcare fraud scheme is part of a nationwide coordinated law enforcement action to combat health care related COVID-19 fraud announced by the Justice Department today." (April 20, 2022).

Myrtle Beach tax fraud case: United States Attorney's Office, District of South Carolina Press Release, "Myrtle Beach family members sentenced to federal prison for tax-related coronavirus fraud scheme." (August 16, 2022).

Allenwood Federal Correctional Complex case: United States Attorney's Office, Eastern District of Michigan Press Release, "Federal inmate pleads guilty to role in stealing more than $2.2 million in pandemic assistance benefits." (May 10, 2022).

Army warrant officer case: United States Attorney's Office, Southern District of Georgia Press Release, "Fort Stewart soldier sentenced to prison for prolific fraud scheme targeting COVID-19 relief programs, student loans." (January 9, 2023).

California rapper case: United States Attorney's Office, Central District of California Press Release, "Rapper who bragged about COVID-related jobless benefits scam agrees to plead guilty to federal fraud and firearm charges." (July 6, 2022).

California reports $20 billion: "California's unemployment fraud reaches at least $20 billion." *Los Angeles Times* (October 25, 2021).

Texas reports 15 percent: Nick Natario, "Texas unemployment fraud soars to $2.5 billion during pandemic: The Texas Workforce Commission is making changes to its unemployment process." *KVUE ABC News* (Austin, TX) (November 19, 2021).

Pennsylvania reports over $4 billion: John Micek, "Pa. says it's investigating 'aggressive and sophisticated' unemployment fraud efforts." *Pennsylvania Capital Star* (January 8, 2022).

Illinois state auditor general report: Beth Hundsdorfer, "Auditor general reports about $2 billion in fraudulent pandemic unemployment claims." *State Journal-Register* (Springfield, IL) (June 17, 2022).

Arizona fraud: Jerod MacDonald-Evoy, "Fraudsters stole $4.4 billion from DES, and it could happen again." *Arizona Mirror* (November 10, 2021).

Maryland fraud ring: United States Attorney's Office, District of Maryland Press Release, "Hyattsville man pleads guilty to his role in a Cares-Act and unemployment insurance fraud scheme involving over 600 victims and caused a loss of at least $2.7 million." (July 14, 2022).

Nigerian national fraud recidivist case: United States Attorney's Office, Northern District of Georgia Press Release, "Nigerian hacker and a repeat offender sentenced to federal prison for unemployment fraud and tax fraud scheme." (September 2, 2021).

Another Nigerian national case: United States Secret Service Press Release, "Nigerian national indicted for conspiracy, wire fraud and aggravated identity theft for fraud on Employment Security benefits." (May 26, 2021).

Fort Lauderdale man: United States Attorney's Office, Southern District of Florida Press Release, "Defendant pleads guilty to stealing $24 million in COVID-19 relief money through fraud scheme that used synthetic identities." (June 29, 2021).

Los Angeles college football player: United States Attorney's Office, Central District of California Press Release, "College football player arrested on federal charges of orchestrating fraudulent scheme to obtain COVID-related jobless benefits." (December 20, 2021).

Florida police officer: United States Attorney's Office, Southern District of Florida Press Release, "Coral Springs police officer charged with COVID relief fraud, using loan money to service and repair his vintage car." (June 16, 2022).

Former president of chamber of commerce: United States Attorney's Office, Central District of California Press Release, "Former Head of Anaheim Chamber of Commerce pleads guilty to federal fraud, false statement and criminal tax charge." (July 1, 2022).

2021 total improper payments: Improper payment data generally is available at PaymentAccuracy.gov. See also, White House, "Updated data on payment integrity." (December 30, 2021).

2022 total improper payments: Improper payment data generally is available at PaymentAccuracy.gov. See also, White House, "Government-wide improper payments declined in FY 2022." (November 23, 2022).

TIGTA report on stimulus checks: Treasury Inspector General for Tax Administration, "Implementation of economic impact payments implementation of economic impact payments." (Report No. 2021-46-034) (March 24, 2021).

Labor inspector general 2022 testimony: Testimony before the US Senate Committee on Homeland Security and Governmental Affairs, Hearing Title: "Pandemic response and accountability: Reducing fraud and expanding access to COVID-19 relief through effective oversight." (March 17, 2022).

Labor inspector general 2023 testimony: Testimony before the US House of Representatives Committee on Ways and Means, Hearing Title: "The greatest theft of American tax dollars: Unchecked unemployment fraud." (February 8, 2023).

House of Commons "eye-watering" remark: UK Parliament committees News Article, "PAC says government 'complacent' about preventing 'eye-watering' levels of fraud in the COVID Bounceback Loan Scheme." (April 27, 2022).

European Union warning: Raf Casert, "EU watchdog: Not enough safeguards on pandemic recovery fund." AP News (March 8, 2023).

CHAPTER 19

Letter to Secretary Pompeo: Letter dated March 19, 2020, from Senator Richard J. Durbin, et al., to Secretary of State Michael R. Pompeo. Available at https://www.durbin.senate.gov/imo/media/doc/March19PompeoCOVID19LetterFINALV3.pdf.

Defense Department warning: US Department of Defense, "DOD works to eliminate foreign coronavirus disinformation." (April 13, 2020), available at https://www.defense.gov/News/News-Stories/Article/Article/2147566/dod-works-to-eliminate-foreign-coronavirus-disinformation/.

RAND Corporation: RAND Corporation, "How truth decay is fueling vaccine hesitancy." (May 14, 2021), available at https://www.rand.org/blog/2021/05/how-truth-decay-is-fueling-vaccine-hesitancy.html.

September 2020 FBI/CISA warning: FBI and CISA Public Service Announcement, "Foreign actors and cybercriminals likely to spread disinformation regarding 2020 election results." (Alert No. I-092220-PSA) (September 22, 2020), available at https://www.cisa.gov/sites/default/files/publications/092220_%20final_PSA_election_results.pdf.

October 2022 FBI/CISA warning: FBI and CISA Public Service Announcement, "Foreign actors likely to use information manipulation tactics for 2022 midterm elections." (Alert No. I-100622-PSA) (October 5, 2022), available at https://www.cisa.gov/sites/default/files/publications/PSA-information-activities_508.pdf.

Top-Secret document leaks: Joseph Menn, "Russians boasted that just 1% of fake social profiles are caught, leak shows." *Washington Post* (April 16, 2023).

Harvard T.H. Chan School of Public Health study: Press Release, "Political ideology of US elected officials linked with COVID-19 health outcomes." (November 1, 2022).

Nancy Krieger, et al., "Relationship of political ideology of US federal and state elected officials and key COVID pandemic outcomes following vaccine rollout to adults: April 2021–March 2022." *The Lancet Regional Health*, Volume 16, 100384 (December 2022).

Senator James Inhofe statements: Eric Garcia, "Former Republican senator who voted against COVID-19 aid resigned over long COVID." *Independent* (February 24, 2023).

US Advisory Commission on Public Diplomacy: "Public diplomacy and the new "old" war: Countering state-sponsored disinformation." Available at https://2017-2021.state.gov/wp-content/uploads/2020/09/Public-Diplomacy-and-the-New-Old-War-Countering-State-Sponsored-Disinformation.pdf.

Johns Hopkins Center for Health Security: "Meeting COVID-19 misinformation and disinformation head-on." Available at https://publichealth.jhu.edu/ meeting-covid-19-misinformation-and-disinformati on-head-on.

EU Joint Research Centre report: EU Science Hub, "Misinformation on COVID-19: What did we learn?" (February 21, 2023). Available at https://joint-research -centre.ec.europa.eu/jrc-news/misinformation-covid -19-what-did-we-learn-2023-02-21_en.

GAO recommendation on improper payments: Government Accountability Office, "Emergency relief funds: Significant improvements are needed to ensure transparency and accountability for COVID-19 and beyond." (Report No. GAO-22-105715) (March 17, 2022).

UK Public Sector Fraud Authority: Additional information available at https://www.gov.uk/government/ organisations/public-sector-fraud-authority.

Australian Commonwealth Fraud Prevention Centre: Additional information available at https://www.coun-terfraud.gov.au/.

UK National Audit Office recommendation: UK National Audit Office, "COVID-19 business grant schemes." (March 23, 2023).

ACKNOWLEDGMENTS

Thank you to my colleagues in the inspector general community, especially Mike Ware, Christi Grimm, Larry Turner, Mark Greenblatt, and Rae Oliver, and their respective teams who help make the magic happen and keep the playing field level. In a media interview I did in December 2020, I was asked what surprised me most. I mentioned the levels of fraud, of course, but I also said that on a positive note I was incredibly proud of the work *you* all were doing with the PRAC *in addition* to your day jobs and how we've come together as a community.

Thank you to all the PRAC staff team, past and present, for your extraordinary work without an instruction manual and under tumultuous conditions. You've heard me say this before: after we got our bearings, I became part astronomer whose job was to simply find incredible talent (stars like you), arrange you into constellations, and then just let you shine.

Even bosses need the occasional boost, and I especially want to thank PRACsters Sharon Smith, Brooke Holmes, Tye Gillins, Ami Schaeffer, Jenniffer Wilson, and Angie Riddick for their selfless service and radiating positive vibes when I needed to recharge.

In writing this book I had the pleasure of getting to know John Kamensky, and I want to thank him for his unique contributions to this book. When you decide to take on a project like this and you end up pouring out a little of yourself onto the pages, you can consider yourself incredibly lucky when you can count on someone like John to look at a rough, unfinished expression and see something of value. John is the teacher I aspire to be. He patiently read my first draft and gave me encouragement and direction in equal measure. He was also the one who suggested the book title.

Thank you to dear old friends from the oversight community, Pam Van Dort, Elise Stein, Brooke Holmes, and to new friends brought together by my editor, who served as beta readers and generously spent time reading an unpolished draft and provided us candid feedback.

Thanks to my production team: Sandra Wendel at Write On, Inc., Mary Anne Shepard, Emily Shepherd, Sam Westbrooks, and Marko Markovic at 5mediadesign.

I owe a massive debt to my wife for the countless hours I spent directly working on pandemic oversight and the selfish hours I later spent mulling over the experience and reducing my thoughts to writing.

ABOUT THE AUTHOR

B ob Westbrooks—a career government watchdog, retired federal senior executive, former inspector general, and the former executive director of the Pandemic Response Accountability Committee—draws on his extraordinary experiences to provide audiences insights on enhancing accountability, promoting innovation and creativity, and building collaborative cultures. At the PRAC, Bob was recognized for

- Building a leading-edge organization from scratch to independently oversee $5 trillion in federal pandemic relief spending;
- Spearheading a collaborative, risk-based, and data-driven approach that has been recognized as the model for future government oversight; and
- Pioneering new agile oversight approaches, strategic partnerships, and shared services.

Bob is a multi-skilled human Swiss Army knife—he admittedly is not the most lethal blade, but he prides himself on versatility and packing as many tools as possible into a compact frame. Bob has certifications and significant experiences as a lawyer, criminal investigator, certified public accountant, certified internal auditor, and certified information systems auditor. He has expert-level technical competency and deep domain knowledge in fraud, oversight, accountability, and compliance.

Prior to his appointment at the PRAC, Bob led organization transformations at two federal offices and has led scores of investigations and audits over his career.

Bob retired from the federal government in December 2022, after twenty-eight years of public service. He began his career as a US postal inspector and later served in leader-ship positions in three federal oversight offices before being appointed inspector general.